P9-DWT-274

World Food Resources

Intext Series in ECOLOGY

ARTHUR S. BOUGHEY, *Editor*
University of California, Irvine

Fundamental Ecology
Arthur S. Boughey

World Food Resources
Georg Borgstrom

Biological Control
Robert van den Bosch and P. S. Messenger

Water Resources
Nathaniel Wollman

Conservation
Archie S. Mossman

World
Food Resources

Georg Borgstrom

Michigan State University

PROPERTY OF
CLACKAMAS COMMUNITY COLLEGE
LIBRARY
WITHDRAWN

Intext Educational Publishers

New York and London

HD
9000.5
.B56

Copyright © 1973 by Georg Borgstrom

All rights reserved. No part of this book may be reprinted,
reproduced, or utilized in any form or by any electronic,
mechanical, or other means, now known or hereafter invented,
including photocopying and recording, or in any information
storage and retrieval system, without permission in writing
from the Publisher.

Library of Congress Cataloging in Publication Data

Borgstrom, Georg, 1912–
World food resources.

(Intext series in ecology)
Includes bibliographies.
1. Food supply. 2. Population. I. Title.
[DNLM: 1. Food supply. HD 9000.5 B734w 1973]
HD9000.5.B56   338.1'9   72-11998
ISBN 0-7002-2367-3

Intext Educational Publishers
257 Park Avenue South
New York, New York 10010

Contents

26544

Series Preface

As we move into the decade of the 70's we are confronted with dire threats of imminent environmental disaster. While prophecies as to the actual doomsday vary from five years to thirty years from now, no professional ecologist seems willing to state categorically that mankind will survive into the next millenium unchallenged by any ecocatastrophe. Some indeed believe that before this time we and most of our familiar ecosystems are inevitably doomed to extinction.

Enough has now been said and written about such predicted disasters to instill in students, governments, and the public at large an uneasy feeling that something may be amiss. Terms such as *pollution, natural increase*, and *re-cycling* have begun to assume a realistic and more personal note as the air over our cities darkens, our rivers are turned into lifeless fire hazards, our domestic water becomes undrinkable, and we have to stand in line for any form of service or amenity.

Politicians, scientists, and the public have responded variously to this new situation. Tokenism is rampant in thought, word, and deed. Well-intentioned eco-activist groups have mushroomed, not only among youth, who are the most threatened as well as the most understanding segment of our societies. More specifically, in the restricted field of college texts, appropriate ecological chapters have been hurriedly added to revised editions. No biological work is now permitted to conclude without some reference to human ecology and environmental crises.

The purpose of this new ecological series is to survey without undue overlap the major fields of our present environmental confrontation at an introductory college level. The basic text for the series presents an overview of the ecological fundamentals which are relevant to each issue. In association with the works listed in its bibliographical references, it can stand alone as a required text for an introductory college course. For such use each chapter has been provided with a set of review questions. For more extensive courses, the base text leads into each series volume, and the particular area of environmental problems which this explores.

This series treats, subject by subject, the main points of impact in this current ecological confrontation between man and his environment. It presents in breadth and in depth the problems of pollution, pesticides, waste materials, population control, and the resource exploitation which imminently threaten to overwhelm us. Each volume in the series is a definitive study prepared by a specialist in the field, writing from an intimate personal experience of his area, relating but not overlapping his subject with other volumes in the series. Uniquely assembled in each volume will be information which presently is not available without extensive bibliographical research, at the same time arranged and interpreted in a more readily assimilable form. Extensive illustrative material, much of it original, still further facilitates a ready comprehension of the matter presented.

This is an exciting series. The urgency and ferment which have been experienced by all those associated with it cannot fail to be transmitted to the reader. The series confounds the prophets of doom, for it illustrates that given a proper understanding of ourselves and our ecological world, there is yet time for action. This time may be short, but sufficient if we exercise now the characteristics of courage and resolution in which, at times of great crisis, our species has never previously been found wanting.

Arthur S. Boughey

Preface

During the past quarter century, public debate has repeatedly centered around the question of how to feed the burgeoning human family, now adding more than 75 million new members each year. Most analyses have focused on either how to raise more food or how to stem the rising population tide. The issue calls for a broader response, one that will inspire programs and actions aimed at a more acceptable balance; reducing the great inequities between the satisfied and the hungry, the rich and the poor. This book takes you behind the scene to survey how, through agriculture and fisheries, man procures the variety of plant and animal commodities which in turn after primitive or elaborate processing all become food. In the distribution of these riches, world trade emerges as an important modifier. Cities and increasing urbanization throughout the world require a profound restructuring of present marketing practices. The nutritional aspects of world feeding are given main emphasis, a matter frequently overlooked in development programs and agricultural planning. Finally, food is discussed as the key element of the present ecology crisis.

Man's quest for food and feed is both epic and drama. This book strives not only to render deeper relief and new coloring to the world food parorama, but also to open wider perspectives in this all-embracing matter. The staggering deficits mirrored in a widening Hunger Gap remain·the overriding predicament.

Special thanks are due my wife Greta for constructive editing, tedious checking of tables and charts, and assiduous help in all stages of the preparation of this book.

World Food Resources

Introduction

Life for more than two-thirds of the 3.7 billion humans on Earth is highly precarious. They are short of most of the necessaries of life: food, water, shelter (clothing and housing), fuel, and metals. Available land for tillage and forestry is inadequate. In a few words: they exist in various degrees of poverty and misery. Some 450 to 500 million people, in contrast to these, live in relative affluence. In between are some 600 to 650 million partly ruled by parsimony but managing to get above minimum needs in most regards.

This intermediate group includes the U.S.S.R., Eastern Europe, and Japan; the top group embraces the United States, Canada, Western Europe, Australia, New Zealand, and the River Plate countries of South America. Together, these groups constitute the *satisfied world*. The *hungry world* covers most of Latin America, Africa and Asia. Around 10 percent within this deficient sphere enjoy good standards, while 10 to 15 percent of the population living in the well-to-do countries suffer from shortages (15 to 20 percent in the United States). Each country has its geographical discrepancies and its internal gaps in socioeconomic structure.

The world has close to one billion children below fourteen years of age. No fewer than 650 million of these will never reach adulthood because of malnutrition and its detrimental health effects. Any marked improvements within this sphere accordingly have far-reaching repercussions on human numbers.

All estimates and projections agree that there is little likelihood the globe will have fewer than 6 billion people by year 2000. Even this figure is predicated upon the assumption that some degree of success can be attained in current measures to curb the population growth. This is highly conjectural and most indications point to 7 billion.

The overpopulation in the rural areas of the hungry world is now so

1

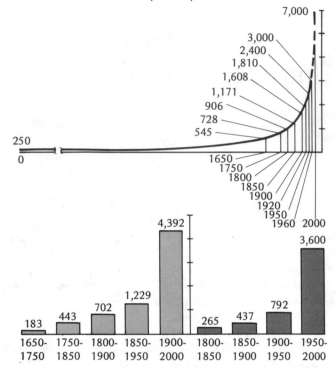

WORLD POPULATION
(millions)

Global population growth from the beginning of the Christian era (with a quarter billion). Note that wars, plagues, and other calamities made no kinks in the general trend of the growth curve. The explosive increase during the last hundred years is best evidenced by the rapid mounting of the increment, as measured in 100-year periods (left section) or 50-year periods (right section), respectively.

critical that it drives the flow toward the cities with added force. Subsistence farms, rarely exceeding three acres and often half that size, offer bleak opportunities for further splitting to accommodate for the next generation of youngsters, soon becoming prospective parents. Almost nowhere are industrialization and urbanization catching up with the added numbers. Yet, cities are almost the only remaining recourse for these unfortunates, in the poor world in excess of 400 million in the 1970's, and these superfluous millions flock into them. The level of gainful employment in expanding industries and services is extremely restricted; only a fraction of those reaching the labor force have a chance. Education and public health are in addition greatly inadequate to prepare the young for jobs. As a result the cadres of unemployed swell, the slums expand. One-fourth of the human family is now estimated to belong to the growing armies of squatters.

This is in a nutshell the status of major portions of the human family. Most noteworthy is the fact that these conditions prevail despite extraordinary measures taken almost everywhere to cope with these calamities by international agencies and foundations, by many governmental bodies, and by a wide array of private activities. Several of these endeavors have been most impressive both in magnitude, tenacity, and perseverance, yet they emerge as having been inadequate to stop effectively the insidious growth of misery. Protein shortages are alarming, yet additional millions are affected by lack of fat, of several minerals, and in particular of vitamins C, A, B_1 (thiamine), and folic acid. Anemias and other blood diseases are prevalent. Intestinal parasites sap the stamina of hundreds of millions. In many countries livestock suffers as much as man through these undermining health hazards.

This ominous trend needs to be reversed. We Westerners cannot expect to remain seated comfortably at ringside while this tragedy unfolds on the world scene. Our food deliveries have mostly been like crumbs falling from the rich man's table. Far more extensive measures, both in time and size, are needed to stem the tide and reduce the enormous dimensions of human misery, not the least in terms of the availability of food.

Two-thirds of those now living will experience a world population exceeding 6 billion. Young people now in school will find their entire lives influenced by this calamity. Within the decade of the 1970's wide-ranging crash programs will have to be initiated if mankind and civilization are to be saved. Only by acting now do we have the slightest chance of moving into the twenty-first century with a population curve level or declining, thus opening up the chance in the next century to reduce human suffering and to improve the lot of man.

This book is designed to bring the global food issue into focus, starting out by reviewing which commodities constitute the basis for our foods. This is done by surveying what the farmlands, the oceans, and the freshwaters deliver to man's larder. This survey is followed by an analysis of the basic prerequisites for crop and livestock production as circumscribed by climate, soils, water, and minerals. Due attention is given to man's foes in the shape of weeds, pests, parasites, and diseases as they threaten these invaluable resources. The oceans, lakes, ponds, and rivers as food producers are analyzed in a similar way. The unique and fragile circumstances for man's quest for food in the tropics and the intimate relationships between food and water are presented in separate chapters. This first section ends by summarizing current advances toward large-scale agriculture and toward ocean cultivation.

The second section of this book describes how this array of commodities is converted into foods and food products through various kinds of processing. Such treatment is in most instances indispensable to making plant products digestible to man. Preservation and storage are key functions in this third dimension of food. The global household is, both in the satisfied and poor worlds, suffering huge losses through waste and spoilage. A relentless battle is raging—with minor let-ups in cold or dry seasons—against rodents, insects, yeasts, molds, and other hostile agents. Many chemical and technical devices aid man in this warfare defending his domain.

To what degree domestic production in some countries is supplemented through global trade in foods and commodities is the theme of a special chapter. This also discusses technical advances—transcontinental railroads, highways, transoceanic shipping—that for the first time in history have made long-distance feeding feasible on a major scale in this century.

Finally, a third section discusses, against the background of man's nutritional needs, crucial repercussions as to public health with particular emphasis on the protein issue, and the relationships between food and the population explosion. A separate chapter traces the neglected key role that food plays directly and indirectly in the current ecological crisis.

There is an urgent need to switch mankind's priorities. But still more imperative is a fundamental reorientation of economics. We not only need a complete and better accounting of our costs, but further we will be forced to much better global economizing and householding on behalf of entire mankind. Man will need to formulate entirely new programs, taking cognizance of the parsimonious conditions ruling life on our limited spaceship. The current frivolity and ignorance will lead us into early disaster—the first signs of which currently are becoming evident in our ecological dilemma. Yet, the global food and water crisis more clearly mirrors the urgent demand for responsive action and responsibility toward others—not only toward ourselves, a minority favored with more land, soil, and water than almost any other peoples. For we Americans constitute, together with the Canadians, a mere 7 percent of the world's population.

It should be occasion for serious reflections that the affluent world, in its armament race between the United States and the Soviet Union together with their allies and satellites, uses more money for those purposes than the entire developing world totally produces. This supreme irresponsibility has had a contagious effect. Many poor countries divert more money to nuclear reactors than the total they use for such other scientific disciplines as agriculture, medicine, public health, or technology.

For such a revitalized program we need to bring into focus, far better than hitherto, the true magnitude and nature of the present world crisis. This will require a massive reeducation within our own midst about prerequisites for human survival in terms of tilled soils, water, fertilizers, and minerals.

We further need to recognize the self-evident limitations of our spaceship, Earth. Such restrictions are felt all the way down to the individual farm. Earth can never feed limitless numbers, nor can individual communities countries, states, nations, or continents. There are rather well-defined limits to how big you can make the cake; and the larger the number that has to share it, the less to each. Gains have in general lagged behind long-range increases in human numbers.

The Technical Aid Programs and various Peace Corps activities have taught us valuable lessons, in particular as related to the many disturbing and detrimental conditions facing crops, livestock, and man in the hungry world. These have had a sobering effect on the euphoria which went with early aid programs. We have further discovered that good lessons could be gleaned from our failures—farms in developing countries are frequently better adjusted within their narrow ecological margins than was earlier recognized. Many of our procedures are deeply disturbing to life's basic frameworks, either through toxic pollutants moving into air or water, or through unmanageable accumulations of waste.

We are now discovering that we have not contrived, and far less explored, all possibilities. We are starting to realize that our western technical civilization is no universal remedy for the world's ills. Its enormous wastefulness in resources—whether water, soil, fuel or metals—cannot be copied on a global scale. Furthermore it carries the dubious feature of economizing with the only resource truly available in surplus, namely man.

Section I

Production

Food Commodities   1

The Earth provides us with food chiefly through agriculture and fisheries. Around the globe shellmounds testify to the fact that major parts of mankind in its infancy lived from snails, mussels, and oysters. During the next stage of human development other animals were hunted and seeds of wild plants were gathered. Through trial and error those that were nutritious and wholesome were selected. Gradually, game and fish were in this manner supplemented with wild nuts, berries and fruits, chiefly from trees and bushes, as well as with seeds from certain grasses, the precursors of cereals. Nowadays agriculture carries almost the entire burden of supplying man with sustenance from the land. Only via pastures does wildlife still render food in certain regions of the globe. Animal husbandry leans to an overwhelming and growing degree on specially cultivated feed crops which thus are converted into meat, milk, and eggs. Fish and other aquatic animals graze, directly or indirectly, the pastures of the seas and other waters as discussed in a separate chapter of this book. All living organisms depend on the production of the plants, and despite tremendous technical progress practically all our food originates from such sources. In the Bible this basic truth is expressed in the revealing sentence: "All flesh is grass."

Plant products provide the total human household with nine-tenths of its caloric intake, and this share will in all likelihood increase as population figures mount. It becomes less and less feasible to take the costly road via animals with the large and unavoidable nutritional losses involved. Obviously only part of what a cow, a pig, or a hen consumes is converted into milk, meat, or eggs. The major part of the feed is required to sustain the life processes of the animal and for the build-up and maintenance of bone structure, skin, and other bodily organs which do not serve man as food.

Three grain crops—wheat, rice, and corn—and as many tubers—potato, yams and cassava—presently provide four-fifths of the world's food calculated in calories. But millions of people depend on other plant crops and even those whose diet is dominated by bread and potato would succumb if they did not supplement their daily food with plant or animal products, rich in protein and fat, and if they did not fill their vitamin and mineral needs through fruits and vegetables. Although grain and starch-rich tubers are primarily energy foods of low protein content, they do contribute considerable protein to the diet by reason of the high volume intake of these products. Special sources of protein among plants are leguminous seeds (pulses), above all beans, and to some degree nuts. Several oilseeds such as peanut (groundnut), sunflower, soybean, and others are also protein sources and in addition figure prominently among the world's fat suppliers.

Sugar crops (cane and beet) were until this century chiefly of local importance in the growing regions such as the Caribbean, but sugar has gradually become an important world-trade commodity. Commercial production on a large scale of vegetables, including mushrooms and onion, is of

GRAIN—GLOBAL PRODUCTION

Annual Average   1969-1970
(millions of metric tons)

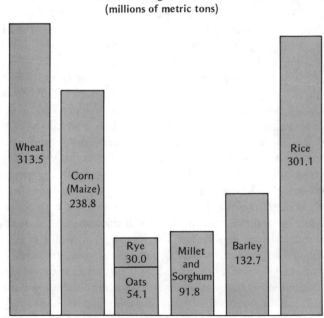

Wheat, rice, and corn dominate world production of cereals.

fairly recent date and almost exclusively a Western undertaking; these are chiefly vitamin and mineral suppliers. Herbs and spices, finally, serve to enhance the flavor and in many cases also the keeping quality of our food.

Without feed crops such as alfalfa, grass, clover, vetch, root crops, and others, our supply of animal products would be severely limited. In addition, grain and potato are used as feed and so are, for the major part, the press residues from oilseeds.

We are inclined to think of most cultivated crops and domesticated animals as more or less universal, but in reality our most important plant crops and livestock animals were internationalized fairly late in the long history of mankind, mostly within the last four or five centuries. The Indians of the Western hemisphere—the world's unsurpassed plant breeders—contributed several major crops such as corn, potato, manioc, beans, groundnut, and tomato. Wheat, barley, and rye originated in the Near East, rice and banana in South Asia, sugar cane in India, and sorghum in Africa.

With the water buffalo and the llama as major exceptions, the Middle East was the cradle of all our domesticated food-producing animals. Reindeer are semidomesticated and belong to the circumpolar area. In the 1530's the first European pioneers brought cattle to the Western hemisphere, more exactly to an area which is part of present-day Argentina, a leading cattle country. That time the cattle stock succumbed in a new environment, but a renewed effort was made in 1569 when horses were also introduced. Cattle reached the North American continent with the early European settlers in 1610 and sheep in 1633. Australia, today's leading sheep nation, received its first sheep as late as 1797 (possibly 1788).

CONTRIBUTIONS FROM PLANT CULTIVATION

Grain products—the dietary mainstay

The common name for grain and grain products is cereals, the name referring to the Roman goddess Ceres, guardian of all grain crops. Most old civilizations have a special grain god. Throughout the ages grain has constituted the mainstay of human diet and will probably always remain so. Practically all people on Earth have every reason to pay homage to the grain crops.

All advanced civilizations seem to have been based on some kind of grain. To the Sumerians, the Assyrians, Babylonians, Egyptians, Carthaginians, Greeks, and Romans, the food grains were wheat, barley, and sorghum. The people of the Orient practiced grain cultivation probably as early as ten to five millenia B.C., primarily sorghum and later rice. India, China, Indonesia, and the Khmer Empire in Southeast Asia all relied on rice. The pre-Columbians, such as the Incas, the Mayans, and the Aztecs, depended on

"Indian grain," maize, or corn, for their daily bread, in the higher Andean regions supplemented with a grain named quinoa. But, as far as is known, sorghum is the oldest of man's grain crops, possibly with the exception of some primitive wheat (emmer) of the Near East and early corn varieties of the American Indians which both are eight to nine thousand years old.

Grain provides mankind with two-thirds of its calories and plant protein. Almost half of the world's tilled acreage is utilized for grain crops. With few exceptions the various types of grain belong to the family of grasses. Wheat and rice are followed in volume by corn, rye, and sorghum. But a major part of mankind can be divided up into rice-eaters and wheat-eaters.

Rice is chiefly grown in the warmer regions of the globe, in those parts which are well provided with water through regularly occurring monsoon periods. Rice and food are almost synonymous to more than 1.5 billion Asians, thus to almost half of mankind, for whom rice makes up from 75 to 85 percent of the food intake. Outside of Asia, Brazil is the only rice consumer of importance, though rice is fairly common food also in southern and eastern Europe, and in some humid areas of tropical Africa. Rice is further cultivated in southern United States, partly for export.

Wheat dominates the temperate regions and is also grown in most subtropical countries and at high elevations in the tropics. Its northward advances belong largely to this century, mainly thanks to successful cross breeding which has produced strains with higher resistance to low temperatures and diseases. Wheat and rye are often designated as bread grain since they are chiefly so used. But the manufacture of noodles and other food items employs considerable amounts of wheat flour. Rye is primarily the grain of the cold northern latitudes and was dominant in Europe and North America until a few decades ago. Presently Europe and the U.S.S.R. together produce nine-tenths of this crop.

In regions which are too dry or too warm for wheat and rye, sorghum takes over as in northern China (under the name of kaoliang), in parts of the high plateaus of India (so-called jowar, with larger acreage than wheat), as well as in tropical Africa. In the southern United States sorghum is locally produced. Sorghum is the least demanding grain in regard to water, soils, and climate and has as a rule a higher protein content than most other grains. It is not suited for baking and the seeds are usually crushed and prepared as mush or porridge. Sorghum is not always clearly distinguished from the millets, which have five clearly related species. This is the ragi of India (also surpassing wheat in acreage). Millets were once—and in most of the hungry world are still—the poor man's cereal, particularly in China, India, the U.S.S.R., the United Arab Republic, and many African regions. Also millets grow under sparse conditions.

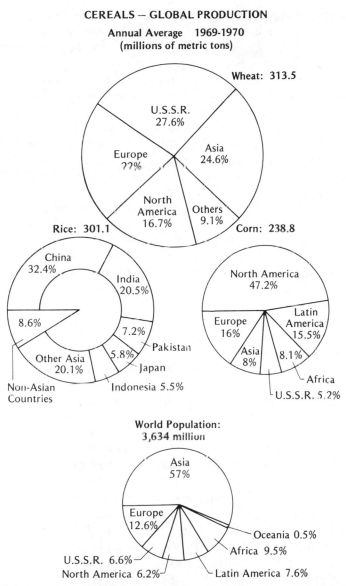

CEREALS — GLOBAL PRODUCTION

Annual Average   1969-1970
(millions of metric tons)

Wheat: 313.5

U.S.S.R.
27.6%

Europe
??%

Asia
24.6%

North
America
16.7%

Others
9.1%

Rice: 301.1

Corn: 238.8

China
32.4%

India
20.5%

8.6%

7.2%

Pakistan

Other Asia
20.1%

5.8%

Japan

Non-Asian
Countries

Indonesia 5.5%

North America
47.2%

Europe
16%

Latin
America
15.5%

Asia
8%

8.1%

Africa

U.S.S.R. 5.2%

World Population:
3,634 million

Asia
57%

Europe
12.6%

Oceania 0.5%

Africa 9.5%

U.S.S.R. 6.6%

North America 6.2%

Latin America 7.6%

Global cereal production (in percent of total) distributed as to continents
and major producers and compared to the distribution of world population.

In Latin America corn has been the chief food item ever since the
heyday of the Indian empires, then as now supplemented with beans. Corn is
also central in the diet of major parts of Africa (in the South, West, and East),

the Balkan peninsula in Europe, and in the southern United States. Almost half the world's corn is produced in the United States, of which four-fifths is used as feed, mainly in hog production. A small part of the crop is exported, chiefly to Europe for feeding purposes.

Barley used to be an important bread grain—note the biblical fable about five barley loaves and two fishes—but is nowadays, for the most part, an ingredient in other food items; at least one-third if not one-half of the world crop goes into the making of beer. It is cultivated in most countries. The U.S.S.R. produces one-third of the world total and Japan about one-fourth. There, as in Korea and other Asian countries, barley constitutes the poor man's rice, but the poorest among the poor have to be satisfied with the still cheaper sorghum.

Oats early entered Central Europe as a weed in the grain fields but achieved the rank of a cultivated crop during the Bronze Age. For centuries it was the favorite crop in regions with heavy precipitation, cold climate, and poor soils, as in Scotland. But the white man carried oats to all temperate regions. Despite the disappearance of the horse, a considerable portion is still used as feed, but oats also provides human food in the form of mush, oatmeal, and flakes.

An old grain type, originating in Central Asia, which was once commonly cultivated on poor soils in Russia and Central Europe, is buckwheat. Not a grass, it belongs to the family of pigweeds. Buckwheat is nowadays cultivated mainly in the Soviet Union and India as well as on small acreages in North America. The seeds are ground into flour or grits, which in the U.S.S.R. is made into a popular mush called kasha, in the United States into certain kinds of pancakes. In China and India buckwheat is used in pastes and noodles.

A few additional grains are prominent as food in restricted regions. Teff (*Eragrostis abyssinica*, Link) constitutes more than half the grain crop in Ethiopia, where it originated. It keeps this position due to its nutritive value and it overshadows most other grains both in protein quality and calcium content. The seeds are milled into flour which is baked into an unleavened bread called injera.

Job's tears or adlay (*Coix lacryma-jobi*, L.) is another source of food among the grasses, cultivated in the Orient for thousands of years. It has been successfully introduced in the São Paulo region of Brazil, where it gives high yields. As to protein quality, it surpasses rice and is milled together with wheat. This flour is particularly suited for the manufacture of crackers. In China it is used primarily in soups, in Japan for a special kind of beer.

In the Inca empire quinoa (*Chenopodium quinoa* Willd.), closely related to pigweed, was the most important crop, followed by potato. Corn ranked

CEREALS — GAINS IN ANNUAL PRODUCTION

(millions of metric tons)

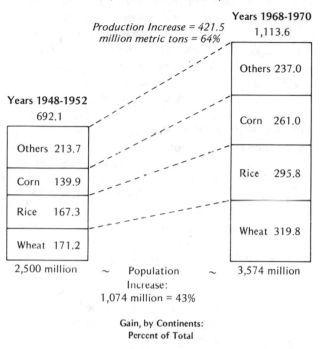

*Production Increase = 421.5
million metric tons = 64%*

Years 1968-1970
1,113.6

Others 237.0

Corn   261.0

Rice   295.8

Wheat 319.8

Years 1948-1952
692.1

Others 213.7

Corn   139.9

Rice   167.3

Wheat 171.2

2,500 million   ~   Population   ~   3,574 million
Increase:
1,074 million = 43%

Gain, by Continents:
Percent of Total

North America —┐   Africa ┐

| Asia   39.5% | U.S.S.R. 17% | Europe 16% | 13.5% | 7% | 5% |

China 15.5%   Latin America ┘

Oceania ┘
2%

Increase in the production of major cereal crops during the period after World War II. Note that the gains have kept pace with population growth. The Chinese expansion is due to a major irrigation drive, encompassing more than 90 million acres. The Soviet Union's gains were achieved mainly through its new breadbasket in Western Siberia and Kazakhstan, also exceeding 90 million acres. Feed grains (corn, sorghum) dominate grains in the Satisfied World.

third. Quinoa was indigenous in the area surrounding Lake Titicaca and first domesticated there. It is mostly cultivated at altitudes between 10,000 and 15,000 feet, where no other grain crop thrives.

Potato and other starch-rich tubers

Far back in history various primitive civilizations discovered that certain plants stored nutrients in subterranean tubers, and the list of starch-rich tubers which have served man as food is lengthy. Turnip preceded potato as food and was important to the poor of Northern Europe. The same applies to rutabaga, which originated along the southern coast of the North Sea. In the past it was cultivated in Germany and Scandinavia and spread from there to other parts of Europe and to England and North America. Like turnip, the rutabaga today chiefly provides feed but both roots are still cultivated as table vegetables in Europe and North America.

Among the food tubers the potato in our days dominates the temperate regions while cassava and yams compete in the warm regions. In Europe the breakthrough for potato cropping came as late as in the eighteenth century, two hundred years after the Spanish colonizers brought the potato from South America across the Atlantic. The potato had a great social impact. From Central Europe it migrated north, west, and east. In Ireland it replaced the parsnip which for centuries had been the most important tuber crop on the island. White potato, also called Irish potato in the United States, penetrated toward the east, all the way to the chilly agricultural regions of northern Siberia. Three-fourths of the world crop is produced in Europe and the Soviet Union. About half is used as animal feed. Bread and potato still dominate the diet in large parts of the U.S.S.R., as they did in Central and Northern Europe until well into this century.

Japan, Taiwan, and Southeast Asia have a corresponding diet combination in rice supplemented with sweet potato. The latter is also highly important for the warm countries. It is largely grown on a subsistence basis or for local markets and hardly figures in world-trade statistics. When other food crops are destroyed through pests or diseases, the sweet potato becomes the chief source of starch and calories, being highly resistant to such attacks. When typhoons damage the rice paddies in Japan, the Philippines, and Taiwan, sweet potato again becomes the savior since the tubers in the soil are protected against such calamities. It is therefore a reliable reserve crop and an emergency food. The sweet potato was early introduced in China and reached Europe before the white potato; in the southern United States sweet potato is also important.

Sweet potato originated in the Caribbean and tropical South America, where it has been cultivated for thousands of years. It belongs to the bindweed family and has a higher nutritive value than the white potato, especially in regard to vitamins A, B, and C as well as calcium. It is often confused with yams, another tropical tuber, closely related to the lily plants and probably of East Asian origin. Yam is not as common as sweet potato. It is cultivated in parts of tropical Africa, the Caribbean, and South America.

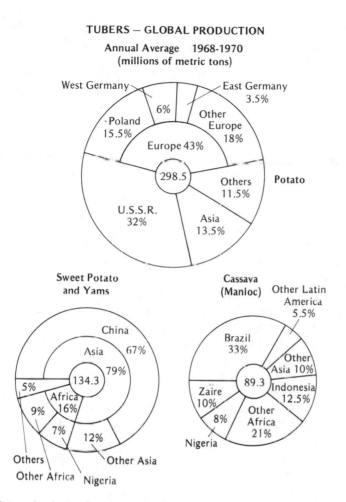

TUBERS — GLOBAL PRODUCTION

Annual Average 1968-1970
(millions of metric tons)

Potato dominates the tuber crops—larger than all others together.

In the Pacific Islands and East Asia the dominant tuber is taro, which like sweet potato exceeds white potato in content of calcium, phosphorus, and vitamins A and D. The Polynesian and Hawaiian poi is made from taro root.

In Brazil and large sections of tropical Africa both white and sweet potato are grown but manioc, also called cassava, has the predominance among starch-rich crops. In many areas cassava takes the place of grain, especially displacing sorghum. The tubers are toxic; they must be ground fine and the "flour" carefully washed in order to remove hydrocyanic acid before being used as food. Here is one of many examples of so called "natural" foods that are not wholesome. Indeed, most plant products, including grain, must be processed in one way or another to make them acceptable as human food.

Among other tubers Jerusalem artichoke, carrot, parsnip, table beets and others have been known for centuries but are commercially grown primarily in Europe and North America. The carrot is common all over the world, particularly in temperate regions. It was a favorite among the ancient peoples. In Japan the carrot is second only to the radish among the vegetables. One variety of radish is more than a yard long. A salt-fermented radish called daikon is eaten daily by the Japanese as a condiment with rice. The radish, original in China, was common in Egypt before the time of the pyramid builders.

Sugar crops

While grain, potato, and other tubers consist mostly of starch, quite a few plants exist which primarily contain sugar. Among them sugar cane and sugar beets are commercially grown on a large scale. India is the country of origin for the sugar cane; this plant impressed the soldiers of Alexander the Great during his Indian campaign and thus dates back more than two thousand years in European experience. The sugar beet is one of the results of Europe's search for food during the nineteenth century. These two plants nowadays contribute most of the world's sugar, two thirds through sugar cane, prevalent in warm regions, sugar beet in the temperate zones. Sugar is also manufactured from the stem sap of several palm trees. The American Indians used to tap the sap of the sugar maple, and this practice continues in Michigan and New England, especially Vermont.

Honey

Until the present century honey was the chief sweetener in Europe in home preservation as well as in candy and cookies. Although sugar largely has taken its place, honey still constitutes an important food item in Mexico, Argentina, East Africa, and the countries around the eastern part of the Mediterranean. Honey is a combined plant and animal product. The bees gather the nectar from thousands of flowers, then preserve and concentrate it by fanning away one-third of its original water.

Protein seeds

Legumes characteristically carry nitrogen-fixing bacteria in their roots, thus readily making protein. They therefore constitute the most valuable protein source among the plant crops. Their seeds provide excellent and necessary

SUGAR — GLOBAL PRODUCTION

Annual Averages
(millions of metric tons)

1967/1968-1970/1971

Beet   29.9

1948/1949-1952/1953

Beet   12.3

Cane   53.6

Cane   25.5

2:1   *Ratio*   1.8:1

Cane/Beet

France   7%
West Germany 6.5%
Poland   6%

Cuba   10%
Brazil   9.5%
Mexico   5.5%

Europe
49%

Latin
America
41%

Others
18%

U.S.S.R.
31%

Others
20%

India   20%
China   5.5%
Pakistan   4.5%
Philippines   3.5%

United
States
9%

Asia 41%

United
States
4.8%

**From Sugar
Beet**

**From Sugar
Cane**

Global sugar production is led by cane output; sugar beets are chiefly grown in Europe and the Soviet Union, but are gaining in relative terms.

supplements to grain protein, but never as such surpass in food value the animal proteins. For this reason a large portion of mankind, forced to subsist on a one-sided grain diet, depends for growth and health on beans, peas, lentils, and other leguminous seeds. Without these they would succumb to protein deficiency.

Several types of beans play a cardinal role in the world's protein supply. As they do with corn and potato, the American Indians distinguish themselves as benefactors of mankind since they bred most bean varieties. In the Andes, in large parts of Brazil, and in the countries surrounding the Mediterranean, beans constitute indispensable daily food. In Spanish (*carne de pobre*), Italian (*carni di poveri*) and Portuguese their designation is "poor man's meat," referring to the fact that they are the protein sources of the poor. In India and Pakistan, various kinds of so-called gram beans are the chief protein food. Among the Chinese and the Japanese the soybeans fill this place. There this crop is not, as it is in the West, primarily a source of fat, but is above all a life-sustaining source of protein. Beans and dried peas are still cherished protein-rich menu items in several Western countries despite the ample availability of animal products which has followed with affluence.

The United States is today the largest producer of soybean. Nine-tenths of its soybean protein used on the domestic scene goes to animal feed. The oil from more than half the crop constitutes the backbone of North American margarine manufacturing; the protein residue from the pressing is the basis of the milk production of the United States and Canada and to a considerable degree in Europe. Soybean is exported to Europe and Canada, mainly for the dual purpose of providing fat and animal feed.

Nuts

Many kinds of nuts may also be included among protein seeds. In order to utilize them fully, bitter substances (tannins, hydrocyanic acid) have to be removed and the kernels milled into flour. Peanut soup is a highly valued and nutritious daily food in tropical Africa for those who can afford it and are not forced to deliver too much of their crop for export. Pastes are also made from the flour, among them our popular peanut butter. In addition, beverages similar to milk are produced from several nuts. Chestnut was once an important food, but is now mostly regarded as a seasonal delicacy, as evidenced by street-vending of roasted chestnuts in Italy, Spain, and France. Unlike most other nuts, chestnuts contain starch.

Coconuts consist of a fat-rich tissue and highly nutritious "milk." Coconut protein is especially high in quality. The coconut palm provides the basis for daily life in many parts of the wet tropics. Its nuts were early spread around the equator with ocean currents. In addition to food, this palm yields building material and fibers. The leaves are utilized as roof cover. Highly delectable cheeses are made from the coconut seed endosperm (white flesh) by growing fungi. Coconut constitutes the mainstay of the diet in parts of India and Indonesia, in the Philippines, and in the South Pacific Islands. But an increasing share of the world harvest is being exported to the United States and Europe as dried coconut meat (copra) and as oil pressed from the nuts. Like several other palm oils, coconut oil is used in the manufacturing of margarine.

Fat sources

In the Bible we read much of the olive tree, supplying oil through extraction from its stone fruits. It is still the predominant food fat around the Mediterranean, but cooking oil is nowadays also produced from other sources, especially corn germ and the oilseeds. The soybean is the most important source of fat in China and Japan while tropical Africa relies on the peanut (groundnut). Since the end of the nineteenth century, North America and

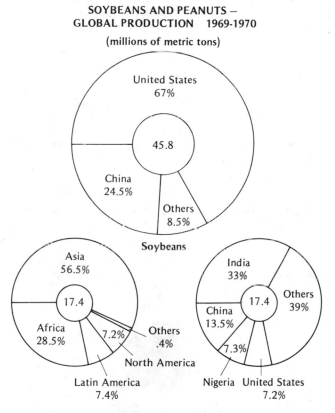

SOYBEANS AND PEANUTS —
GLOBAL PRODUCTION   1969-1970
(millions of metric tons)

Soybeans

Peanuts (Groundnuts)

Soybean production is dominated by the United States and peanut production by India.

Europe have become increasingly dependent on margarine for their fat supply, with vegetable oils now the chief ingredients. This fat derives from soybean, peanut, coconut, and sunflower seed. The oil is pressed from the seeds; the residue, the press cake, was originally discarded as waste. Gradually its value as animal feed was recognized, but so far the West channels very little into direct human food. The emergence of imitation meat, discussed in Chapter 8, may eventually change this.

During the last two hundred years and especially during the twentieth century large acreages around the globe have been planted to oil crops. Western Europe's production of vegetable oils is very limited and it leans heavily on imports: soybean from the United States, peanut from Africa, and coconut oil from the South Pacific Islands. The Soviet margarine industry is almost exclusively based on domestic sunflower crops. The butter of India, the so-called ghee, is produced from buffalo and cow's milk. India's margarine counterpart bears the name of *vanaspati* and is made from vegetable oils, chiefly peanuts.

Fruits and berries

Fruit did not become an important item in the world diet until this century. Citrus fruits dominate the subtropics; mango the tropics. India has more than two thousand varieties of mango. Apples and to some degree pears are the fruits of the temperate regions. Commercial orchards are almost exclusively a phenomenon of the West and even when located elsewhere in the world they are mostly under Western control and intended for export to North America and Western Europe. Fruits and berries are primary sources of water-soluble vitamins and minerals but otherwise as a rule have low nutritive value; a few exceptions are banana, pinapple, dates, and breadfruit.

The banana (*Musa sapientum* L. and *Musa cavendishii* Lamb) appears in several shapes and varieties and seems to have many origins, such as India, South China, and the South Pacific Islands, and has spread into Africa. Bananas were grown in India as long ago as 600 to 500 B.C. and were early brought to the island of Madagascar from Indonesia by the Arabs. This fruit is mentioned by Pliny, the Roman historian, in his *History of Nature* (70 B.C.). The Spaniards and the Portuguese introduced the banana to the West Indies and Brazil. In the tropics it is probably the chief food after cereals and provides mainly starch. A related species called plantain (*Musa paradisiaca* L.), called "mealy banana" because of its texture, is quite common in the wet tropics. It is fried or otherwise prepared before eating.

Banana plantations had their centennial in the 1960's; the first one was established in 1866 by Germans in Panama. A few years later the United Fruit Company, the giant North American corporation, started such plantations in Central America. At the turn of the century the African Fruit Company established banana plantations in Cameroun, West Africa.

Pineapple (*Ananas comosus* L.) is another important fruit plantation crop which even more exclusively serves the Western world, and this despite the fact that it would be most needed in the producing countries, by and large undernourished, since its nutritive value is high. It is especially rich in sugar. The pineapple originated in Brazil and early spread from there to other parts of the world. Columbus found it in the West Indies. Nowadays, large pineapple plantations are located in many tropical regions including Hawaii, the Malay peninsula, Taiwan, the Philippines, Ecuador, Brazil, and several other countries. Plantations on the Azores supply Western Europe with up to half a million pineapples annually from four thousand greenhouses.

In the dry sub-tropics the date palm (*Phoenix dactylifera* L.) plays the same role as the coconut palm in the coastlands of the wet tropics. With the fig tree, the date palm shares the honor of being the first fruit tree cultivated by man, by the Sumerians in Mesopotamia as early as 3000 B.C. The date palm is the chief tree of the desert oases and its fruits, in combination with camel milk, provide a well-balanced diet to the Bedouins. This tree has the capability, invaluable to man, of thriving even where the water has a rather high salt content. It is as versatile as the coconut palm and supplies fibers and timber in regions devoid of other trees. The dates, often sun-dried on the tree, have a sugar content between 60 to 70 percent and are especially rich in iron and potassium. The tree stem may also be tapped for sugar sap, sometimes made into wine. The date palm is cultivated commercially in southern California and Arizona, but the largest plantations are found in the Middle East and North Africa.

Mango (*Mangifera indica* L.) is the most common fruit in India, and the mango tree is cultivated on two-thirds of the fruit acreage. It is one of man's oldest crops, more than four thousand years, and exists in thousands of varieties since it is propagated from seed. The fruit is highly nutritious and constitutes the chief item in the diet of Southern and Eastern India, particularly in years when the monsoon is weak and the grain harvests poor. The mango is for the most part eaten raw but is also canned; it is used also as an ingredient in the preparation of India's famous piquant sauces, chutney, and other foods. The fruit kernel is dried and roasted like chestnut. In hard times it is ground into a flour, used in mushes. The mango fruit is also common in Southeast Asia and tropical East Africa.

Breadfruit of various kinds is highly cherished food all over Southeast Asia and is also an important food along the Mexican Gulf and in the Caribbean. In the Mediterranean region and in several Arab countries, breadfruit is the poor man's food. The true breadfruit tree (*Artocarpus altilis*

Fosberg) is native to the South Pacific Islands and to the Malay peninsula and was the dietary mainstay for many tribes into the present century. This tree does not yield fruit until twenty years of age but remains productive over a long period of time. The fruit, which has a high sugar content (7 to 44 percent) and a protein level of 2 to 7 percent, is sun dried. Several other kinds of trees have similar fruits and are important food sources for the poor in Southeast Asia and India. The fruits are harvested when ripe or earlier and are either boiled, baked, or fried after slicing. The seeds are also cooked and eaten. The breadfruit was introduced to the Caribbean in the eighteenth century and, particularly in Jamaica, is eaten by everyone. When dried, the fruit is pounded into flour. The blossoms are made into a preserve.

Mexico's poor often have reason to praise the thorny, reddish-yellow fruits of cacti. In times of drought they were frequently the only food available. Such cactus figs, "tunas" as they are called, are common all over the arid tropics, not the least in the Middle East, and are generally regarded as an invaluable food reserve.

Vegetables

Cabbage is probably the world's most important leafy vegetable, especially because of its high calcium content; but it is also rich in vitamins, particularly vitamin C which is highly stable. At least twenty kinds are used as food, among them broccoli and cauliflower, of which the inflorescence is eaten. Fermented white cabbage, sauerkraut, provided continental Europeans with vitamin C and calcium during the winter months, long before milk became everyday food.

The American Indians excelled in the cultivation of pumpkin and over the centuries bred many new varieties, several of which are still being cultivated. The fruit pulp made a refreshing dish and the seeds supplied additional nutrition.

Among the fat-rich fruits avocado is eaten as a vegetable. This fruit originated in tropical America and is cultivated in many regions on plantations. It is sometimes called alligator pear.

The eggplant, belonging to the potato family and indigenous to India, is also an important food. It is at present the most important vegetable in the tropics for rich and poor alike.

Spinach, celery, endive, lettuce, parsley, and artichoke are grown worldwide. The Romans harvested leafy vegetables and preserved them through salting and drying. The new sprouts of many plants are cherished food and may be designated vitamin concentrates; examples include asparagus in our part of the globe, and bean sprouts in China and Japan. Bamboo and palm sprouts are tropical counterparts. In India and in several other countries cultivated vegetables are luxury items but people, especially the poor, use several wild plants as vegetables.

The tomato is one of the many contributions of the American Indian to the world household. It was cultivated by the Aztecs, the Incas, and the Mayans. In Europe, the Italians started tomato cultivation as early as the mid-sixteenth century but it became widespread only in the past century. The tomato was little appreciated to begin with and only gradually did it become an important commercial item. The tomato today constitutes a key source of both vitamins A and C. Tomato-growing has advanced as far as the northern parts of the U.S.S.R. and China, where part of local needs is raised in heated greenhouses.

Union (*Allium cepa* L.) was a staple in the Egyptian diet at the time of

WHEAT YIELDS (100 kg/ha)
Annual Average   1967-1970

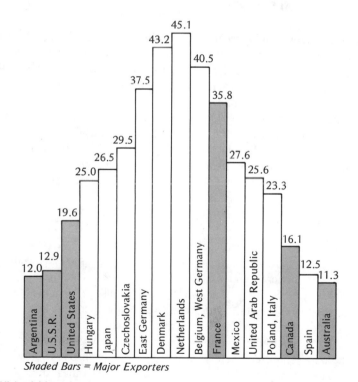

Shaded Bars = Major Exporters

High yields only attained in humid climate or when irrigated. (See pages 63-64.)

Moses and the pyramid-builders. Wild onion and barberry berries are assumed to have been the C-vitamin source that kept the scurvy from the Vikings during their far-reaching sea voyages. They as well as the Celts hauled onions from the Mediterranean. Garlic early enjoyed the reputation of staving off infectious diseases and was compulsory food for the Roman galley slaves. In Japan and China, rakkyo (*Allium chinensis* L.) is the most important onion variety, cultivated for centuries. It is salt treated and lightly fermented. It vies with radish in popularity as a vitamin-C condiment with rice.

In the United States and Europe large mushroom cultivations are found, but the Chinese and the Japanese started long ago to cultivate several species of fungi. They have other methods than the West but have of late started to copy its methods. Thanks to high content of protein and vitamins, mushrooms constitute an important food.

CONTRIBUTIONS FROM DOMESTIC ANIMALS (LIVESTOCK)

Our livestock supply milk, meat, and eggs by converting the plant feed they consume. Their total intake of feed exceeds considerably what agriculture produces in the way of plant products for direct human consumption. Yet animal food, including fish and shellfish, provides only one-tenth of the world's calorie consumption. But owing to their high content of first-rate protein the animal foods are significantly important in the world household, accounting for one-third of the global protein intake. Chiefly due to cost, animal protein remains largely the privilege of the rich and satisfied nations while the poor world is forced to resort almost entirely to plant protein, at best supplemented by fish.

Milk

Cow's milk consists of roughly equal parts of protein, fat, milk and sugar (lactose), together almost 15 percent; the remainder is mostly water and a few percent of minerals and vitamins. The cow is the leading milk supplier. No less than four-fifths of the world's cow's milk is produced in North America, the Soviet Union, and Europe, which together have one-quarter of the world population. In Chapter 8 the wide spectrum of dairy products resulting from industrial processing of fresh milk is discussed.

The cow cannot compete with the plants as fat producer. One acre of oilseed (rape or soybean, for example) yields six times the fat that a high-producing cow can make on the feed from the same acre. Butter making is therefore not competitive. For this reason not even the United States, much less Europe, could revert to provide food fat exclusively through butter. Available soil would not suffice for such a return to an older consumptional pattern. Margarine based on plant fats has thus become incorporated into the diet of the rich world.

The hungry, who for the most part live in the warm regions of the globe, are largely dependent upon milk from animals that are better adjusted to the prevalent climatic conditions than the cow. In high-rainfall areas the water buffalo is the chief milk animal. In regions with sparse vegetation the goat is unsurpassed as a milk producer. But milk consumption is extremely low in most developing countries, usually a mere one-fourth to one-twelfth of the minimum need. Many peoples in the northern cold regions, such as the tundra Eskimos, the Lapps, the Yakuts, and the Samoyeds, get their milk from reindeer. In the Tibetan highlands the yak has the same function.

Most milk-using cultures convert a large portion of their milk into cheese.

Meat

Meat is about one-fifth protein. The fat content in the muscle tissue and surrounding it varies a great deal. Cattle are the world's chief providers of meat, followed by pigs. But many dairy cows are also meat suppliers, and in addition are often draft animals. Sheep and goats were probably domesticated long before cows. Sheep nowadays contribute less than one-tenth of the world's meat supply. Australia, New Zealand, the Mediterranean area, and the British Isles are the major sheep raisers. In the desert region of the Middle East, the fat-tail sheep is found; in addition to meat this creature also yields fat. Camels are nowadays threatened with extinction through overslaughtering, a consequence of the rapid population growth and increasing demand for meat, though in some degree due to motorization.

The mechanization of agriculture released a great deal of horse meat to the food market in North America, Europe, and the Soviet Union. In Central Asia horses have long been raised chiefly as meat providers, as they still are in the U.S.S.R. (Kazakhstan and other regions) and in parts of Europe. A hairless dog, bred in old-time China, is a meat provider in certain parts of that country and in Southeast Asia. The Aztecs also had such a meat dog. Rabbit meat is commonly used in some parts of the world. But poultry, especially the hen, is much more important; so is turkey, duck and goose. In several countries such as Italy, Germany, England, and the United States, pigeon— called squab—is the poor man's poultry. At least two-thirds of the world's meat is eaten by one-fourth of its people, largely Westerners. Their needs are not satisfied with what is produced domestically and in additon they buy practically all meat that moves into world trade.

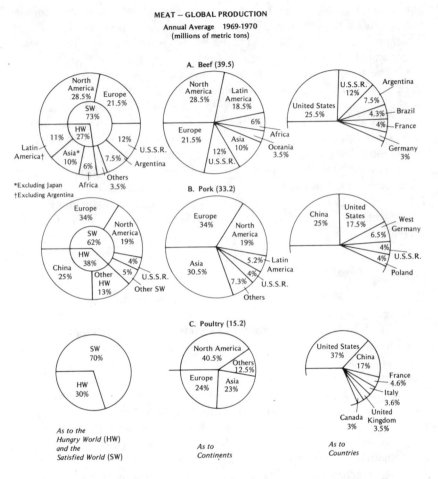

MEAT – GLOBAL PRODUCTION
Annual Average 1969-1970
(millions of metric tons)

A. Beef (39.5)

B. Pork (33.2)

C. Poultry (15.2)

As to the
Hungry World (HW)
and the
Satisfied World (SW)

As to
Continents

As to
Countries

Poultry production is half that of beef or pork. Note China's pork standing.

Blood

Blood is excellent protein-rich food and the Germanic peoples have for centuries prepared sausages, pudding, and other foods from the blood of slaughtered animals. Dried blood is also used as animal feed. Some tribes in Sudan and East Africa tap blood from cattle each tenth day on a regular basis and drink it mixed with goat milk. The cows give little or no milk but are utilized in this ingenious manner for providing protein until they are slaughtered and provide some meat.

Eggs

Owing to the ideal composition of their protein, eggs are extremely well adapted to man's needs. The hen is almost everywhere the chief egg layer for human consumption, but the temperate regions offer the best protection against diseases and therefore assure higher productivity. This explains why egg production by and large remains the privilege of the well-to-do. One-

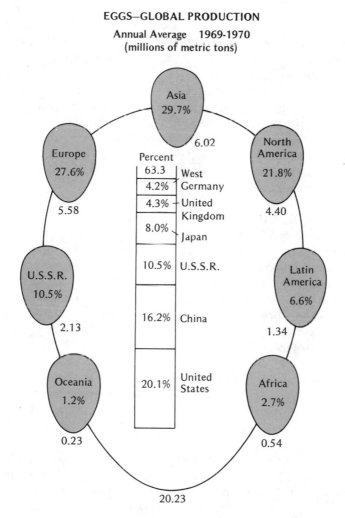

EGGS—GLOBAL PRODUCTION

Annual Average   1969-1970
(millions of metric tons)

The **notable** dominance of Asia is due to China (second) and Japan (fourth).

fourth of the world's people, living in Europe, North America, and the U.S.S.R., consumes three-fifths of the world's eggs.

WILDLIFE CONTRIBUTIONS

Mushrooms, game and wildfowl probably first come to mind in terms of the role of wildlife as a source of human food. Elk, deer, pheasants, wild duck, and many other species are still utilized as food but are gradually diminishing in relative importance because of the population increase. Many wild animals have simply been eradicated through hunting. The most startling example is the extermination of the North American passenger pigeon. In millions it confronted the pioneers on the prairies and even late in the nineteenth century it was sold in large quantities in big cities, especially New York. Being an excellent meat bird it would presumably have become a valuable addition to our supply of poultry meat. The buffalo, which roamed in millions on the virgin prairies, was saved from extinction only by the creation of reserves; there is no longer room for the buffalo in the wild. The auks of Spitsbergen and Greenland met the same destiny as the passenger pigeon in North America when this rather timid bird was captured by the thousands and salted to serve as a provision for the whalehunters.

Especially in East Africa, big game still constitutes an important food source. In those regions, cattle raising gives unacceptably low yields, partly because of diseases and partly because of scarce feed; game cropping has therefore been introduced. The herds of antelopes, elephants, giraffes, and several other animals are cropped in a well-regulated manner so that the stock is maintained at a reasonable level based on appraisals of the carrying capacity in each region. Thereby man takes over the role of the predator as a regulating and balancing factor in nature, and in so doing obtains supplies of meat for his own use.

Several other animals have, however, been much more important as a source of human food than big game: insects and their larvae, frogs, turtles, lizards, snakes, and reptiles. Locust swarms are not welcome in view of the havoc they cause by destroying crops, but they are nevertheless looked upon as a godsend food in many areas of South America and tropical Africa. Several kinds of larvae are regularly eaten as food in Indonesia, Central Africa, Central America, and Mexico. Wood-boring shipworms, which in a destructive way affect both fishing and transport vessels in the South Pacific archipelago as well as in India, constitute invaluable food to many poor people. Frogs are raised in the United States, Japan, and Southern Europe and the legs produced are considered delicacies.

A great number of wild-growing mushrooms are regularly collected in the forested areas of the temperate and tropical zones. In addition, many temperate lands are regularly harvested for berries, such as lingonberries, blueberries, bilberries, and cloudberries. Bogs are scanned for cranberries. The tundra Eskimos of Alaska preserve cloudberries as a source of vitamin C for the long winter season. Good harvest years provide the needs for years of low crops.

Wild fruits and seeds were more significant to human feeding in early days. Acorns often served as food in Asia, North America, and Europe. An expert in the field even presented the hypothesis that acorns once were more important than grain to the human diet. Several seeds, especially nuts, used to be ground into flour after extracting bitter substances (tannins). In years with poor harvest, tree bark was used for the same purpose. In certain Siberian regions a milklike beverage is made from pine-cone seeds. Cone seeds have been and still are food for several North American Indian tribes and are currently on the market as piñon nuts. Earth almonds, the fat-rich tiny tubers of a tall rush plant, serve the same purpose in the Mediterranean region. In Spain a refreshing beverage called horchata is made from such tubers. They are also eaten directly and constitute important supplementary food in Ethiopia, in tropical Africa (zulu nuts), and in India.

In principle, aquatic foods—both fish and shellfish—belong to the wild-life contributions. They are discussed in Chapter 6.

REFERENCES AND RECOMMENDATIONS
FOR FURTHER READING

Aykroyd, W. R., *The Story of Sugar.* Chicago: Quadrangle Books, 1967. 160 pp.

Bodenheimer, F. S., *Insects as Human Food.* The Hague: Junk, 1951. 352 pp.

Child, R., *Coconuts.* London: Longmans, 1964. 216 pp.

Coursey, D. G., *Yams.* London: Longmans, 1967. 230 pp.

Dassman, R. F., *African Game Ranching.* Oxford: Pergamon Press, 1964. 152 pp.

FAO, *Indicative World Plan for Agricultural Development.* 2 vols., 1970. 672 pp.

FAO, *The State of Food and Agriculture.* Annual Report of the Food and Agriculture Organization of the United Nations.

Grist, D. N., *Rice.* London: Longmans, 1953. 308 pp.

Hartley, W. W. S., *The Oil Palm.* London: Longmans, 1967. 706 pp.

Jones, W. O., *Manioc in Africa.* Stanford: Stanford University Press, 1959. 315 pp.

Ovington, J. D. (ed.), *The Better Use of the World's Fauna for Food.* London: Institute of Biology, 1963. 175 pp.

Riedman, S. R., *World Provider: The Story of Grass.* London, New York, Toronto: Abelard-Schuman, 1962. 191 pp.

Simmonds, N. W., *Bananas.* London: Longmans, 1959. 460 pp.

Simoons, F. J., *Eat Not This Flesh.* Madison: University of Wisconsin Press, 1967. 241 pp.

Stefansson, V., *Not by Bread Alone.* New York: Macmillan, 1946. 239 pp.

REVIEW AND RESEARCH QUESTIONS

1. Discuss the role of cereal grains (*or* the tuber foods, *or* the pulses) in world feeding.

2. Sugar has been called both a malefactor and benefactor to mankind. What are some of the reasons for these differences of opinion?

3. What kind of foods were available to the American Indians, which crops did they give the world, and what did the white man introduce to the Americas?

4. What are the advantages or disadvantages of tuber foods with respect to their growth, storage, and nutritional characteristics?

5. Discuss whether honey is a plant or animal product.

6. What are the nutritional characteristics of nuts and what kind of nuts and nut products are available on the food market in the United States?

7. Review what fats are available to the well-to-do world and the hungry world, respectively.

8. Why are fruits (or vegetables) generally included in human diets? Discuss some kinds which are particularly important to people in the United States, Latin America, India, or the Mediterranean region.

9. Define "milk" and discuss its composition.

10. What kinds of meat are used as food? Are there regional differences in this regard?

11. Review what wild sources of food are currently exploited in the United States or in some other part of the world.

Prerequisites for Crop Production 2

The transition from the hunting and gathering stage to controlled crop production is often presented as the most important dividing line in human history. Undoubtedly the emergence of organized agriculture meant the beginning of an entirely new era. From obtaining his food by collecting wild plants, especially their seeds and fruits, in forests and grasslands, by game hunting, or by a nomadic existence with grazing livestock, man settled down and relied upon what the soil produced of food and feed crops under his management. In all likelihood, centuries of empirical experiences provided the basis for this development. Climate and the condition of the soils determined the yield. To begin with the plains and grasslands were cultivated. In many climate zones agricultural land was conquered from the forest. The slash-and burn technique was employed in both warm and temperate regions. Naturally the transition to organized agriculture did not take place simultaneously all over the globe, and in some remote areas tribes still live as hunters and gatherers or as nomadic cattle raisers.

THE LAND

The topsoil

Topsoil is necessary for the growth of plants. Different kinds of soil have emerged through the degradation of the rock and in interplay with the climate during thousands of years. Complex soil classification systems have been developed both for temperate and tropical regions. In principle all soils consist of a series of layers (horizons) in various stages of weathering. The upper layer, called the topsoil, is of prime importance to field crops. But the subsoil layers also exert influence. Below the topsoil a densely packed layer called hardpan is sometimes found; this is little penetrable to the roots and may affect the movement of water.

Distinctions are made between clay soils and sandy soils, arid soils and moist soils, porous soils and compact soils. Soils are characterized by their particle sizes: sandy soils have large and clay soils minute particles. The compact soils impede the movement of water and air. These basic differences influence plant productivity. The development of the plants, in particular the roots, depends upon the availability of water and the amount of dissolved nutrients. The spread of the roots is decisive for the nutritional uptake of the plant. Root growth and metabolism are also affected as well as movements of soil animals. Heavy equipment may induce compaction and reduce root and water penetration.

Humus and microorganisms

The ability of the soil to retain water depends to a high degree on its content of organic matter, humus. Soil poor in humus lets the water readily through and stores little for the needs of the plants. This type of soil easily dries.

The topsoil is a living world in itself. It is woven through with organic life, inhabited both by animals and billions of other organisms, primarily microorganisms, drawing their sustenance from plant residues and dead animals. The animals are insect larvae, worms, and in some regions rodents, badgers, and others. The topsoil surface is mostly covered with tiny plants called soil algae. They take part in the production of organic matter by the soil. Blue-green species function in addition as nitrogen fixers. Such algae play a key role in rice paddies.

The roots of most plants are surrounded by a galaxy of microorganisms—the rhizosphere—which most probably cooperate in protecting the plants against parasites and other intruders. Furthermore, numerous microorganisms are of utmost importance to crops by reason of their transferring minerals from the soil into their own bodies, releasing them when they die and thus making them available to the plants. Some free-living bacteria, present in many soils, have the capacity of fixing nitrogen. The total weight of the microorganisms in the topsoil may reach two or three metric tons per acre.

Man is dependent for his food upon this invisible living world within the soil. This dependence is often overlooked, as also is the fact that these invaluable helpers of his must be fed. In many instances they require more than the decomposing roots and other crop residues. To sustain these soil microorganisms man has resorted to green manuring, the plowing down into the soil of growing crops such as vetch, beans, and others. This flora of the

SOIL ORGANISMS

(metric tons per hectare)

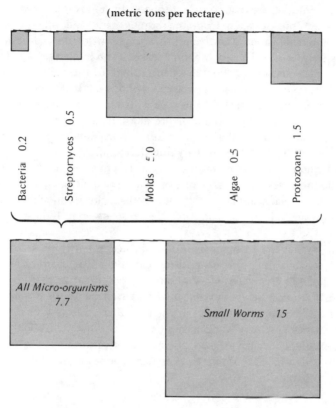

Bacteria 0.2

Streptomyces 0.5

Molds 5.0

Algae 0.5

Protozoans 1.5

All Micro-organisms 7.7

Small Worms 15

Secondary producers dominate the soil fauna and flora.

topsoil has the significant role of breaking down organic matter and releasing minerals. A rich fauna (worms, larvae, springtails) also plays an important role in this process of making nutrients available to the crops. Organic matter might otherwise accumulate in the soil and impede productivity. Yet, the humus level of the soils must be maintained not only to hold water but also in order to bind together the soil particles. Without this cohesive force the soils may be more readily eroded and carried away by rain and wind.

Minerals in the soil

The amount of minerals available to the plants for their growth and development is another factor that determines soil productivity. Primarily phosphate, potassium, and calcium are needed but in addition a score of other minerals though in lesser quantities. With each harvest considerable amounts of minerals are removed from the soil through the crops. Nitrogen is equally indispensable but is taken from the humus bank and other organics via microbial mineralization. On the subsistence farms of the old pattern these minerals were returned through animal manure and human sewage. Urbanization created a continuous and expanded tapping of these mineral reserves in the soil. To avert critical depletion these withdrawals had to be compensated through commercial fertilizers. (See the illustrations on pages 37 and 48.) Certain minerals, present only in minute amounts and therefore named trace elements, hold a key position in soil productivity. Molybdenum is a prerequisite for nitrogen fixation, cobalt for the development and growth of microorganisms, and zinc, boron, manganese, and copper are involved in several metabolic processes in plants. If one or other trace element is missing in the soil or is inadequate in quantity, it must be brought in and added to the soil. Otherwise even soil that is good in other respects may remain poorly productive or useless.

The availability of minerals in the soil hinges partly upon the mineral-releasing capabilities of microorganisms. Consequently, chemical analyses of soils do not tell the whole story about the potential for plant production. Other tests are necessary to establish what is available to the plants; there are a great many binding phenomena in the soil; there may also be disturbances of the balance, whereby various minerals affect the utilization of others. Thus, absurdly, deficiency of iron, phosphate, or calcium may appear in crops raised on soils which according to chemical analyses are fairly well provided with these compounds.

Nitrogen fixation

Nitrogen, the key ingredient in protein, has its origin in the air and thus in the pores of the soil; the soil furthermore carries several organic and inorganic nitrogenous compounds. Specific microorganisms do the trick of binding the free nitrogen, transforming it into compounds readily available for the nutritional uptake of plant crops. Leguminous plants, to which the pea and bean belong, support such nitrogen fixers in their roots, providing feed for their microbial helpers. These plants are thus independent of the erratic occurence of such bacteria in the soil. The free-living nitrogen-fixing species take their nutrients from the soil and often require for their metabolism up to one metric ton of organic matter per acre. This is a section of man's food front frequently overlooked. In modern agriculture the nitrogen fixers may be provided or supplemented through inoculating the seeds or the soil. Nitrogen-fixing blue-green algae supply irrigated rice. This presumably explains the feasibility of growing rice persistently through centuries on the same piece of

COMMERCIAL FERTILIZERS — GLOBAL USE*

Annual Averages   1962/1963-1969/1970
(millions of metric tons)

Plant Nutrients: K_2O, Potassium; P_2O_5, Phosphate; N, Nitrogen

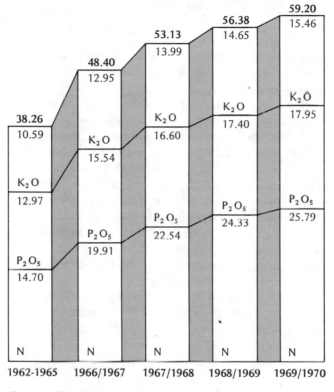

| 1962-1965 | 1966/1967 | 1967/1968 | 1968/1969 | 1969/1970 |

*Excluding China

Fertilizers replenish and supplement soil minerals.

land. Other blue-green algae, including waterblooms, have similar characteristics. In bygone times they were sun-dried into food and represented cheap protein in the diet of the poor in China, among Saharan tribes of Lake Chad, and among the Aztecs.

Soil erosion

For modern cropping, which entails extensive cultivation after sowing and between plant rows, soils without cover vegetation are a prerequisite. A consequence is increased exposure to the erosive effects of rain, wind, and drought. Where rainfall is persistent, soil minerals are leached. But the sheer mechanical force of raindrops, especially in heavy downpours, as well as that of strong winds, directly carries away soil particles. The drier the soil, the more is lost to the wind. These phenomena, resulting in removal of topsoil and loss of fertility, are termed soil erosion. In consequence of man's intervention considerable damage has been done this way throughout history, which in turn has led to the demise of many a flourishing civilization. FAO (the Food and Agriculture Organization of the United Nations) estimates that about one-sixth of the world's agricultural land suffers from wind and water erosion.

The best protection against this soil degradation is provided by maintaining a plant cover. The roots weave through the soil and tie together the particles so that they are not easily carried away. But when the fields are plowed and left exposed during a fallow season or immediately before and after sowing, they are in particular exposed to the vagaries of the weather. This is in contrast to regions with a natural vegetation cover. The forest plays a significant role in protecting the soil moisture not only by breaking winds but also by catching precipitation (rain, fog, and snow). It thus helps collect moisture in its own soil and facilitates a more even distribution of water to soils surrounding groves or forest lands. In a few instances forests return to the atmosphere through their own growth more water than they manage to receive or collect and are then desiccating to the soil.

The unrelenting increase in human numbers has forced man to expand his tilled acreage in order to procure more food. Beginning in the plains and fertile river valleys he was gradually forced to plant up the hillsides, to break the pastures through plowing, and above all to clear the forest. In both Australia and sub-Saharan Africa too many livestock on natural pastures were allowed to overgraze and destroy the vegetation cover. Many deserts and wastelands have been created in this way. This is still happening, evidenced by deserts expanding and intruding into such overused borderlands.

Forest once covered major parts of the Mediterranean region and the Middle East. These areas were, however, filled with people by the beginning of the Christian era. On the plains of India and China, once forest covered, only lone trees remain. On the European continent the forest acreage has diminished steadily and little is left in inhabited regions. The forests in the northern United States, in Michigan, and in many other regions were virtually stripped off during the past hundred years. The same destiny befell forested enclaves on most of the Caribbean and African islands. Not the least drastic was the burning and removal of the forests of New Zealand, the greatest wholesale forest destruction in history. Large-scale stripping of the virgin forests of tropical Africa, southeastern Africa, and South America is now underway. Only the U.S.S.R., Canada, Sweden, and Finland have a reserve left of any magnitude that counts. Disregarding the value of the forest as such as a source of timber, food, and lumber for paper products, man has thus through forest devastation lost his best ally in the battle against soil erosion. Yet more than 40 percent of the forest outtake (in the developing world 80 percent) is still used as fuel, often for cooking food.

The most important countermeasure against soil erosion in noncultivated soils is therefore, in most areas, reforestation. On slopes the soil is easily leached of its mineral content and also swept away by wind and water. In order to check erosion in cultivated soil, man early resorted to contour plowing, (making his furrows follow the terrain gradients in lieu of running straight) or to terracing (a practice extremely costly in manpower for main-

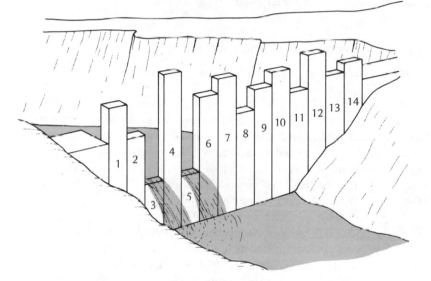

1. Light
2. Water
3. Farm Management
4. Carbon Dioxide
5. Soil Fertility
6. Fertilizing
7. Weed Control
8. Plant (Row) Distances; Rotation Schemes
9. Varieties (Selection of Crop)
10. Disease and Pest Control (Spray Programs)
11. Seed Control, Choice of Variety and Kind of Crop
12. Time of Harvesting (Sowing)
13. Climate (Rain, Temperature, etc.)
14. Equipment

Each stave indicates a major factor crucial to crop results. If one such factor fails to be put into play, this limits the holding capacity of the dam. The optimal fulfillment and coordination of those needs constitute the embankment, catching the productive flow from the sun's energy into the feed crops.

tenance). Contour plowing is sometimes used also on large open fields. Soil management has become a science but despite large-scale measures in many countries, the world's annual loss of tilled land due to erosion is estimated at 15 million acres, maybe more—equivalent to twice the tilled acreage of Sweden or to the total tilled land of Japan. Many more millions of acres are damaged to a greater or lesser degree, resulting in lower yields.

Most modern agricultural methods have been developed for application in temperate regions. When introduced to tropical or subtropical areas with entirely different climatic conditions, they frequently cause serious damage via erosion; witness the big losses of soil from banana and coffee plantations and the like. If we are to give effective aid to the developing countries, most of which are in the warm latitudes, we must employ cultivation techniques which maintain the soil productivity under those particular conditions. We often discover that our methods are less applicable.

Fallowing and double cropping

With the slash-and-burn technique of early days, the ash from burnt forest trees and bush as well as humus from the disintegrating roots offers good additional mineral fertilizing. As a rule the yield from burnt-over fields was initially high, but after a few years the productivity declined noticeably. The land was then abandoned and a new plot obtained in some other area by repeating the same procedure of burning the vegetation cover. Subsistence agriculture in many parts of the tropics (Malaysia, Indonesia, Brazil, Venezuela, Congo, for examples) still hinges upon shifting cultivation. The Indians of Central and South America, as well as many tribal Africans, still practice such shifting cultivation, but with one major difference: due to the rapid growth of the population it has become necessary to return to previously used land much earlier than before, often after as few as three years, when the soil has not as yet had time to build up its fertility again. In far too many instances cultivation has become permanent, thus jeopardizing the future of the soils.

Even in regions where agriculture has gradually become more permanent, it is frequently difficult to maintain the productivity level. Growers then resort to fallowing—leaving the soil untilled for one or two seasons. This method, still prevalent in many parts of the globe, has one or two chief aims, namely to give the soil a chance to collect enough water to ensure a normal yield or to give microorganisms and organic decomposition a chance to release minerals. This latter kind of fallow has gradually disappeared from all regions where full-scale commercial fertilizing is being practiced. By contrast, water-restoring fallows are still to be found in many arid and semiarid regions, among them the grain-producing prairies of North America, particularly

RICE YIELDS (100 kg/ha)
Annual Average   1967-1970

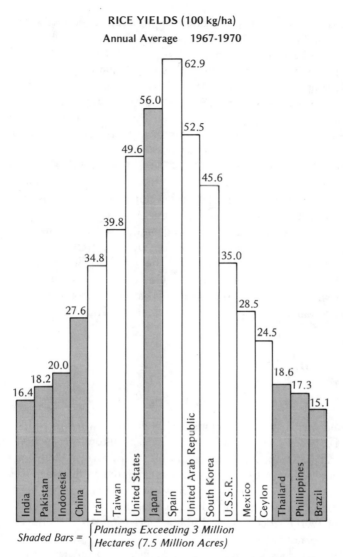

Shaded Bars = { Plantings Exceeding 3 Million / Hectares (7.5 Million Acres) }

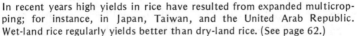

In recent years high yields in rice have resulted from expanded multicropping; for instance, in Japan, Taiwan, and the United Arab Republic. Wet-land rice regularly yields better than dry-land rice. (See page 62.)

Canada, but also in precipitation-short Mexico, in parts of Argentina, and in East Africa.

The practice of fallowing is an important factor to keep in mind when comparing acre yields in regions with diverse climates. Knowing the tilled acreage is not sufficient to evaluate crop productivity correctly. The percentage of tilled land lying idle each season and thus temporarily out of cultivation needs to be acknowledged.

In areas where the climate allows year-round cropping the situation is quite the opposite. And American Indians still employ the age-old method of growing two crops simultaneously on the same field. Such double or multiple cropping is generally practiced in regions that have no winter and are well provided with water through irrigation or high precipitation. This factor, like fallowing, has to be taken into account when comparing yields between countries. Double-cropped land yields more than the figure for each individual crop would indicate.

Judged in global terms, the development during this century has brought about a steady decline of acreage under fallow. In far too many instances this has meant a more rapid depletion and dessication of the soil, in particular in regions where irrigation or adequate fertilizing have not been applied. What has happened can also be expressed in the following way: long-range benefits have been sacrificed in favor of short-range gains. Agriculture has shied away from recognizing limitations in cropping as imbedded in inadequate water resources and inadequate mineral nutrients.

THE CROPS

Seed control and seed dressing

Improved seed material, combined with purity control, is undoubtedly the most significant contributor to increased agricultural production during recent decades. Stalin, the Soviet chief of state from 1924-1953, emphasized in a nocturnal conversation with Winston Churchill in the Kremlin during the fall of 1942 that according to his view such seed control had been the single most important advance in Soviet agriculture during his lifetime. Further gains for world agriculture could be achieved in many countries where such control does not yet exist.

In early days, seed was set aside at harvest for the next year's sowing. It was rarely sorted out as to quality and was naturally often impure, mixed with seeds of various weeds. As a result yields were affected. A still graver drawback was that many soil microorganisms, especially fungi, readily invaded the seed. In many instances it became contaminated before it could be sown.

Modern seed control is a major measure in efficient weed control through the checking of purity and removal of extraneous seeds. The seed is furthermore prepared through so called seed dressing, being coated with fungicides to impede fungal attacks in the soil. In the developed world practically every country has sizeable industrial plants for such seed preparation. This constitutes a battlefront of mankind, rarely considered in the debate about the world's food, but one which may very well be one of the most important.

Plant breeding

In bygone days seeds and tubers from especially well-developed plants were set aside for the next year's sowing and planting. Breeding was achieved through selection. Modern genetics made it possible to combine and even create plant and animal strains with desirable qualities. Plant breeding had two important consequences. First, by building into crop plants greater resistance against frost and drought, it was instrumental in pushing the boundaries for cultivation toward colder as well as drier regions which earlier did not yield food. The second major consequence was the development of strains with better resistance against diseases, whereby losses due to attacks by fungi and insects have been greatly reduced.

These advances have been most significant with major crops, the most spectacular being the battle against rust fungi. This is alluded to in the Sermon on the Mount in the Bible. Reference is there made (Matthew 6:19-20) to this scourge of cereal crops and not to the rust formation on iron, as many may think. "Moth" stands for damaging insects in general, not only for moths that attack wool. Rust diseases have periodically caused famines by damage to grain crops. Without the achievements of the plant breeders, North America at the end of World War II would have been facing serious food shortage due to rust fungi. During the period 1948-1952 a new strain (15B) of wheat rust raced across the prairies with a devastating effect. If the plant breeders had not then been ready with new wheat varieties resistant against this new intruder, the situation might have gotten out of hand. Man's conquests over his foes in nature are never final. A relentless battle goes on where renewed attacks always follow upon counterattacks and where victory and defeat succeed each other in a never-ending sequence.

In connection with plant breeding most people think of increases obtained in yield per acre. They have been considerable, but not so significant as improvements in the armor against drought, frost, pests, and diseases. Augmented yield potentials usually have to be supported with larger inputs of water and nutrients, among other things. By and large, only technologically highly developed countries, located in the temperate regions and with favorable conditions for cropping, have been in a position to apply sufficient fertilizers to take advantage of the production potentialities made feasible through plant breeding. It remains to be seen whether the recent "green revolution" of Asian lands can be sustained with adequate input of water and fertilizers.

Crop rotation

Quite early in the history of plant cultivation it was discovered that the same field gave higher yields of one particular crop if preceded by some other particular crop. On that basis so-called crop rotation was introduced: the crops were arranged to succeed each other in specified sequences. Gradually it was found that seven-year to three-year cycles were the most favorable. Leguminous plants, distinguished as we have seen by the presence of nitrogen-fixing bacteria in their root system, release nitrogenous compounds to the soil and provide an excellent extra fertilizing. Such nitrogen gains are often large enough to allow for the needs of next year's cereal or root crop.

The foremost benefit of crop rotation, is, however, that it reduces the incidence of soil pathogens. If one crop is grown for several years on the same piece of land, disease agents readily build up. When the sequence is broken by inserting other crops, there is less of an increase. In several cases microorganisms surrounding the root sphere of a certain crop directly attack invading fungi or bacteria. The mineral content of the soil is also utilized more completely under rotation since the requirements of individual crops differ as to the relative amount of each mineral nutrient.

Unfortunately, the modernizing of agriculture has hampered the application of such strict crop rotations. The pressure exerted by the never-ending need to provide more people with food, be it for export or domestic consumption, has forced the raising of the same crop year after year. This is the principle behind plantations, which was first applied in the tropics. Under the pressure of more people this has gradually become the pattern also in temperate regions. In several instances crop rotation has vanished. Such monocultures favor the development of pests and diseases which specialize on a particular crop. This has forced persistent chemical fumigation of the soils, which in turn often has negative side effects in removing also such desirable organisms as earthworms and nitrogen fixers.

THE ENVIRONMENT

Chemical warfare

Modern agriculture is waging a relentless battle against invading weeds, pests, and microorganisms. Only by maintaining an almost permanent chemical barrier is it possible to hold them reasonably at bay. Yet various harmful agents frequently break through and cause substantial losses even in countries with highly developed agricultural techniques. The total loss to world agriculture on this account is enormous, never below 10 percent and frequently 20 to 30 percent or more. In Latin America annual losses from weeds, pests, and plant diseases amount to some 40 percent of the total crop.

Despite efficient spraying, losses in the field in United States agriculture rarely stay below 10 percent. The United States crop losses to weeds, pests, and diseases are rated above $8 billion annually on the average. Our victories over such foes are not final. They may go to attack in new formations, primarily through new strains with resistance to our chemicals. Since so many of their competitors are eliminated through this all-out chemical warfare, the field is often left open to such survivors. As a result such tough species or strains may become stubbornly entrenched (for instance, wild oats in cereal crops). Yet chemicals so far remain man's most potent weapon against harmful invaders.

Agricultural chemicals are costly and most poor countries cannot afford this kind of protective warfare except possibly for certain cash crops for export such as bananas and cotton. Without the benefit of a cold winter season, which checks and incapacitates harmful agents, these predominantly warm countries are inherently worse off than those located in temperate zones. Dry periods used to hamper or eliminate many of these marauders, but extended irrigation removes this control.

Weeds

Weeds infest almost every farm around the globe. Though many easy-growing weeds in the past were developed into crop plants, weeds rob the food crops of water and mineral nutrients, absorb sunlight, and compete for space. Thereby they deprive millions of people of needed food. United States agriculture spends about $2.5 billion annually on chemical spraying against some 600 kinds of such infesting plants and yet, the loss in yield on this account is estimated at about the same sum, making the total annual loss on the weed account reach $5 billion. In the hungry world, lack of chemicals and modern seed control does not mean capitulation to the weeds. On the innumerable small subsistence farms, which in poor countries account for most of the food, the campaign against these enemies is very intense. Not the least does this apply to the rice paddies where every intruder is removed by hand through almost daily inspection tours.

Microbial diseases

Not only fungi such as cereal rusts but also several bacteria attack crops. Rice crops in Japan and India are often ravaged by rice-blast disease, corn in India by stem decay and blight. Ring rot is common on potato in South America, Africa, and Asia; both India and China suffer huge annual losses from this particular disease. Gum flow and redstreak disease are two major enemies of sugar cane in the Caribbean, India, and Australia. Late blight affects beans in India and Africa. The losses caused by these agents in afflicted regions are often stated as 30 to 60 percent.

Both fungi and bacteria are themselves involved in a two-front battle. They have their own "diseases" and are in turn attacked by virus. These may also develop independently in living tissue. Such viruses are responsible for a great many severe maladies of crop plants and livestock. Best known are the virus diseases of potato and sugar beet. Others cause devastating attacks on orange groves (tristeza) in South America and cocoa plantations (swollen shoot) in Africa, often killing the trees.

Bacteria constitute attractive food to the unicellular protozoans, the most primitive of all animals. They devour bacteria both in the rumen of the cow and in the soil. Protozoa may also invade plant crops, livestock, and fish with ruinous effects. Among diseases caused by protozoa are sleeping sickness in man and livestock as well as malaria.

Pests

Recurrent crop attacks by locusts, descending in huge swarms, are described in the Bible. They still threaten man, and a persistent battle is going on, also from the air, against their breeding grounds, particularly in tropical Africa, the Middle East, Pakistan, India, and parts of Argentina and Brazil.

But the locust is not the only insect menace to man's crops. Entomologists have listed about 20,000 insect species as destructive crop pests somewhere in the world. They are attracted by different crops, on which they feed. Boring insects thrive on rice and corn, others like potato leaves. In the United States no commercial crop is produced without some protective means, and yet, the losses caused by insects amount annually to about $4 billion. Insects destroy one-twentieth of the United States wheat crop on the average—about 1 million tons of wheat a year, enough to make 2 billion loaves of bread. Many insect specimens are carriers of livestock diseases.

In many countries seed-eating birds ravage crops, in particular grain, and they frequently take a very big toll. Repellent or scaring devices are not too efficient against major attacks. Most serious, is the quelea, a bird of tropical Africa. Despite the killing of more than 100 million queleas in one year (1965), its numbers were little affected. Attacks on fruit orchards by some birds appear to have increased with more effective removal of weeds.

Many worms intrude as parasites into roots and tubers of crop plants. Best known are the tiny threadlike nematodes. Sometimes they get so prevalent that soils have to be abandoned. This menace may make it necessary to fumigate with chemicals at intervals in order to kill off these intruders, their eggs, and their larvae.

Other animal pests are rodents (rats and mice). They are a constant threat not only to stored grains but also to many growing crops. Crabs often invade wet-land rice fields. Sometimes they attack coconut palms in plantations.

THE RETURN

Productivity

Crop yields are normally measured in pounds or bushels per acre without taking into account the nutritive composition of the harvested product. Potato contains five times as much water as grain. Weight figures are thus misleading when comparing crops. Such data give no indication of nutritive value. A great deal of the yield increases in this century have involved considerable changes in the nutritive composition of the crop. The protein content has, as a rule, been declining or in any event has not mounted in step with the increase of total yield. The size of the harvest as such grew, but the cells were deceptively filled with fat or carbohydrates. The starch in the United States corn crop would suffice to provide the calorie requirement for the entire nation. If sugar beets were grown in the north and sugar cane in the south, the United States could by itself supply the entire world with calories. In both instances a catastrophic protein shortage would be the result, inducing deficiency diseases and death. In essence, it is the protein production which demands the most acreage and which sets up narrow limitations for how many the Earth can feed. Rarely do the crops yield more than 500

Crop productivity—cereal and potato

	Approximate yields from 20 metric tons		Comparable approximate yields from 1 acre, metric tons	
	Cereal	Potato	Cereal	Potato
Starch and sugar (carbohydrates)	14.00	3.80	0.70	1.43
Protein	2.40	0.40	0.12	0.15
Fat	0.40	0.02	0.02	0.008
Total organic matter	17.00	4.20	0.85	1.58
Minerals	0.46	0.20	0.023	0.075
Water	2.60	15.6	0.13	5.85
Total harvest	20.0	20.0	1.0	7.5

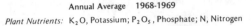

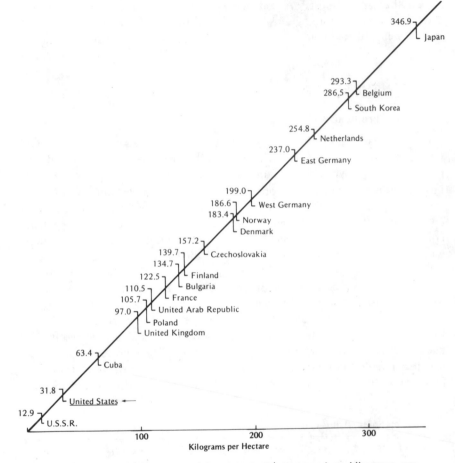

FERTILIZER USE

Annual Average   1968-1969

Plant Nutrients: K_2O, Potassium; P_2O_5, Phosphate; N, Nitrogen

346.9 ⌐ Japan

293.3 ⌐ Belgium
286.5 ⌐ South Korea

254.8 ⌐ Netherlands
237.0 ⌐ East Germany

199.0 ⌐ West Germany
186.6 ⌐ Norway
183.4 ⌐ Denmark

157.2 ⌐ Czechoslovakia
139.7 ⌐ Finland
134.7 ⌐ Bulgaria
122.5 ⌐ France
110.5 ⌐ United Arab Republic
105.7 ⌐ Poland
97.0 ⌐ United Kingdom

63.4 ⌐ Cuba

31.8 ⌐ United States ⬅

12.9 ⌐ U.S.S.R.

100   200   300
Kilograms per Hectare

Current use of fertilizers (plant nutrients) expressed as kilograms per hectare and kilograms per person. Note the very high rate of application per hectare in Japan and South Korea and per person in Scandinavia, Eastern Europe, and Oceania, in both cases above United States levels (indicated by arrow). Compare this illustration with the one on page 37.

pounds of protein per acre; the average is 240 to 290 pounds. In terms of calories many more people can be provided per acre. The lower limit for protein in man's diet is 12 percent of the calorie intake. As was pointed out in Chapter 1, the conversion losses in meat, milk, and egg production are considerable: from 90 to 50 percent of the calories and 70 to 20 percent of

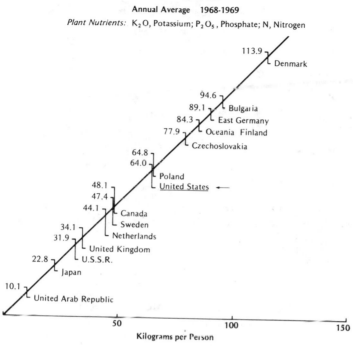

FERTILIZER USE

Annual Average   1968-1969

Plant Nutrients: K₂O, Potassium; P₂O₅, Phosphate; N, Nitrogen

Current Use of Fertilizers (Continued)

the protein. The approximate figures for crop productivity in temperate regions in two key crops, cereals and potato, picture the composition of the harvest and the yields per acre.

Measures to attain higher yields

—Land reform in the sense of either combining farms into larger units or dividing up large farms into self-owned small farms

—Improved agricultural implements

—Protection against erosion (terracing, reforestation, grass seeding, or other measures)

—Fallowing

—Seed control

—Crop rotation

—Improved strains, such as high-yielding, or resistant against drought, low temperatures (frost), fungi, insects, etc.

—Chemical seed treatment (seed dressing)

—Manuring or application of fertilizers

—Closer planting

—Weed control

—Fighting plant diseases, insects, and other pests, chiefly through spraying of chemicals

—Irrigation and water-saving devices

—More efficient harvesting methods with less field losses

—Better transportation facilities (rivers, roads, etc.)

—Water management, such as flood control and protective precautions against floods and other natural catastrophes, in particular typhoons

—Drainage

REFERENCES AND RECOMMENDATIONS
FOR FURTHER READING

Alexander, M., *Introduction to Soil Microbiology.* New York: Wiley, 1961. 472 pp.

Bear, F. E., *Soils in Relation to Crop Growth.* New York: Reinhold, 1965. 297 pp.

Bunting, B. T., *The Geography of Soil.* Chicago: Aldine, 1965. 214 pp.

Carefoot, G. L., and E. R. Sprott. *Famine on the Wind—Man's Battle against Disease.* Chicago: Rand McNally, 1967. 230 pp.

Comber, N. M., and W. N. Townsend. *An Introduction to the Scientific Study of the Soil.* London: Arnold, 1962. 230 pp.

Farb, P., *Living Earth.* New York and Evanston: Harper, 1959. 178 pp.

Hopkins, D., *Chemicals, Humus and the Soil.* New York: Chemical Publishing Co., 1957. 288 pp.

Kevan, D. K. McE., *Soil Animals.* New York: Philosophical Library, 1962. 237 pp.

Krebs, A. H., *Agriculture in Our Lives.* Danville: Interstate Printers and Publishers, 1964. 696 pp.

Leonard, W. H., and J. H. Martin. *Cereal Crops.* New York: Macmillan, 1963. 824 pp.

Murton, R. K., and E. N. Wright, *The Problems of Birds as Pests.* London and New York: Academic Press, 1968. 254 pp.

Rose, G. J., *Crop Protection.* 2nd rev. ed. New York: Chemical Publishing, 1963. 190 pp.

Wayte, M. E., *Mining the Soil.* Toronto: Claren, Irvin Co., 1963. 63 pp.

Whyte, R. O., *Crop Production and Environment*, 2nd ed. London: Faber, 1960. 392 pp.

Wilsie, C. P. *Crop Adaptation and Distribution.* San Francisco: Freeman, 1962. 448 pp.

REVIEW AND RESEARCH QUESTIONS

1. Discuss how pre-agricultural man obtained his food.

2. How would you define topsoil? List its many functions in crop growth.

3. Review the significance of roots to plant growth and crop development.

4. How is humus defined? What problems exist concerning its relationship to soil fertility and to the growth of the food crops?

5. What is meant by the rhizosphere? What are some of its possible functions?

6. Review soil biota (flora as well as fauna). What is the function of the major elements?

7. Why is application of fertilizers indispensable to modern agriculture?

8. How is nitrogen removed from the air by nitrogen fixers in agricultural fields?

9. Describe how rain (water) and wind may carry away soil (soil erosion) and discuss its relevance to cropping and food production.

10. Explain how removal of forests has changed climate, water balance and conditions for crop growth and pastures.

11. What is meant by "fallows"?

12. What role does double cropping play in raising yields?

13. Reliable yields are generally dependent upon pure seed. How is such purity achieved?

14. Give some examples of significant advances in crop production due to the breeding of new varieties.

15. How are gains in yield attained by the chemical spraying of weeds, against insects and disease fungi?

16. Can you visualize what role birds play in checking pests on crops?

17. Review the significance of one or more of the production factors listed on pages 49-50.

The Tropics 3

TROPICAL CLIMATES

Rainfall

The hot zone of the globe is generally called the tropics, sometimes defined as the regions lying between the equator and the Tropics of Cancer and Capricorn. Climatically the tropics are better characterized as those parts of the globe where the daily average temperature stays above 80°F. High-altitude areas of both South America and Africa that have pleasant, cool, characteristically temperate climate yet are located right on the equator; altitude overrules latitude.

Most significant from the point of view of food is the distinction that can be made between the *arid tropics* with possibly one brief rainy season and the *humid tropics* with regular daily downpours. Tropical lands thus may differ profoundly as to the amount of rainfall.

Short day length

One common characteristic for the entire tropics is the short day length, around 12 hours, with small fluctuations between seasons. In the rainy zones, cloudiness reduces sunshine and creates less favorable conditions for crop productivity. For this reason the arid tropics, when irrigated, produce far better than the humid tropics, where rain clouds assembling each day for afternoon rain curtail the flow of sun energy.

The high night temperatures sustain an intense metabolic activity in the plant tissue, mainly respiration, using up much organic matter accumulated through photosynthesis (light action) during the day. Hence, generally, the net yield per acre is less in the tropics than in temperate regions.

The short days and high temperatures of the tropics reduce productivity. The United States Midwest provides much more favorable conditions for cropping because the influx of sunlight during the vegetation period is larger.

THE LAND

Soil features

Deep in a tropical rain forest, where evaporation acts as a perpetual cooling agent, the temperature is as a rule lower than in the sun-drenched tree canopies. Down in the soil it is still cooler, thanks to the many insulating layers of leaves and other organic waste accumulating from the trees. When such a forest cover is removed, the soil becomes exposed to the direct radiation of the sun. As a result, the soil temperature often rises by 20° to 40°, even by as much as 60° Fahrenheit. The soil microorganisms are well adapted to the cool conditions in their domain. When the soil temperature mounts their development is at first speeded up, but their tolerance levels are soon exceeded. In the beginning the degradation of organic matter is accelerated and the soils rapidly drop in humus content. New humus forms too slowly to replace this, and the soils finally become almost dead, showing little microbial life. A series of chemical oxidation processes gradually become a dominant feature and less favorable conditions develop for plant growth. Furthermore, such soils easily fall victim to destruction through water and wind. Despite intense research, it has so far not been possible to find agricultural techniques which sustain the productive capacity of tropical soils when permanently cultivated. Paddy rice in fields with abundant water resources is one notable exception, but with many unique features.

Soil nutrients

When the organic matter that binds soil particles together is lost or is in jeopardy, poor cohesion results. Wind and water therefore often operate more destructively in the tropics, eroding away the topsoil. Daily heavy downpours in particular leach out minerals rapidly, often as fast as they are released from decaying plant matter or organisms such as worms, larvae, insects, and mites dying off in the topsoil. Fertilizers, when added, are lost in the same way, and the growing crops have accordingly less time to pick up the nutrients for growth. Because of these complications a sack of fertilizer is as a rule far more effectively utilized on a Michigan or Iowa farm than for instance in central Brazil.

In contrast, many tropical soils show peculiar binding phenomena, withdrawing such essential nutrients as phosphates from ready availability to growing plants. Some tropical soils are persistently replenished with nutrients through volcanic ash, rich in minerals. The regular rains contribute in this instance to rapid fertilizing through the air. This factor is the key to the rich soils of Java as contrasted to most of the outlying Indonesian islands, which are nonvolcanic and as a result less fertile and less populous.

Soil quality

Tropical crops have to sustain high soil temperatures. The lush vegetation of the jungle misled early colonizers into believing that these soils were far superior to those of the temperate regions. The greenhouse conditions which characterize these lands would seem to create ideal conditions for luxuriant foliage and rich crops. This is largely a deception. Much of the apparent richness is due to large amounts of water in the leaves; the net content, measured in dry matter, is low. Seemingly lush pastures poorly sustain cattle grazing. Not only do cattle get too little substance, but they also trample down much more than they eat. In the dry tropics the seasonality restricts the usefulness of pastures to a very brief period. In both instances livestock has to be provided with extensive supplementation. On the whole, grazing becomes a questionable procedure. The costly technique of temperate regions, with harvesting coupled to drying or silaging, becomes advisable despite the apparently ideal climate.

COMPETITORS IN THE ENVIRONMENT

Foes on the rampage

The most detrimental feature of the tropics is the fact that man's foes in the shape of pests, diseases, and weeds almost constantly are on the rampage. Those who have the privilege to live in a temperate climate do not realize the invaluable asset winters are, wiping out or at any rate incapacitating insects, larvae, fungi, bacteria, and other harmful agents. In the tropics there is little letup. In arid regions with only a brief rainy period, the shortage of water used to exert a similar salutary effect. But as irrigation spread over such areas, this advantage was lost. Most pests and diseases of man, livestock, and crops have as a result gained a firm foothold through man's intervention, or at any rate become a greater menace.

This ever-present threat partly explains why plant diseases and livestock epizootics frequently are far more disastrous in these warm lands. Among examples are the rust fungi that eradicated coffee in Ceylon, the rinderpest that wiped out millions of cattle in tropical Africa, coffee blight in Brazil, and several diseases that time and again threaten to eliminate bananas. Another factor has been the introduction of large-scale crop-raising in plantations and the creation of big herds of livestock. In both instances little time or chance remains to build up gradually a countervailing resistance. In the name of efficiency also, small farm operations were switched from the traditional pattern. Several crops of different kinds used to be mixed on their small lots, often temporarily grabbed from the forest through a slash-and-burn technique. In the name of efficiency the number of crops was reduced and cultivation was made more permanent. Both circumstances favored invasions by man's foes, whether rodents, birds, insects, or fungi. Big fields with one single crop (monoculture) and huge establishments for the raising of livestock have even in cooler latitudes greatly compounded the hazards for large-scale attacks. In warm regions, with no letup in the propagation of disease agents, this menace is even greater.

Animal husbandry hampered

Unfortunately, the narrow margin of existence for livestock in the warm belts of the tropics has so far been poorly recognized. The grasslands rarely allow grazing as in temperate regions, and the feed supply is often inadequate. The heat forces nighttime grazing, which is not efficient. Frequently the animals are forced to walk over considerably larger pasture areas than are optimal in order to find the nourishment they need. Hungry weeks often stretch out into hungry months for the animals before the rainy season comes. Diseases are spread by various kinds of insects to such a degree that in many regions, as in the pampas and llanos of South America, animals must be dipped in chemical baths as often as each tenth day; otherwise pests and parasites retain their foothold. In many areas sheep, cattle, swine, goats, and even ducks are walked to the stockyards over long distances. This means high transportation costs, directly measureable in weight losses and diminished meat output.

There are thus numerous reasons other than backwardness why the livestock of the developing countries produce so much less than ours. The average age at slaughter for beef cattle in Africa is two to four years; in the United States it is less than two years. In warm Brazil meat animals must be kept twice as many years as in the cooler Argentina. Despite the higher slaughter age, the meat yield is lower: 135 to 155 pounds in Africa, 45 to 80 pounds in Pakistan, as against 350 to 400 pounds in the United States. In several developing countries the milk output of the cow is scarcely one-tenth to one-twentieth of the yield reached in dairy countries such as Holland and Denmark.

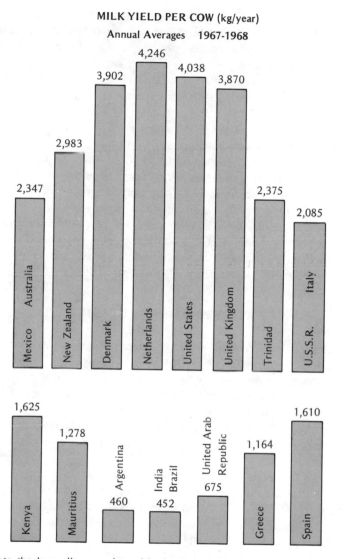

MILK YIELD PER COW (kg/year)
Annual Averages 1967-1968

Note the huge discrepancies, with the United States almost top-ranking.
Compare with tables on pages 213 and 214.

A TREACHEROUS PARADISE

What has been said above suggests why the tropics are no paradise overflowing with abundance. There are no shortcuts, magic tricks, or technical gadgets whereby man could easily overcome the hazards raised by Nature. Through bitter experience he has learned that he has to tread carefully. Western man has also gained great respect for the many civilizations that early flourished in these regions, but through the centuries their populations grew and decline set in—they became too many. The tropics offer less opportunities to the future billions of the world than the temperate regions. Their potentialities are as a rule grossly overrated. History and the fragile basis for life in those latitudes give man many a basic lesson which he ought to heed.

Even so, the few remaining potential areas for expanded cultivation by man lie in the tropics. The rain-forest lands of the Congo and the huge Amazon basin constitute the two major assets. Decades of studies by the Ford Foundation in the Amazon and by Belgian agronomists in the Congo have strongly confirmed the fragility of these regions when confronted with modern techniques of cultivation. Entirely new procedures need to be devised, with better awareness of the subtle interplay between climate, soils, and living nature. This will take time and patience, partly entirely new approaches and partly incorporation of time-tested devices.

HUNGRY WEEKS AND WORN-OUT SOILS

A characteristic feature of many tropical lands, largely relying on regional production, is the inadequacy of total food production. When drought, diseases, floods, or typhoons reduce output, the crops easily become too small to last—even when storage facilities are adequate—until the next harvest. People go hungry for weeks, sometimes for months. This phenomenon is a clear indication of the shortcomings of production. It leads to recurrent migrations as in the northeast of Brazil, and to extended stays of migrant workers in the factory cities of South Africa.[1]

In many regions of Latin America, tropical Asia, and Africa, the pressure of growing numbers has forced subsistence growers to shorten the resting periods for their soils; forest or shrub is cleared again for tilling before it can recover. Malnutrition and hunger become more severe and reach a crisis stage when such clearings are worked permanently. Depletion and erosion may then accelerate the destruction of the topsoil.

REFERENCES AND RECOMMENDATIONS
FOR FURTHER READING

Caswell, G. N., *Agricultural Entomology in the Tropics*. London: Arnold, 1962. 152 pp.

---

[1] F. Muhlenberg, *Wanderarbeit in Sudafrika*. Stuttgart, G. Fischer, 1967, 267 pp.

Davies, W., and C. L. Skidmore. *Tropical Pastures.* London: Faber, 1966. 215 pp.

Garlick, J. P., and A. W. J. Keats (eds.), *Human Ecology in the Tropics.* Oxford and New York: Pergamon Press, 1970. 112 pp.

Gourou, P., *The Tropical World* (transl. from French). New York: Wiley, 1966. 196 pp.

Hodder, B. W., *Economic Development in the Tropics.* London: Methuen, 1968. 258 pp.

Millikan, N. F., and D. Hapgood. *No Easy Harvest.* Boston: Little, Brown, 1967. 178 pp.

Phillipps, J. F. V., *The Development of Agriculture and Forestry in the Tropics.* New York: Praeger, 1961. 163 pp.

Steel, R. W. and R. M. Prothero (eds.), *Geographers and the Tropics.* London: Longmans, 1964. 375 pp.

Taylor, C. J. *Tropical Forestry.* New York: Oxford University Press, 1962. 163 pp.

Webster, C. C. and P. N. Wilson, *Agriculture in the Tropics.* London: Longmans, 1966. 488 pp.

Whyte, R. O., *Milk Production in Developing Countries.* London: Faber, 1967. 240 pp.

Williamson, G., and W. J. A. Payne, *An Introduction to Animal Husbandry in the Tropics.* London: Longmans, 1965. 447 pp.

Wrigley, G., *Tropical Agriculture.* London: Faber, 1969. 376 pp.

REVIEW AND RESEARCH QUESTIONS

1. Why did the tropics appear to be a green paradise to early explorers?

2. What are the advantages versus disadvantages of the short tropical day?

3. Discuss microbial life in the soil under tropical conditions.

4. Why are pests and diseases as a rule more destructive and persistent in the tropics than in the temperate world?

5. Review some of the complications facing animal husbandry in the tropics.

6. Why are areas with tropical rain forests difficult to put under the plow and retain in agricultural use?

7. Discuss signs of inadequacies in providing food in the warm lands.

Crops and Water   4

Water is the decisive and in most instances the chief limiting factor in the growing of crops and raising of animals. Practically all life processes of the plant depend on water. This is pumped via the root hairs into the vascular strands of the roots; thence, through special mechanisms, it is carried further up into the stem and the leaves; finally it evaporates into the air. Alongside this physiological process, the *transpiration*, a direct *evaporation* is taking place from soil and plants. The magnitude of this is determined by the temperature of the air and its content of water. No clear-cut differentiation can be made between these two processes. They are, as a consequence, difficult to measure separately. The term evapotranspiration was created for this very reason. Many factors determine its volume, such as how close the plants stand and how intensely they transpire. This in turn depends on active physiological processes such as respiration and photosynthesis. The size of the plants, their structure (both as regards leaf anatomy and the overall build-up of the plant), and the position of the leaves in relation to the light inflow are also vital. Leaves often arrange themselves into mosaic patterns that cast a minimum of shadow on each other. Other critical factors are the pumping efficiency of the roots and—not least—the sun-energy influx.

WATER FROM THE ATMOSPHERE

The rainfall pattern

Wheat and rice are both harvested somewhere on the globe every month of the year, not only because of the season reversal between the northern and the southern hemispheres but also because of characteristic features of the rainfall, whether dependable, regular, or intermittent. Seasonality of rain in relation to crop-growing periods is furthermore crucial. Although precipitation is essential to crop yields, rainfall may nevertheless put harvesting and sowing into jeopardy. These are factors not always taken into account by persons habituated to the rather regular seasonal changes of temperate latitudes.

Other peculiarities may affect yields. Annual rainfall may be quite plentiful, yet be insufficient to grow acceptable crops. Rain in off-season periods, when no products grow, becomes useful only under two conditions: either if the soil can soak it up and hold it for later use or if it can be collected in dams and reservoirs.

Another kind of fluctuation is also decisive, namely the distribution of the precipitation over years. Once again, though mathematically calculated average rainfall may look reassuring, cropping can be very hazardous if the average is the result of precipitation-rich years interspersed with dry years; both may be harmful. In the one, destructive floods may occur; in the other, droughts may be devastating to crops and livestock.

Snow features

Snow is a form of precipitation with its own features, not always reflected in amount of melted water. Over large portions of the temperate region snow renders excellent protection to the soil, its microorganisms, and growing plants. Snow insulates against extreme temperatures and desiccating winds. Winter grains get warm protection this way. In areas short of rain, as in major parts of the U.S.S.R. and in some parts of the prairies, snow can be collected by placing fences across the pathways of its drift. Snow when melting becomes more readily available to the soil below if the thaw extends into the topsoil. Otherwise run-off may erode surface topsoil. When snow stays on the ground too long, some cold-loving fungi may attack the young plants of winter grain.

WATER NEEDS

Two kinds of rice and wheat

Rice of the lowland or wetland type is in general cultivated on permanently irrigated soil. Highland or upland rice manages on rainfed areas or through temporary irrigation, but as a result its yields are lower than those of wetland strains. In many parts of India and Indonesia highland rice is common; most rice grown in Japan belongs to the wetland type. For this very reason acre-yields of India and Japan cannot be compared on a nationwide basis.

There are likewise two distinct kinds of wheat, namely winter wheat and spring wheat. Winter wheat, sown in the fall, enjoys a ten-month vegetation period that includes a rest period when the plantlets are covered by snow. The vegetation period of spring wheat, sown in the spring, is limited to four months. Winter wheat is much more demanding as to climate. To protect it against excessive frost and desiccating winds, it requires less severe winters, guaranteeing an adequate frost-free period, or else efficient insulating snow cover so long as frost remains in the soil. Spring wheat needs a frost-free period of 90 to 100 days. As a rule winter wheat renders higher yield per acre than spring wheat. This is only reversed in case winter wheat is killed by extreme winter temperatures, by harsh drying winds in the spring with little snow protection, or by fungal attacks under the snow cover. There is always the risk of late frost damaging spring-sown crops.

When comparing wheat yields between countries, it is important to check that the same kind of wheat is involved. Highly misleading comparisons are for this very reason made between Soviet and United States wheat yields. The United States crop is dominated by winter varieties and that of the U.S.S.R. by spring types. (See the illustration on page 25.)

The water requirements of crops

Both winter and spring wheat uses as a minimum 12 to 14 inches of rain for a regular crop. To assure this, the annual precipitation needs to be considerably higher, around 25 to 30 inches; in India 60 inches or more since more evaporates. Any additional water boosts the yield; in Kansas 0.5 inch produces an extra bushel per acre. In case of heavy precipitation wheat may become lodged through excessive growth, seeds start to germinate and mildew diseases or root rots gain ground.

When shortage of water intervenes, growth is impeded and in later stages seeds are shed. In some parts of the world (Pakistan, sections of India, and parts of Mexico) wheat is irrigated although basically a semiarid crop. In rain-short areas water is collected through fallowing, still commonly practiced in the dry prairies of Canada.

Lowland rice demands a minimum rainfall of 40 to 50 inches per year. As a rule this requires irrigation and in many cases the rice fields are placed under water permanently. Corn needs primarily heat and at least 20 inches of water for acceptable yield, implying far higher rainfall. Few regions of Europe and the Soviet Union are warm enough to be suited for the raising of corn. Millet is the least water-demanding grain crop and thrives in areas too dry or too warm for other cereals, for instance northern China, central India, and parts of Central and South Africa.

Most cereals originated in semiarid regions and are ecologically tied to this type of climate. In general, arid conditions or drought cause drastic yield curtailments as compared to years with normal rainfall. Water is, in other words, the cardinal factor in crop yields. In plant cropping, as in most phases of animal production, the water use is consumptive; that is, the water evaporates into the air and becomes part of nature's hydrological cycle.

By and large, the wheat yields of the temperate regions require 300 pounds of water (35 to 40 gallons) to produce one pound of organic matter. For each pound of kernel there are about three pounds of leaves and stems above the soil surface and about three pounds of roots, all demanding corresponding amounts of water. These ratios mean that for every harvested pound of wheat about 2,000 pounds (250 gallons) of water is needed. A one-pound bread loaf accordingly requires at least 250 gallons of water or 15 to 16 gallons for each one-oz. slice of bread. Lowland rice is the most water-demanding among the grain crops and requires 10,000 pounds (1,200 gallons) per pound of rice kernel. Such a high water requirement is a crucial matter in many Asian countries. Potato is another crop which consumes considerably more water than wheat, 800 pounds (100 gallons) per pound of dry matter.

Grass crops are in particular voracious in demand for water—1,000 to 1,500 pounds (125 to 200 gallons) per pound of harvested green bulk matter. This partly explains why animal products demand seemingly unreasonable amounts of water. The well-being of animals and their productive capability is both directly and indirectly affected by the availability of water. About 1,200 gallons of water is required for the production of one quart of milk, and 3,700 gallons for one pound of beef.

In the warm regions of the globe evaporation is more intense. A good rule of thumb is that in such parts of the globe the rainfall available in runoff or to crops is thus reduced by about half. Therefore 20 inches in Michigan corresponds in productive efficiency to 40 inches in Brazil, the Congo, or Indonesia. This can also be expressed by saying that for the same amount of organic matter twice as much water is needed in warm as compared to temperate climates. This discrepancy becomes still greater in truly arid regions under irrigation.

IRRIGATION

When natural precipitation is inadequate for obtaining acceptable yields but other prerequisites for cropping are favorable, recourse may be had to irrigation from lakes, rivers, or groundwater. Another procedure practiced since ancient days is to collect excessive rain in reservoirs, in extreme cases to store such water from one season to the next, mostly from a rainy period to a

WATER REQUIREMENTS FOR DAILY FOOD
IN THE UNITED STATES

Water for Selected Items (gallons)

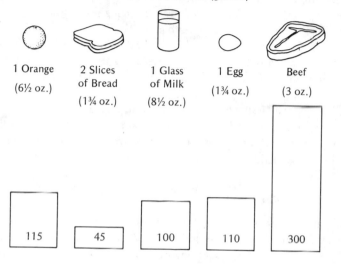

1 Orange (6½ oz.)	2 Slices of Bread (1¾ oz.)	1 Glass of Milk (8½ oz.)	1 Egg (1¾ oz.)	Beef (3 oz.)
115	45	100	110	300

Water for Average Daily Food Intake

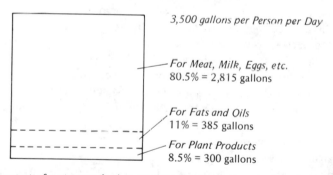

3,500 gallons per Person per Day

For Meat, Milk, Eggs, etc.
80.5% = 2,815 gallons

For Fats and Oils
11% = 385 gallons

For Plant Products
8.5% = 300 gallons

Amount of water required to produce five major items in daily food (top). Total amount of water required to raise the average daily food in the United States (below). The figures take into account the water needed to grow the required feed.

subsequent dry season. In some tropical and subtropical countries, double cropping or even multiple cropping may be made feasible by applying irrigation.

It was not until the past hundred years that large-scale irrigation was instituted and became a cornerstone of world agriculture. China has the largest irrigated acreage of all countries, three times more than second-ranking India, which also is showing major extensions during the period since World War II. During the 1950's, China greatly expanded its irrigation by improving the service to land earlier irrigated and by bringing water to additional fields, the two efforts together serving more than 100 million acres.[1]

The West, the Soviet Union, Africa, and Latin America have followed suit. Even regions with good rainfall are resorting to supplementary irrigation since every yield increase has its water price and natural precipitation no longer is enough.

Although this century has seen a fourfold increase in irrigated lands and through present major projects further project a doubling prior to the year 2000, man on the whole has, in his quest for food, created far more desert lands than the arid lands he has made blossom.

Complications of irrigation

In many parts of the globe new land has been made available for agriculture through irrigation but there are limitations. In developing countries water is not always available in adequate amounts and moreover the soils are often poor in minerals and do not respond to irrigation. To obtain an adequate return in yield, an appropriate amount of fertilizer must also be supplied. In addition, the high evaporation in warm latitudes from open reservoirs and canals must be taken into account. Finally, reservoirs and canals frequently are short-lived since they get filled with silt and sand carried by the water; this is an especially acute consideration when upstream areas have been stripped of their forest cover in the quest for tillable land.

Groundwater sources are everywhere tapped for cropping purposes, often excessively. As a result the water table has fallen to critical levels where pumping becomes uneconomic or the wells dry up.

In many instances there is no adequate replenishment from rains. The improved crops use more of the rain than the unirrigated vegetation, hence less is available for seepage and for refill of the groundwater. In large parts of the world, water shortage has therefore become the most serious obstacle to increased yields. Though availability of water unquestionably determines the final limit to what can be accomplished through development, only rarely have such studies been made; water has almost always been taken for granted.

---

[1] Buchanan, V., *The Chinese People and the Chinese Earth.* London: Bell & Sons, 1966. 94 pp.

It is most unfortunate that Western man assumed that his agricultural procedures, in general developed in temperate zones of the globe where they served him well, would be equally effective in the tropics. Nature's rebuffs were smarting and have taught would-be developers many useful lessons, some of which have been only tardily recognized. Several of these are discussed in the chapter about the tropics.

In summary: These lessons as to water were that many complications affect the soils, variously by extensive leaching in the humid parts, by rapid salination in arid regions, and by greater susceptibility to erosion. Ecologically the seemingly favorable parameters for luxuriant plant growth and thriving animal life extend to man's competitors and foes weeds, pests, and diseases. Both droughts and floods are more destructive in the tropics than in temperate regions. Life on the whole operates on a much more fragile and hazardous basis in the tropics, and so far experience proves in these regions that man's dominion is much more difficult to sustain.

REFERENCES AND RECOMMENDATIONS
FOR FURTHER READING

Borgstrom, G., *Too Many—A Study of Earth's Biological Limitations.* New York: Macmillan, 1969. 368 pp. (Paperback: Collier Macmillan, 1971.)

Furon, R., *The Problem of Water—A World Study,* (Transl. from French). New York: American Elsevier, 1967. 208 pp.

Hillel, D., *Soil and Water.* New York: Academic Press, 1971. 288 pp.

Hogan, R. M., H. R. Haise, and T. W. Edminster (eds.), *Irrigation of Agricultural Lands.* Madison: American Society of Agronomy, 1967. 1180 pp.

Kramer, P. J., *Plant and Soil Water Relationships.* New York: McGraw-Hill, 1969. 482 pp.

Walton, K., *The Arid Zones.* London: Hutchinson, University Library, 1969. 176 pp.

REVIEW AND RESEARCH QUESTIONS

1. Define evapotranspiration and discuss its significance to crop production.

2. Review different kinds of fluctuations in rainfall as affecting crop yields.

3. Is snow valuable to subsequent crops?

4. What are the differences between wetland (or lowland) as against upland rice?

5. What distinguishes winter wheat from spring wheat?

6. How much water is required for the production of an average daily food supply to each American?

7. Discuss how much of the rainfall becomes available to crops in temperate regions as contrasted to tropical areas, recognizing the distinctive features of arid and humid regions.

8. Review the disadvantages which reduce the efficiency of irrigation dams in arid regions.

Livestock
and Poultry

5

General statistics indicate that livestock are approximately as numerous as humans, around 3.5 billion. To this may be added an equal number of poultry. But such figures are not adequate to convey clearly the place of livestock in each individual country and what is needed for their production. Total weight varies with breed and country, amount of feed, and how efficiently feed is utilized. Additional information is needed, requiring thorough studies which are not always available. In most cases we can, however, get a general idea of the animals' role as competitors with man for plant feed. Employing available data as to the average size of the animals and their nutritional needs, I have computed, for countries as well as for continents, their equivalence to humans as consumers of the world's key nutrient protein, often in crucially short supply. Estimated in this way, as protein consumers, the world's cattle corresponded in 1967 to a number approximately twice that of man. The horses, despite the decline in their numbers because of mechanization, still correspond to 675 million people. The hogs correspond to half the number of people; the sheep barely exceed the equivalent of a billion; the poultry, somewhat more than a billion.

Through the feed they eat in the form of plant products, such as grass, hay, silage, feed grain, oilseed, livestock utilize an amount of organic plant matter four times the direct human consumption. The meat, milk, and eggs produced, however, benefit only a small portion of the world population. And much animal produce does not feed people—the well-nourished part of the world allows itself the extravagance of feeding its livestock such products as nonfat milk solids, skim milk, fish meal, meat meal, and whey. In professional language this is called tertiary production, while the animal production based on the primary plant production is termed secondary.

BIOMASS IN THE BIOSPHERE OF MAN   1968-1969

(millions of population equivalents)

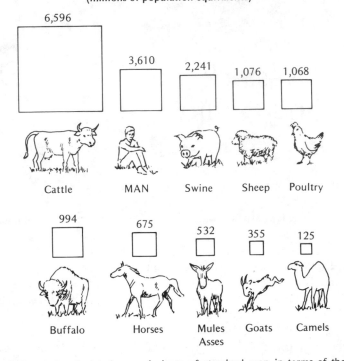

All livestock calculated as equivalents of standard man in terms of their protein intake. The cattle correspond to 6.6 billion population equivalents, almost twice that of man; and swine to 2.2 billion, more than half that of man.

MODERN ANIMAL HUSBANDRY

Man early broadened his food basis by keeping cattle, which are capable of utilizing many plant constituents that the human intestinal system cannot digest, such as cellulose, hemicellulose, and lignin. They can therefore stay alive and thrive in many regions where plant cropping with the techniques hitherto applied does not yield a satisfactory return. Ruminants—such as cows, sheep, goats, and camels—have in their rumen an almost miraculous food factory in which they make additional protein for themselves with the help of huge armies of microorganisms (bacteria and protozoans).

In the past, both pigs and poultry lived like the ruminants on plant

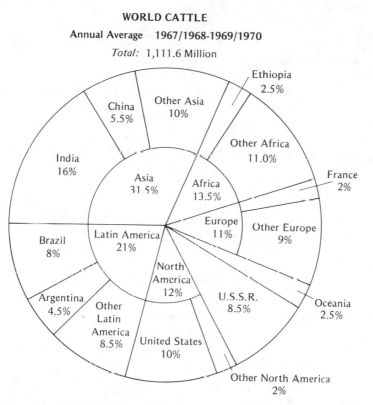

WORLD CATTLE

Annual Average 1967/1968-1969/1970

Total: 1,111.6 Million

Note that one-third of the world's cattle are in Asia (half of this number in India) and one-fifth in Latin America; the United States a mere one-tenth.

products which were not well suited as human food. Pigs, for instance, were let loose in oak and beech forests to feed on beech nuts and acorns. Poultry picked up what they could from insects, seeds, and weeds. The pig was also a scavenger, fed on waste and swill from man's own kitchens, and remains so in many parts of the world, in particular in China, where he also performs the service of converting sewage into meat. In modern animal raising both pigs and poultry, and to a lesser degree cows, have increasingly become man's direct competitors for food and this to the degree that it has been found economically profitable to put them on scientifically formulated feeding regimens. The feed of hogs and poultry is considerably better controlled, in particular as regards detailed content of nutrients, than the food we in the United States give our own children.

Feed conversion

Though some eat or are fed animal products, our food-producing animals are plant eaters, herbivores. The transformation of plant material into animal products, called feed conversion, takes place with a varying degree of efficiency. In the end, all life on Earth gets its energy from the sun, but the animals, including man, cannot utilize this energy directly. They are in this basic respect dependent on the green plants. Assisted by the green compound, chlorophyll, in the leaves, plants catch sun energy, primarily for the transformation in the living cells of atmospheric carbon dioxide into organic substances, above all starch and fats. In other words, they convert light energy into chemical energy.

The plants must use part of the energy to sustain their own metabolism, respiration, transpiration, translocation of water to the various parts of the plant, and other life processes. Similarly, and to an even greater degree, animals use up a sizable portion of their feed intake not only to sustain their metabolism but also for moving around and in some cases for serving man with traction energy. The major portion of the feed is used up in the growth and build-up of their bodies and in sustaining life. The net yield produced as food for man is, as a result, much lower than that from the plants. In short, animals convert only part of their feed into food.

The dairy cow is unsurpassed as a feed converter, returning on the average in the milk up to one-third of the protein in the feed; indeed, high-quality protein used to top feed mixtures may return on a one-to-one

STOMACH CAPACITY OF LIVESTOCK
(gallons)

Cow	Horse	Sheep	Swine
40–50	4.5–5.0	7.8–8.0	2

There are considerable differences in the holding capacities of the stomachs of livestock animals, one factor determining feed-conversion efficiency. The polygastric ruminants need the greater volume for their predigestion. The manufacturing of feed has meant primarily a reduction in nondigestible matter (bulk); poultry and swine have benefited the most from this development. The cow, on the other hand, is capable of producing some of its own feed in the rumen.

basis. Modern broiler production attains almost the same impressive degree of conversion efficiency. A dairy cow produces from the same amount of feed at least twice and often three times as much food as a beef animal. On the other hand, it requires more supervision and must be milked at least twice a day.

More than photosynthesis is needed, however, for plants to make food and feed, as is discussed in Chapter 10. It is well to be reminded here, however, that life hinges on the microbial world, especially the microbes in the soil, which catch nitrogen and a whole galaxy of minerals, including trace elements, which are then taken up by plants. Even the microbes in animal bodies help supply nutritive needs, vitamin B_{12} especially — see page 164.

Animal breeding

Throughout the centuries many different breeds have evolved, adjusted to various climates and living conditions. Modern breeders of animals and crops have created animals which produce more food from a given amount of feed. They have also created special meat and milk breeds of cattle and have developed poultry strains specialized as egg layers or meat producers. But, as in plant breeding, the greatest gains have been made by building in greater resistance to various diseases. In this way animal husbandry has extended geographically into new areas.

INTENSIVE PRODUCTION

Animal raising in the temperate zones is characterized by intensive production. This involves meticulous control of feed intake for high yields, strict health control with early vaccination against common diseases, and abundant availability of water and feed. The result has been increased yields of meat, milk and eggs. As was pointed out above, the cattle are bred with the aim of getting the highest possible return, either meat or milk, though a compromise may be made through the rearing of double-purpose animals. This last is especially common in poultry, from which both eggs and meat are desired. Such animals do not reach top yields in either product.

A few striking examples show what has been achieved in modern animal production:

—Dairy cows yielding 5,000 gallons of milk a year or, measured in butter, almost twice their own weight.

—Brood sows which can produce fifteen piglets which after eight weeks have reached a total weight of 900 pounds and after six months more than two tons. The economic return is in this case determined by the growth rate.

—Poultry pushed to yield close to one egg a day all year round. The current average production figure is much lower, about 220 eggs annually.

—Broiler chickens reaching a weight close to 3 pounds within less than eight weeks.

These achievements have their price in large feed inputs, costly vaccinations and other disease-control measures, controlled growth conditions through heating and air conditioning, major service organizations for the production of hatching eggs and breeding chickens, insemination centers, factories for commercial mixing of feeds, and the like. Moreover, the body metabolism of these animals does not function without creaking. The strain is considerable, especially in the milk-producing udder of the cow. The end products are often influenced as to composition and quality. A good example of this is the structure of the eggshell, as to number and distribution of pores as well as thickness.

Even in the developed nations, meat, milk, and eggs must be subjected to continuous sanitary inspection. Diseases and parasites easily spread from animal to man. Tuberculosis transmitted via milk was for long a serious menace. This motivated the introduction some 70 years ago of pasteurizing, rapid heating of milk in dairies, in order to eliminate pathogens. In many countries the spread of disease agents from livestock to man has not been fully checked and constitutes a hazard. Trichinosis in pork and tapeworms in beef provide examples of parasites that can be averted only through rigorous sanitary inspection of feed and final products.

Modern man in the affluent world is largely unaware that such a relentless vigilance is a necessity for his own health, as well as for that of his livestock. This lack of awareness about the significance of sanitary control measures leads to misjudgment of conditions in less developed countries, where sanitary legislation may be inadequate and poorly implemented. Even nations with well-organized health and food control suffer losses in animal production through diseases and parasites. Such losses are not completely avoidable. The lay public of advanced countries is only rarely reminded of this fact through brief mention in the news media. Only when foot-and-mouth disease, a major virus disease of cattle, takes on epizootic dimensions or when hog cholera is on the rampage do such happenings reach the headlines.

STEPS FOR INCREASED PRODUCTION OF ANIMAL FOODS

—High-yielding animals (breeding associations)

—Improved feed regimens

—Veterinary sanitary control of animals

—More and better water

—Breeding of animals with higher resistance to diseases and parasites

—Vaccination

—Improved control of diseases and parasites

—Well-organized slaughter practices and improvements in the utilization or disposal of waste

ANIMALS IN HUNGRY COUNTRIES

Most livestock in the hungry world have a precarious existence. When food is scarce, so also is feed, usually. When drought occurs, grazing cattle and sheep often die in the thousands as their pastures dry up and die. This may even happen in countries that normally are well provided with water but where precipitation is erratic (Argentina, Uruguay, South Africa), or where drought with some regularity reaches catastrophic proportions (Australia, the North American prairies). In many hungry countries such calamities are commonplace.

Even under relatively favorable conditions in the hungry countries,

Annual yields of animal protein in different regions (pounds of protein per acre)

	Temperate regions		Developing countries and warm regions	
	Favorable conditions	Average conditions	Favorable conditions	Less favorable conditions
Beef	40	25	20	10
Pork or chicken	80	45	30	15
Milk	100	60	40	20
Eggs	60	40	30	12.5

animals yield less protein than they yield from the pastures of the satisfied world under average conditions.

CLIMATE AND MILK PRODUCTION

Despite these many advances, it has proved difficult to obtain cattle capable of producing milk in warm regions of the Earth in quantities comparable to those obtained in the temperate zones. The water buffalo, closely related to the cow, remains unsurpassed in this regard. After grazing, the water buffalo during the hot hours of the day submerges her body in the water closest by, thereby cooling the milk factory in her udder. The water buffalo plays a significant role as milk provider in India, the Philippines, Indonesia, in southern China, and in parts of the Nile Valley. In addition it is an invaluable beast of burden.

In India, through centuries of hot climate, debilitating diseases, and shortage of feed and water, a special breed of cattle emerged, the zebu (in the United States called the Brahman). This breed is remarkably resilient. It has several inherent advantages: its sweat glands are more numerous and better developed than those of other cattle strains. Its light-colored pelt reduces heat absorption and lies in deep folds over neck and abdomen. Large pendent ears and many short hairs in the pelt further contribute to a greater surface area

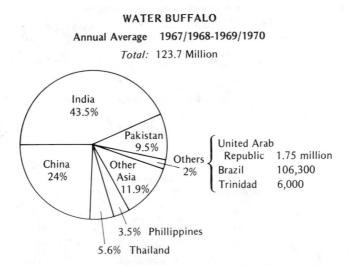

WATER BUFFALO

Annual Average   1967/1968-1969/1970

Total: 123.7 Million

The water buffalo is chiefly an Asian animal, employed both as a beast of burden and as a milk producer in hot regions with swampland. The biggest group outside Asia is in the Nile Valley.

SHEEP AND GOATS
Annual Averages 1967/1968-1969/1970

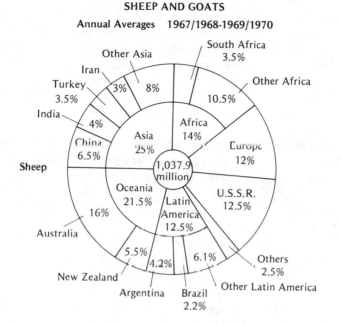

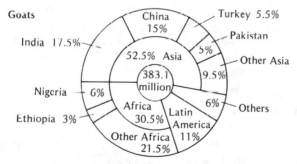

Global goat and sheep population. The goat is regarded around the world as the poor man's cow. Nevertheless, its meat is more significant to India and North Africa than its milk. The Angora goat provides fine wool (mohair) in Turkey and other Near East countries. Australia is the country with the most sheep. In Africa, Europe, and Central Asia, sheep render some milk, besides wool. The fat-tail sheep provides fat in North Africa.

per unit of weight, all contributing to a better body-temperature regulation, also aided by a lower heat production within the animal. These invaluable traits have now been crossbred into more than half of the world's cattle stock.

Heat as a negative factor in milk production may best be illustrated with experiences from the United States. At first the dairy cow did not manage very well in North America except in the cooler northern regions, hence the South was for centuries largely dependent on the North for its dairy products. For the same reason warm Spain concentrated more on meat than milk production. Not until man had conquered disease-spreading ticks and developed feed crops adapted to this warm climate was it possible for the South of the United States to build up a dairy industry of its own with satisfactory productivity. But even more important was the attainment of hardy and vigorous stock. Through long-range breeding efforts and selection, the heat-tolerant zebu cow from India was crossed with domestic breeds to develop a new dual-purpose milk and meat breed, the Santa Gertrudis.

In arid regions with sparse pastures the goat, the most frugal animal, is the favorite, followed by the sheep. Especially the Mediterranean nations, the entire Middle East, the Soviet Republics of Central Asia, and large parts of India and Pakistan rely on the goat for their milk and meat supply. In some of these regions the buffalo, camel, and sheep provide some supplementation. The Caribbean islands are becoming increasingly dependent upon the goat, since their pastures are rapidly declining. In extremely dry lands, fat may be produced through the fat-tail sheep. On saline marshlands, Merino sheep is the only domestic animal which can survive and produce, thanks to its high tolerance for salt. The camel is in particular well adapted to desert conditions.

For the northern regions of the globe a new kind of cattle is presently being bred. Both in the Soviet Union and Canada efforts are under way to cross the yak with common cattle in order to obtain an animal that yields more milk and meat under these rigorous climatic conditions. Similar experiments are in progress with the musk ox.

DISEASES AND MALNUTRITION

Malnutrition of both man and livestock undermines their resistance to ever-present disease agents (in air, water, food, soil, and elsewhere) or to intruding parasites. Contamination, infection, or infestation may also originate with living creatures, wild, domesticated, or—like rats and flies—living in the shadow of man. This is a vicious circle: shortage of food reduces the capability to stave off pests and diseases; these enemies deprive man and livestock of their capability to fully utilize food or feed.

Diarrheas are very common among infants or children. They may be both the cause and effect of ravaging malnutrition. To remove the prime cause may be very difficult, almost impossible. Anemia is another very common defect caused by sickness and malnutrition. Deficiencies of several

COSTS TO PRODUCE ANIMAL FOODS

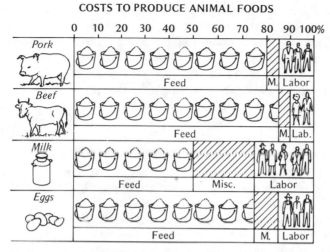

Approximate cost breakdown for animal production. Feedstuffs are the biggest cost item. Milk requires the most labor and machine investment (milking machines, bulk tank cars, refrigeration installations, and the like), included in "Miscellaneous" (M.) above.

minerals (among them phosphorus, calcium, magnesium, sulfur, iron, copper, zinc, manganese, cobalt, and vanadium) are reflected in the composition of the blood and cause anemias to develop. Livestock suffer the same types of afflictions.

Even more serious than such deficiency disturbances, directly attributable to one or several elements, are poor health conditions in general, aggravated by scarcity of food and feed. Epizootics and other contagious diseases still ravage livestock to an appalling extent In the hungry world. History records that during the latter part of the eighteenth century the cattle disease called rinderpest killed more than 200 million cattle as it spread over Europe from Asia. Towards the end of the nineteenth century it struck in tropical Africa, again killing cattle in the millions. Much control has been achieved, but a continuing watch against rinderpest is required, especially over remaining foci for the plague in Tanzania from where frequent outbreaks spread both north and south. As late as the 1960's rinderpest claimed larger losses to the world household than any other animal disease.

We could discuss cholera among pigs and poultry, contagious pneumonia among cattle, tuberculosis, and many other diseases which, despite man's countermeasures, take a large toll of both food-producing and work animals, to great detriment to the human economy besides suffering and death among the animals. In a broad belt across tropical Africa, the tsetse fly persists despite large-scale efforts toward eradication. This fly spreads sleeping sickness (nagana) to cattle from carriers among disease-resistant hoofed wild animals. Destruction of both vegetation and animals on a major scale, massive spraying against the fly, and medical remedies against the disease as well as vaccination efforts have all failed or provided only partial or temporary relief.

Parasites of all kinds still constitute the prime menace to animal husbandry around the world. Lung worms, tapeworms, and hookworms are only a few of numerous parasites that plague livestock and spread to man. In Ethiopia the cattle are so generally infested with tapeworms that most people are afflicted, the more so since many persist in eating raw beef.

Animal diseases and parasites cause an annual loss of meat, milk, and eggs of 17.5 percent, or close to one-sixth of the total production, in the developed world. In the developing countries this loss is twice as large, often even higher. The world food issue cannot therefore be grasped in its entirety if we do not take into account these enormous losses. No less than 4 million metric tons of animal protein is lost on the affluent side of the hunger curtain; on the other side where man already finds himself in a desperate shortage situation, especially with regard to first-rate protein, the loss has been estimated at 7 million metric tons despite the fact that the number of food-producing animals is much smaller.

REFERENCES AND RECOMMENDATIONS
FOR FURTHER READING

Anderson, A. L., and J. J. Kiser, *Introductory Animal Science.* New York: Macmillan, 1963. 800 pp.

Cardand, L. E., and M. E. Nesheim, *Poultry Production.* 10th Rev. ed. Philadelphia: Lea and Febiger, 1969. 400 pp.

Faust, E. C., P. C. Beaver, and R. C. Jung. *Animal Agents and Vectors of Human Disease,* 3rd ed. Philadelphia: Lea and Febiger, 1968. 462 pp.

Lerner, J. M., and H. P. Donald, *Modern Developments in Animal Breeding.* London and New York: Academic Press, 1966. 294 pp.

Porter, A. R., J. A. Sims, and C. F. Foreman. *Dairy Cattle in American Agriculture.* Ames: Iowa State University, 1965. 330 pp.

Warden, A. N., K. E. Sellers, and D. E. Tribe (eds.), *Animal Health, Production and Pasture.* London: Longmans, 1963. 360 pp.

REVIEW AND RESEARCH QUESTIONS

1. The Bible (Isaiah 40:6) says "All flesh is grass." Comment about the validity of this statement with particular reference to man and his livestock.

2. Discuss in which ways livestock animals compete with man for food.

3. What is the ratio of feed conversion among livestock animals? Discuss some factors affecting this kind of efficiency.

4. What are the goals of animal breeding?

5. Review the difficulties encountered in producing milk in warm countries.

6. Why is the goat well suited for arid regions?

7. Review some of the measures and precautions required to raise healthy and efficiently productive cattle, hogs, or poultry.

8. Discuss some persistent animal diseases that frequently hamper production on a global scale.

9. Review the role of parasites in livestock and the risks of their being transmitted to man.

What Oceans and   6
Freshwaters Provide

Since time immemorial the seas and freshwaters have been harvested by man. Archeologists have found and dated ancient dumps; shellmounds from prehistoric eras are encountered in several parts of the world. Mollusc shells and to a lesser degree fishbones make up the bulk of these mounds. Aquatic ecosystems have become increasingly important to man as he has multiplied and experienced the limitations of the soils. More than two-thirds of the Earth's surface is covered with water and the ocean is indisputably man's last continent. The race for its treasures has already started and becomes increasingly acute.

Until the mid 1950's, fisheries were largely conducted as hunting enterprises and always had an element of chance since catches were affected by fish movements and heavy winds. This is changing. Modern science and technology have provided better tools, making fisheries more like organized and controlled hunting. The next step, which long ago was taken in many parts of the world, although in a rather limited and groping way, is direct cultivation of the sea—the raising on a large scale of fish, shellfish, and other organisms of food value. Fish cultivation in ponds and other freshwaters is of long standing. In Asia this procedure has thousands of years of tradition behind it; in Europe it has existed since the Middle Ages, preceded by the holding ponds of the Romans where fish were fed while awaiting festive eating. Yet, we still know far too little about the seas to be able to evaluate to what extent they may be exploited by cropping; neither do we know the return which would accrue from such big investments; nor do we know the extent of organizational efforts required in terms of hatcheries, raising ponds, feeding, and weeding.

PROTEIN YIELDS—GLOBAL COMPARISON

Average   1967-1968
(millions of metric tons)

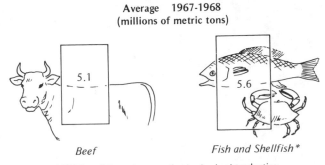

Beef   Fish and Shellfish*

*38% into fish meal, supporting land animal production

The relative standing as protein sources of the global aquatic harvest and
the world's beef production.

THE OCEANS

In the race for the food riches of the oceans, the Soviet Union and Japan hold
the lead among the nations as to the size of their fishing fleets and their wide
global roamings. In catch volume, Peru presently holds the top-ranking
position, but this is almost exclusively based on coastal fishing of one single
sardine species, the anchoveta. This operation is mostly directed by fish-meal
manufacturers, and only a small share of the catch (less than 3 percent)
reaches the Peruvians as food.

China and Japan come next in total catch; in which order is hard to tell
since reliable figures are lacking about the Chinese aquatic harvests. Not until
quite recently (1959) did this land giant start ocean fisheries in a real sense.
The Soviet Union follows behind Japan as to size of its marine catch.
Nevertheless Western Europe and North America get the lion's share of the
ocean harvests but exhibit a wastefulness similar to what we have seen with
regard to agricultural products. Half the ocean catches of fish are channeled
as fish meal into the feeding troughs of the well-fed world. The oil from the
pressing of the fish flows the same way, chiefly to the margarine industry of
Western Europe.

The food chains of the sea

As on land, all life in the ocean hinges on sun energy, which green plants
catch and transform into chemical energy. But in the sea there are few
conterparts to cows or sheep, that is, animals that live from the pastures of
the sea or underwater plants and which man utilizes directly as food. The

GLOBAL AQUATIC CATCH

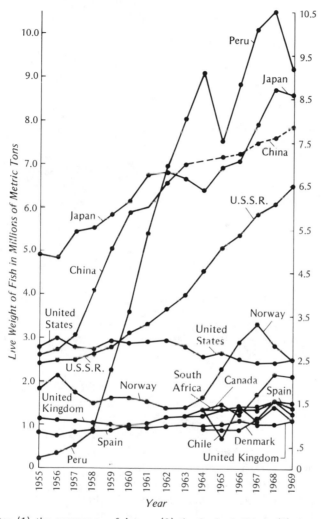

Note: (1) the resurgence of Japan; (2) the Soviet build-up; (3) the rapid rise of Peru—almost exclusively in anchoveta for fish meal; (4) the rise of Norway to exceed or hold equal with United States production; (5) the absence of increase for the United States and the United Kingdom. Totals for recent years are: 1964, 52.8 million metric tons; 1965, 53.7; 1966, 57.4; 1967, 61.1; 1968, 64.3; 1969, 63.1; 1970, 69.3.

basis for the oceanic fauna consists of microscopic plant algae, phytoplankton, that live down to a depth of about 200 feet—as far down as the sunlight penetrates. The phytoplankton are grazed by microscopic crustaceans, the

MARINE FOOD CHAIN

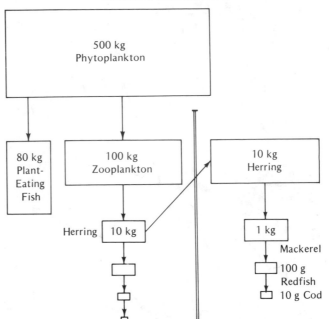

The major food chain in the ocean, starting with phytoplankton as the initial stage. A few fish are herbivorous (plant eaters), and constitute alternatives to zooplankton.

zooplankton. These in turn constitute the feed for certain fish species, such as herring and salmon, and for other aquatic animals. Consequently they constitute the third link in the nutritional chain of the sea. The fourth link is the meat eaters, sea carnivores which live from fish and other aquatic animals. But there are at least two more links of carnivores to which the meat eaters in the previous link constitute the chief food.

As on land, losses occur in feed conversion since the food chains are much longer in the ocean. A great deal is lost in the conversion process from one link to the next in the chain, as a rule nine-tenths. In the first link, however, the step from plant to animal plankton, the losses are less, presumably only four-fifths. At best, 500 pounds of phytoplankton yields 100 pounds of zooplankton, and this provides 10 pounds of herring, which in turn can yield 1 pound of mackerel. But the same original quantity of phytoplankton (500 pounds) in the end only renders 3½ ounces (0.2 pound) of haddock or a tiny 1/3 oz. of cod.

For the oceans to produce 1 pound of cod, 12 short tons of phytoplankton are required. Bottom fish and other fish living deep down also get their sustenance directly or indirectly from the producing surface layers of phytoplankton and take care of what "rains" down from above such as dead plankton and some fish. Lakes and other freshwaters have a corresponding nutritional chain.

More than 40,000 fish species are known, about twice the number of mammal species, but at the most one thousand are used as food and no more than ten species carry real significance in world feeding. An acceptable economic return can be achieved in commercial fisheries only from species that appear in large shoals or are individually big (such as tuna, weighing 50 to 200 pounds). The majority of man's important food fishes are meat eaters and belong to the third, fourth, or fifth link in the food chain. With present catches man therefore avails himself indirectly of a considerable portion of the plant production of the oceans. He is, in other words, depending on a producing machinery far bigger than is normally recognized.

What world fisheries yield

From 1955 to 1970, the world's fish catch has more than doubled, from 28 million metric tons (1955) to more than 69 million (1970). Fisheries have been far more effective than agriculture in increasing outputs, in consequence of the race for the ocean riches under the pressure of growing numbers and markets. The seas provide nine-tenths (87 percent) of the catch. The remainder comes from freshwaters (8.9 million tons in 1969). So far, fish cultivation yields less than one-fiftieth of the total aquatic catch. In addition, subsistence fishing around the globe is estimated to yield around 6 million metric tons. This is not included in international statistics.

As a calorie supplier, fisheries do not contribute very much—a mere couple of percentage points of the global consumption. But fish is rich in protein, the prime shortage nutrient of the world. When the total catch is calculated in terms of this vital commodity, the picture changes considerably. Fish and other aquatic animals then contribute almost one-fifth of the animal protein—moreover, of first-rate quality—even more than the world's registered meat-producing cattle (beef). In many countries devoid of the prerequisities for large-scale cattle raising or not able to afford this, fish is the chief source of animal protein; examples are Japan, Southeast Asia and Portugal, and many parts of tropical Africa. Fish is above all the poor man's animal protein, both in the poor and the rich world.

But not all fish that is caught is directly utilized as human food. A

AQUATIC CATCH

Annual Average   1968-1969

Total: 63.7 Million Metric Tons

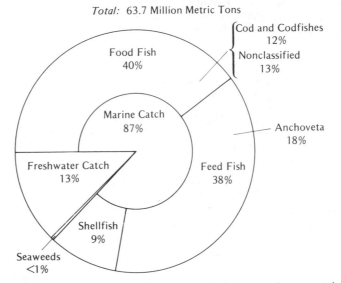

Note the modest role of freshwater fish and that the anchoveta catch is larger, exceeding 47 percent of all feed fish.

distinction needs to be made between food and feed fish, the latter some-times called trash fish. This is channelled to factories for the pressing of oil and the manufacture of fish meal. Most of the oil goes to the making of margarine, chiefly in the West. Fish meal is mixed with other ingredients in feed factories to be used primarily in the raising of poultry and swine in Western Europe, the United States, and Japan. During the 1950's more than one-fifth of the world's ocean catch was processed this way, but during the 1960's this portion grew persistently to reach the fifty-fifty mark in 1969. Viscera and other waste, together with the species of fish considered less suited for human consumption, are channelled this way. Even first-rate food fish such as herring passes in considerable quantities (as in Norway and Iceland) via margarine factories and land animals to the already overflowing tables of the Westerners. First-rate nutritional riches thus bypass the world's poor and protein-hungry millions. This is the more remarkable since a great deal of this fish is caught right outside their own shores—in the Peruvian Current off the Pacific coast of South America and in the Benguela Current of the Atlantic, off the coast of Southwest Africa.

In recent years several new species of fish have been incorporated into world food fisheries: ocean perch, also called rosefish and redfish in the North Atlantic and rockfish in the North Pacific; furthermore hake in the South Atlantic and the Northeast Pacific; mackerel-pike in the Northeast Pacific; and the previously mentioned anchoveta in the Southeast Pacific. Of all fisheries the tuna catch has increased most dramatically both in the Atlantic and the Pacific, although in total quantity it does not reach a million metric tons per year. Several fishing nations take considerably larger catches of herring and sardine than earlier. Atlantic herring surpasses three-quarters of a million metric tons. The shellfish take has also increased all around the globe, especially of shrimp, in particular from the Gulf of Mexico. Gains have also been registered for rock lobster in Australia and South Africa, mainly shipped canned or frozen to Western Europe and the United States.

The revolution in fisheries since World War II

An impressive technological development is behind the large increases in the world's ocean catch. From having been largely confined to coastal waters and continental shelves, usually close to the home country, fishing has advanced its positions out on the high seas and far away from home shores. In other words, distant and high-seas fishing is now being pursued on a grand scale. Fleets travel thousands of miles to fishing grounds, bringing along the process- ing facilities either on board or in separate floating factories. Most fishing nations have introduced modern vessels capable of making much higher speed and equipped with radar and other navigational innovations. Specialized types of vessels have been designed for different kinds of fisheries. Most coastal fishing vessels have been modernized to enlarge their operational range.

Ocean fishing is no longer a game of chance. Oceanographers have mapped the sea currents and the biologists are thoroughly investigating the living habits of individual species, their migrations, and their schooling. They are detected and located through echo sounding and by aerial reconnaissance from helicopters. Telecommunication systems signal the location of the fish schools, their speed, and their course to the catching vessels. Nylon and other synthetic fibers, some invisible in water, are increasingly used for nets and lines. These are lighter in weight and require less care and maintenance than earlier ones made from natural fibers. The catches are hauled on board with hydraulic winches instead of manpower as in the past. This practice facilitates the work and in addition makes it possible to take much larger and faster catches than before. The nets can therefore be filled many more times during a given time span. Fish schools can be attracted with light or be directed with electronic impulses and then pumped on board through tubes, eliminating the use of nets and lines altogether. These are only a few examples of significant modern technical advances incorporated into the vessels and gear used in modern fishing. Cooling and freezing installations aboard the catching vessels have furthermore made possible the storing of the fish for much longer periods of time. Fishing vessels do not have to visit port as frequently for unloading. The space needed on board for salt and ice has as a result been much reduced.

The geographical expansion of fisheries

Concomitantly with this modernization, fisheries have expanded geographically. Earlier large-scale fishing took place almost exclusively in the North Atlantic and the North Pacific while the fish riches of the southern hemisphere were left less exploited. The intensification of the fisheries in traditional waters has now been extended to all oceans. Behind this development lies, in addition to the population growth accompanied by grossly increased needs for animal protein, a pollution problem. The release of waste from industries and communities into adjacent waters has impaired the productivity of inland and coastal waters so that the catches in most instances have diminished drastically or entirely as pollution wiped out living stocks of fish. To compensate for these reductions in catches it has become imperative for fishing vessels to venture further out.

Many nations have copied the U.S.S.R. and Japan, the front runners in this transformation, often in cooperation with these two superpowers of modern ocean fishing. The Soviet Union cooperates primarily with East European countries, North Korea, North Vietnam, Cuba, and Egypt; Japan renders aid and advice to South Korea, Taiwan, the Mediterranean countries, and also some African and South American states. Norway assists India in developing its fisheries. Poland gives technical aid to the fisheries of tropical West Africa and Ceylon; Sweden similarly supports Tunisia.

Even before World War II, Japan was the leading fishing nation but she then largely kept to her own coastal waters in the North Pacific and to the adjacent seas along the Asian mainland. During the war her entire fishing fleet was practically destroyed and when peace came, Japan's fishing rights in her traditional fishing waters were severely curtailed. After the signing of the peace treaty in 1952, the operational range of the Japanese fishing fleet was gradually extended and finally encompassed almost the entire Pacific from the Bering Sea in the north to the waters surrounding the South Sea Islands and reaching down to Australia and New Zealand. Japanese fishing fleets also reached the Indian Ocean and worked further south around Africa into the Atlantic. Now they operate in all oceans. A large fleet has been created for long-distance fisheries and Japanese catchers participate in fisheries off Iceland and the Faeroe Islands and on the Newfoundland banks in the North Atlantic. They even appear in the Norway Sea. They catch in the Caribbean Sea and the Gulf of Mexico as well as in the Mediterranean and the Middle and South Atlantic. They take large catches in the Bering Sea close to the Alaskan coast. Ever since the 1930's they have taken part in the whaling in Antarctic waters.

To support these wide-ranging fishing operations, Japanese fishing enterprises have acquired a world-encompassing net of support bases. They have leased handling and storage facilities in the fishing ports of a great many countries. Their vessels go to these bases to obtain provisions, to get repairs done on ships and equipment, and to unload catches. These ports also provide the crews rest and recreation. Important bases in the Mid-Atlantic are in the Canary and Cape Verde Islands and the Azores.

More remarkable than the Japanese success, however, is the sea empire created by the Soviet Union during the period since the 1950's. This constitutes in many ways a true revolution. This land colossus traditionally used to receive four-fifths of its fish catch from inland waters and had very limited coastal fisheries. In the 1950's a large-scale ocean drive was launched. From an average annual catch of 1 to 1.5 million metric tons up to the end of the 1940's, the U.S.S.R. attained an annual catch exceeding 7 million tons in 1970—one-tenth of the total world catch. Fish has thereby become an integral part of the protein intake of this big land mass. An impressive, multifaceted fishing fleet has been created, composed of numerous types of vessels with ultramodern equipment. Some have highly automatized units for catching operations, in some cases employing light and electric attraction by low-voltage current. Many of these ships were built in domestic shipyards, but the U.S.S.R. also placed large orders for fishing vessels both in East and West Europe and in Japan.

In contrast to Japan, the Soviet Union relies almost exclusively on home bases for its fisheries and operates with large fleets functioning as coordinated units. Such a fishing fleet may be composed of 20 to 25 catching vessels. One or two special search ships are equipped with elaborate echo-sounding equipment for locating fish schools. Most importantly, these fleets are served by processing units, also called mother ships. In the later 1960's high-speed transport vessels were added. These bring the catches back to home base and, on the return trip, frequently deliver food, fuel, and other commodities to the fleets, which often remain on the fishing grounds up to three months. Special repair and maintenance ships may also be servicing the fishing fleets. The mother ships are equipped for freezing, canning, salting, and other handling of the fish. They may have movie installations, libraries, and recreational facilities as well as hospitals for the benefit of the crews, which for a fleet unit of 40 to 70 ships may amount to 20,000 to 25,000 people, both men and women. Mother ships may also carry on deck smaller catching vessels and helicopters for the reconnaissance of fish shoals.

Soviet fleets, large or small, are encountered on almost all major fishing grounds of the globe, often close to the territorial limits of other nations where good catches may be taken—in the Arctic Sea; off Greenland and Newfoundland in the Atlantic; off the North American continent from New England in the north to Florida in the south; in the Mid-Atlantic, and along Africa's west coast all the way down to Capetown. In the Pacific all the fringe seas along the Soviet Asiatic coast are intensely fished, as are the waters around the Alaskan penisula and the Aleutians, where the Soviet Union vies with Japan as a leading whale-hunting nation.

Western Europe, the United States, and Canada, which are so well-provided with animal protein from land animals have so far not modernized and enlarged their fisheries to a corresponding degree. They have lagged behind and may never catch up—the resources of the oceans are not inexhaustible. However, United States tuna fisheries have grown considerably since World War II. Earlier the United States got enough tuna from its own waters off the Pacific coast, but gradually supplementary quantities had to be bought from Japan. Simultaneously United States catchers went further and further southward, all the way down to the coast of Chile, in order to secure tuna for the insatiable domestic market. After World War II a new base for the Pacific tuna fisheries was established on the Samoa Islands. In the 1950's, the Atlantic was invaded and a base with new modern canning factories was erected in Puerto Rico. Tuna for these plants is procured through purchase from a network of Japanese bases in the Caribbean, via Dakar from French and Spanish catches, and also through United States tuna vessels operating in the Middle Atlantic. In the 1960's, a new tuna-processing center was readied in the Boston area to receive catches from adjacent Atlantic waters. The United States population growth requires an additional catch of 10 to 11 million pounds of tuna each year to sustain the present annual consumption approaching 3 pounds per person. There is little margin for a second tuna giant the size of the United States. Catching quotas—very severe for yellowfin tuna—have been introduced in recent years as signs of overfishing emerged. Currently plans for similar restrictions are contemplated for the Middle Atlantic. Besides these extensive measures, the United States buys supplementary quantities of tuna, frozen and canned, from Japan.

Shellfish and other seafoods

Man uses many seafoods other than fish.

Molluscs such as clams, mussels, and oysters constituted daily food in prehistoric days, as was mentioned in Chapter 1. Shellmounds encountered almost in all continents and on the shores of all major waters testify to this fact. As early as in the fifth century A.D., the Chinese and Japanese started to cultivate molluscs, the first step toward the clam and oyster beds which today almost exclusively supply the food market.

Shrimp, lobster, and crabs, caught in increasing quantities, are primarily luxury foods. In the North Pacific, the gigantic king crab, up to 12 feet across, is the basis for large-scale canning on huge floating factories (9,000 to 14,000 register tons). These belong to the Soviet Union, which markets the canned product on the world market under the brand name of Chatka, and to Japan, using Geisha and Aku as brand names. Furthermore, Alaskan plants freeze king crab for delivery by air to the United States mainland and to Western Europe.

Japan catches more than three-fourths million tons of squid a year. Cephalopods are also caught in the Mediterranean. In China, sea cucumbers (holothurians) are a cheap and appreciated food, especially for elderly people. The domestic catches of squid and sea cucumber are supplemented through their importation in a dried state.

Seaweeds have been utilized since far back as food and feed, especially in Asia. They are prepared for human consumption by drying, fermentation, and other processing. China has the lead in the cultivation of seaweed along its entire coast. Japan also raises many species.

The tragedy of the whales

Whale hunting was practised in ancient times both in the Mediterranean and along the coast of China. Whales were then abundant in all oceans and latitudes and man hunted these giants with almost ferocious ruthlessness. In the nineteenth century, this carnage culminated in the northernmost Atlantic, around Spitsbergen and Greenland. The stock faltered and many species became extinct. With Norway in the lead, the harpoons were then turned south, and the Antarctic became the stage for the large-scale onslaught on the whales in this century. The peak in this major whaling operation was reached after World War I, when huge, newly built factory ships of more than 40,000 gross register tons joined the older fleets. Biologists warned, but restrictive catch quotas were introduced too late. The blue whale, the largest and most remarkable creature on Earth, seems to be threatened by extinction due to man's unscrupulous quest for food and feed. The oil became margarine in the Soviet Union and Western Europe, the meat, food for Japanese, Russians, Norwegians, and others. A sizable portion of the flesh was converted into meat meal. Some became pet food in the United States and Europe.

For Eskimos and coastal Indians, seal and walrus made up the bulk of their food for centuries. Dolphin has been hunted for food purposes since times immemorial. But none of these animals can compete with the blue whale, which used to reach an adult weight of 75 to 120 metric tons. The young whale normally suckles for two years and grows each day by about 165 pounds, the weight of an average human adult. The mother blue whale has to manufacture several hundred quarts of nutritious milk daily containing 20 percent fat. Her feed in turn is tiny crustaceans, krill, which she strains from the water in a quantity reaching several tons daily—truly a producing miracle.

Several other kinds of whales, particularly sei and humpback, felt the brunt of man's onslaught when strict quotas and finally prohibition were introduced against further blue-whale hunting. They are now rapidly falling in number. Only Japan and the U.S.S.R. remain as whaling nations in the Antarctic. Further restrictions were introduced in 1972.

THE FRESHWATERS

Lakes, ponds, and rivers give food for the many people who live far away from the sea coast in China, Africa, Europe, and North America. Even though freshwater fisheries today amount to a mere one-eighth of the aquatic catch, they have throughout history played an important role as a local source of first-rate protein food. Not until modern fast rail and highway transportation were developed and modern methods of preservation, such as icing, freezing, and canning emerged, did it become feasible to bring the ocean harvests to the interiors of the continents. Freshwater fisheries then yielded their key position as food providers. In China, Southeast Asia, tropical Africa, and in parts of Eastern Europe and the Soviet Union they have, however, retained their standing. In inland Africa dried freshwater fish is a common trade item.

CROPPING THE WATERS

Fish cultivation

Early in history, with China probably the pioneer, fish, especially carp, were cultivated in ponds. Stocking natural waters with fish fry was also practiced quite early. Feeding and fertilizing of fish in cultivation ponds is done in many nations. In the warm latitudes of China, in Southeast Asia, Indonesia, and other countries, annual yields as high as close to one ton of fish per acre are obtained. Fish has thus become a new category of livestock, but obviously as with land animals only a portion of the feed is returned as food. Both cultivated and natural waters produce about five to ten times more in the tropics than corresponding ponds and lakes in the temperate zones with low temperatures and sharp seasonal changes.

Besides carp of several different kinds, a few other species have been subject to major cultivation. Mention should be made of the eel and (the only species introduced in later years) various tilapias from African lakes. Milkfish, raised in Southeast Asia, is the only major marine species also adapted to brackish waters, and was brought under cultivation 2,000 years ago. Catfish farming has caught on in the United States in the 1960's. This production is, however, based on the high yields obtained through supplementary feeding. Yields of 500 to 1,500 pounds per acre have been reported, but this involves added acreages to raise the feed. Taking this into account, the true productivity is in general only around 150 pounds per acre. Another requisite is the availability of water from nonpolluted sources.

Ocean lagoons have also been cultivated for centuries in Italy, Indonesia, and the Philippines and the return has been good. This constitutes an early beginning of the cultivation of the sea previously discussed in this chapter.

Fish management

Few natural waters of any magnitude are nowadays left unmanaged. Conservation and control of fisheries have become common practice in Europe, North America, and the Soviet Union. Hatcheries have been built by the hundreds for the raising on a massive scale of fry from salmon, sturgeon, pike, carp, and pike-perch. Nonetheless, the higher the number of humans, the less important the freshwaters become in relative terms as a food source. In industrialized areas they are increasingly jeopardized through pollution to the degree that fish and shellfish vanish. This is currently happening in the Great Lakes of North America.

A single, modern ocean freezer-trawler of 2,700 gross tons, with an annual catching capacity of 10,000 metric tons of fish, harvests more fish than well-tended cultivation ponds of 125,000 acres yield in favorable locations of the temperate regions. In the tropics the corresponding pond acreage would be approximately 25,000 acres. Man in the era of the billions is thus being forced to go to sea in order to survive. As we will see in Chapter 11, fish cultivation will, however, have a different and new key mission in the overpopulated world of the future.

REFERENCES AND RECOMMENDATIONS
FOR FURTHER READING

Bardach, J. P., *Harvest of the Sea.* New York: Harper, 1968. 302 pp.

Chapman, V. J., *Seaweeds and their Uses*, 2nd ed., New York: A. S. Barnes, 1970. 304 pp.

Christy, F. T., Jr., and A. Scott, *The Common Wealth in Ocean Fisheries.* Baltimore: Johns Hopkins Press, 1965. 281 pp.

Gullion, E. A., (ed.), *The Uses of the Seas.* Englewood Cliffs: Prentice-Hall, 1968. 202 pp.

Hickling, C. F., *Fish Culture.* London: Faber, 1962. 295 pp.

Idyll, C. P., *The Sea against Hunger.* New York: Thomas Y. Crowell, 1970. 221 pp.

Jackson, D. F., *Algae, Man and the Environment.* Syracuse: Syracuse University Press, 1968. 554 pp.

Mackintosh, N. A., *The Stocks of Whales.* London: Fishing News, 1965. 232 pp.

Russel-Hunter, W. D., *Aquatic Productivity.* New York: Macmillan, 1970. 306 pp.

Wimpenny, R. S., *Plankton of the Sea.* New York: American Elsevier, 1966. 426 pp.

REVIEW AND RESEARCH QUESTIONS

1. Discuss major advances in techniques among leading fishing nations in the postwar period.

2. Review some of the longer food chains of the ocean.

3. Discuss the role of fish in worldwide human nutrition in terms of protein and calories.

4. Review major advances in fish-catching techniques and gear since World War II.

5. Review major features of the Soviet deployment of widely ranging fishing fleets.

6. Discuss United States tuna fishing and its significance to United States diet and world fisheries.

7. Discuss some significant shellfish catches other than shrimp and crab.

8. What is the difference between a molluscan and crustacean shellfish?

9. Which whales are threatened by extinction and why?

10. What is the relative significance of freshwater fish catches as compared to ocean harvests?

11. Survey which aquatic species are currently subject to cultivation by man.

12. What is meant by fish management?

Visions of the Future 7

Let us briefly consider the food issue when judged from the narrow horizon of the affluent world in the age of computers, electronics, and nuclear energy. Mass prodution also of food has taken on entirely new dimensions. One Jules Verne vision follows the other in the fairy tales about food of the future. Tissue cultures emerging from huge growth tunnels on endless conveyor belts are continuously cut into slices, molded into steaks, pork chops, poultry rolls, and fish fillets and flavored for full simulation through the simple addition of taste and aroma substances. In this fantasy world agriculture and fisheries have become superfluous but man still is caught in conventional concepts about food and food commodities.

SYNTHETICS

The fallacy

There is a next imaginary step where man has freed himself completely from traditional sources of food and is sustaining himself on chemical compounds in strictly specified combinations, all in accordance with guidelines presented by nutritional science. This is the promised land of pure nutrients and tablets. To avoid having the number of pills zoom to many hundreds a day, only vitamins, minerals, and essential amino or fatty acids can be presented in this form. The remainder is drunk or spooned into man via oil, sugar concentrates, or liquefied proteins. In this paradisiacal world of chemistry, fisheries and agriculture have been reduced to recreational hobbies; neither is any longer required for the provision of food. Old-time meat, poultry, milk, and cheese are looked upon as piquant luxury dishes or costly savorings to a main dish composed of factory-made chemicals.

INTENSIVE ANIMAL PRODUCTION

Animal factories

One step toward this streamlined and synthetically fed society is the exten-sive mechanization of agriculture and fisheries to achieve mass production. Utilizing to the hilt all the devices of advanced technology, man in this stage would still depend on the creative forces of crops and livestock but would squeeze them to the last degree of rationalization and economization. Mod-ernization would be carried to the extreme in order to meet the needs of the human anthills created by the forthwelling millions. In this alternative, most food is being produced in what best could be described as factories, relying however on living organisms, crops, and livestock—eventually to include microbial crops such as molds, yeasts, and algae, both terrestrial and aquatic. Feed, in the shape of peas or other forage crops for dairy cattle, is produced in gigantic towers where the many floors are equipped with endless conveyor belts carrying cultivated plants and exposing them to different temperatures, humidity, and artificial illumination.

Eggs, broiler chickens, pork, and beef already originate from such installations. Basic elements in this new phase of advancement exist in experimental model farms and even large commercial units in the United States, Europe, and the Soviet Union. Raising chicken in cages in order to save feed and to facilitate and mechanize the collecting of eggs has been the practice for several years; such establishments have constantly grown in size, until they have now become huge complexes; single examples in the United States and the U.S.S.R. have a million chickens. Still larger units are in the planning stage, carrying close to 2 million egg layers. The entire United States demand for eggs could be covered from 200 such factories, sometimes designated instant egg plants. The largest operation is located in California, turning out a million eggs a day from a flock of 1.7 million birds. The hens are fed scientifically composed diets, and each hen is producing close to one egg per day. Hens are held in cages, with five birds to each, arranged in tiers 10 to 20 cages high. The cages are rigged around a central scaffolding rotating slowly from darkness into light. Each hen gets six 4-minute watering periods and six 4-minute eating periods in 24 hours. The feed formulas are adjusted to ensure maximum production. Eggs are carried on conveyor belts from the cages to the cooler, where they are brought down below 50°F. The droppings are mechanically collected and made into fertilizers or recycled and upgraded to food, as also are cracked eggs. High-volume ventilation cleans and deodor-izes the air.

These huge establishments are built on the economy of size. Unques-tionably this trend will be pursued further and the commercial flocks will increase still more in numbers. The intermediate next stage is the computer-ized coordination of major producers.

Broiler assembly lines

When it comes to the raising of broiler chickens, thinking moves into still larger dimensions. Present complexes in the United States, England, and the U.S.S.R. carry one-half to three-quarters of a million animals. Slaughtering takes place at the age of six weeks. Still larger establishments are being planned, covering 300 acres, each one of which would give 14.5 million broilers for slaughter per year. Chickens are hatched within the establish-ments, and all slaughtering and primary processing takes place on the prem-ises. Feeding is automatic. Around 150 people will be employed in such an establishment when everything is automatized: feeding, watering, slaughter, and preparation of the chicken for sale. The whole establishment can easily be put into a skyscraper with elevators taking care of all vertical transporta-tion. The roof will become the landing platform for helicopters.

These examples present a picture of trends currently prevalent in a rich world with its almost unlimited availability of cheap energy and technical devices. It remains to be seen if these huge units will be followed by still larger complexes now on the drawing boards.

Cattle and hog skyscrapers

The trend is similar when it comes to the raising of hogs and beef cattle. High-volume production centers with thousands of animals in each unit and pork factories with 30,000 to 50,000 swine are already in operation both in the United States and the Soviet Union. Outside Hamburg in Germany, tower skyscrapers are producing hogs at the rate of 156,000 per year.

Nor is meat the only product of such factories. Millelactaries—milk-producing complexes—with 1,000 to 5,000 dairy cattle in each unit have been tested in the United States for some years but only in the 1960's were they copied in other places, primarily in Australia and some cities of India. In one United States operation, six towers are equipped to handle more than 6,000 milking cows with shifts operating around the clock. Herd groups of 130 cows are run through the milking line at one time. As soon as one batch is milked another takes its place. The milking time for each herd is one hour, broken only by brief intervals for washing. Prior to milking, the cows are shower-sprinkled for the cleaning of udders, feet, and hoofs. Pipeline milking is practiced. All milk is piped to 7,000-gallon tanks which are picked up twice daily. Trucks haul the tanks to the dairies.

Artificial ovulation

Cattle-embryo transfers will presumably become a subsidiary commercial practice. Fertile ova from a superior cow will be transplanted into common cows, allowing a superior cow to be the mother of as many as a thousand calves in her lifetime, compared to today's average of ten. This practice is the next step from artificial insemination, which has for decades been distributing high-quality genes from a few select breeding males to countless numbers of females.

Land scarcity

As the world's population increases, suburban developments infringe on farm lands. Industries, highways, airports, and recreation areas do the same. In order to exist, the farmer must be able to operate profitably in a strictly confined area. The trend of future farming is unmistakably toward multistory complexes tended by computer, controlled evironmentally and located within or close to urban areas. As indicated above, farmers are in many instances already installing multistory feeding plants for livestock, computer-controlled greenhouses rendering year-around production, and multistory poultry farms, all with rigorous control of ventilation, humidity, and temperature. There is a great diversity of blueprints for such huge food factories of the future.

Underground housing for the raising of animals has also been suggested, permitting surface land to be used for major crops and homes. This will permit more complete control of environmental factors such as temperature, ventilation, and lighting, as well as a more effective control of birds, flies, rodents, and other disease vectors.

INTENSIVE CROPPING

Tomato factories

Normally an acre of good farm land will yield 5,000 pounds of tomatoes per year. In Texas, a company now operating a farm of 5 acres in glass-fiber greenhouses obtains 200,000 pounds per acre per year, or 1 million lbs. of tomatoes. This yield, about 40 times the outdoor average, is primarily attributed to the environmental control center, regulating lighting, heating, cooling, watering, and spraying. Fertilizers are automatically injected into the watering system. Ceiling blowers send warm air to the plants through perforated plastic tubes, keeping the tomatoes at the ideal temperature in each stage of their development. Not even pollination is left to nature. Flowers are vibrated electrically to cause pollen to fall and thus to fertilize the plants. The

...uch greater than natural pollination by the
rt of control two harvests are feasible per
on the day of harvest, the tomatoes are
vegetables and also berries can be

so grown under huge plastic
controlled glass greenhouses
nvironment is regulated by
circulated within each house.
or lighting and for pumping
up and desalt the water from
the fresh water goes into the
coolant. A test installation in
ering 4,600 square feet.

Master crop control

A farmer in this streamlined world may never get his boots dirty. He will control his big acreage and high-profit farm sitting at a control console in a central tower using monster multipurpose machines or remote control for feed operations. Information to help him farm will be fed by television and memory computers from multiple sources. Cybernetic reminders will indicate when irrigation is needed or sprays should be scheduled. Built-in machines will do this work at the push of buttons. The soil may be broken to a perfect tilth by ultrasonic waves beamed from low-flying hovercrafts. In other cases a single machine will harvest a crop, recondition the soil, and plant seed-fertilizer pellets coated with time-release chemicals to hold the seed dormant until correct growing time. Machines are further envisioned with electronic eyes and computerized fingers for picking, grading, and packaging fruit and vegetables, and for the stripping of cereal crops by ultrasonic sound, then moving the grain by air streams into silos or elevator storage.

COMPLICATIONS

So far these visionary ideas about the future have been described as if they were without complications. This is not the case. Huge establishments of this kind have a high degree of mechanical complexity. A smooth, dependable operation also hinges upon an uninterrupted flow of energy.

One important question as to livestock units is the location of feed production in relation to these operational centers. It becomes essential to weigh the cost of feed transportation against the cost to deliver finished products. The feed normally has a volume or weight six to ten times that of the produced foods together with the waste. Such a coordination is not too difficult to arrange, although a lively debate still prevails as to the location of such large animal factories.

In many instances subsidiary power plants for emergency situations are needed in case of power failures. The economic risks, with so many costly plants and animals depending on artificial control of heat and temperature of water, reach such dimensions that this kind of insurance is required. Equally essential are the countermeasures against the spread of diseases facilitated by ventilation ducts and compounded by the size of these establishments. The crowded conditions of the animals is another adverse feature.

One difficulty, largely unresolved, is the disposal or, still better, utilization of waste and sewage. Obvious sanitary risks are involved in this regard. The accumulated wastes from these future food complexes can be handled only in ways similar to those practiced by sewage plants. As in space vehicles, recycling is imperative. Such waste, with its invaluable ingredients of carbon, nitrogen, sulfur, and phosphorus, needs to be recycled to produce new foods. Man cannot continue to dump these precious resources. Alternative ways of such recycling or recovery are presented in illustration on page 206. Waste may give food or feed via microorganisms, worms, or insects. It may be converted into algae, plankton, benthonic organisms, or insect larvae. All these organisms may in turn constitute the basis for fish cultivation or for the raising of ducks or other water birds.

HIGH-EFFICIENCY FISHING

Visionary pictures have been drawn about the future exploitation of the ocean, much like those of the agricultural scene. Fishing fleets are described as moving on a broad front, several miles long, across the ocean expanses, sucking in through vast pumps all living organisms, in turn made to congregate by photic, sonic, or electrical impulses. Little would escape these huge ocean rakers. Such catching armadas have been likened to the harvesters moving in lines over the endless prairies.

It is visualized that these catches would be submitted to an automatic electronic rating. Larvae, young fish, and other less valuable species would be returned to the sea. It is, however, anticipated that most of the catches would be utilized and constitute the basis for commercial manufacturing of a diversity of specialized products such as oils, vitamins, proteins, or precious glandular compounds.

The U.S.S.R. has experimented with fishing through vessels under distant control and operating almost entirely automatically. Such tests have been successful and have involved not only capture but also sorting, evisceration, and preparation for final freezing, canning, salting, and drying.

Much has been written about the potentials and feasibilities of cultivating the oceans and finally abandoning what is pejoratively called "hunting." Modern fishing, with its sophisticated technology and efficient organization, does not warrant such a term. Electronic instruments locate fish, machinery sets the nets rapidly, and electronic sensors control the movement of the trawl. These matters were discussed in more detail in Chapter 6.

MARICULTURE

Man is taking the first step towards truly farming the oceans. Soviet and Japanese studies in such mariculture have managed to develop in fish, conditioned reflexes to sonic impulses. Such reflexes remain implanted in the fish and can be used for regular, controlled feeding of fish.

The same kinds of snags and hazards are encountered that were once met on land by agriculturists. Diseases and parasites easily spread among such fish held impounded and crowded together at a much greater density than normally is the case. Competitors for the feed readily appear, upsetting the balance between such scavengers and the fish "livestock." Predators, including birds, must be kept at bay. Future cultivation of the oceans on a major scale will furthermore require expensive hatcheries for the raising of fingerlings. In any major ocean farming man will soon be forced to take over control of most phases of the production, much as he did in the raising of chicken, hogs, and cattle; in other words, he must achieve a mastery of the complete production chain from insemination to catch. This involves policing against parasites, diseases, and competitors for his new foods.

The road to a true farming of the ocean will be a lengthy one and even greater complications than those mentioned will have to be met. Many dangers lie ahead. Time-consuming studies will be required before mariculture can be significantly incorporated into the feeding of the human millions. The chief limitation in the ocean is the solubility of oxygen, a constraint most difficult to overcome. We are regularly reminded of the narrow oxygen margins in the ocean by "red tides," with ensuing mass mortality of fish due to excess of plankton decomposing and using up available oxygen.

As things are now developing in the oceans, man will presumably destroy the marine biosphere long before it will yield to any human endeavor to achieve new levels of productivity or increased output of those particular species man needs. The massive dumping of toxic chemicals, sewage, and oil is not only creating vast dead areas but also jeopardizing the oxygen systems of the oceans.

HOBBIES OF THE WELL-TO-DO?

In summary, it seems that many of these future visions are more characterized by lively imagination than by sober, realistic analysis. In most of these
projects the magnitude of the present critical hunger gap is overlooked. They
may at best yield some supplementary food to people that can mobilize
sufficient capital and energy resources. Such food would, as a rule, become
extremely expensive and would undoubtedly have to be vastly subsidized. In
the foreseeable future such alternatives will in all likelihood remain the
hobbies of the well-fed world.

REFERENCES AND RECOMMENDATIONS
FOR FURTHER READING

Harrison, R., *Animal Machines—the new Factory Farming Industry.*
London: Vincent Stuart, 1964. 186 pp.

Huxley, Elizabeth, *Brave New Victuals—Inquiry into Modern Food
Production.* London: Chatto & Windus, 1965. 168 pp.

Iversen, E. S., *Farming the Edge of the Sea.* London: Fishing News,
1968. 304 pp.

McKee, A., *Farming the Sea.* New York: Thomas Y. Crowell, 1969. 198
pp.

Sykes, G., *Poultry as a Modern Agri-business.* London: Crosby, Lock-
wood, 1963. 242 pp.

Waters, J. F., *The Sea Farmers.* New York: Hastings House, 1963. 120
pp.

REVIEW AND RESEARCH QUESTIONS

1. Why could man not take all his food in the form of tablets?

2. What is meant by animal or crop factories?

3. Discuss the potentialities of egg factories in providing the needs of
the United States.

4. How is modern broiler production organized?

5. What is meant by feed-lot rearing of beef cattle?

6. What are the hazards of large-sized units for the raising of food-
producing animals?

7. Describe some of the feasible operations being forecasted for large-
scale ocean fishing.

8. What is meant by ocean farming?

Section **II**

Utilization

Food Storage, Processing, and Marketing

8

In order to feed the human family it is not sufficient that agriculture and fisheries produce adequate *amounts* of food. The right *kinds* of commodities must be made available to safeguard nutrition and sustain health. This requirement should be self-evident but it has been woefully overlooked in the world economy. Preservation of the products from soils and waters—what could be termed the third dimension of the food issue—is equally important with food production (the first dimension) and population control (the second) but is nonetheless the most neglected aspect. Decomposition through biochemical changes, decay or nondesirable fermentations through microorganisms, and destruction through pests are the three major ways in which foods spoil. The microorganisms responsible are molds, yeasts, and bacteria. The chief pests are insects, mites, rodents, and birds. To avert such ravages, these foes of man must be kept under control. The means include processing of the raw products in various ways, not only to make them digestible in man's intestinal system but also to preserve and package them and thus make it possible to handle and store them.

Processing and storing is the twofold task of the food industry. Processors must trim the products, discard nonedible parts, in some cases enrich the foods by supplementation with nutrients which are in relatively short supply, prepare the foods completely or partially for eating, and also eliminate deleterious ingredients from plant products. The food industry has also taken over packaging in consumer units combined with weighing the foods, operations earlier done in retailing. The packaging of the products furthermore serves the function of protecting food from dust, dirt, infectants, contaminants, and pests.

FROM OCEAN AND FIELD TO CONSUMER'S TABLE

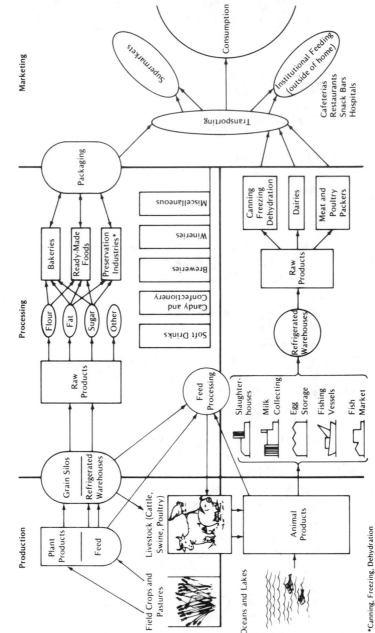

*Canning, Freezing, Dehydration

The food lifeline in a technically highly developed society such as ours—running from production (fields and oceans) via processing and marketing, finally to reach the consumer's table (consumption).

Some people still subsist by hunting, as do the Bushmen of Africa and some Aborigines of Australia. They devour the entire game bag immediately and may then have to live without food for several days. This practice was probably the common rule in the infancy of mankind before the development of special techniques for the storing and processing of food. It was most likely discovered at an early stage that wind and sun dried and preserved meat, fish, grain, fruits, and seeds. When man migrated northward following the receding ice masses, he had to rely on storage and preservation for survival, to carry him through the off seasons between one harvesting season and the next. This was indispensable to the settlement both of the arid and semiarid regions of the world.

The Spanish conquerors were impressed by the well-filled granaries of the Aztecs and the Incas. The Bible tells how Joseph in Egypt placed grain, collected in seven fat years, in storage against seven lean years. Despite modern refrigerated stores and grain silos, even rich countries are no longer able to place in storage food for much more than one year. Man has become too numerous for that kind of operation. The magnitude has become overwhelming.

Since far back in history, lean or hungry weeks preceded harvest time. Millions in tropical Africa, Latin America, and parts of Asia still experience hungry weeks, often extended into hungry months, as the stored food nears exhaustion and can no longer provide an adequate daily ration. The closer the time approaches for sowing the next year's crop, the greater is the risk for shortages. Unfortunately this hungry time coincides with the peak need for heavy work—weed removal, soil preparation, and other chores requiring extra strength and energy. Yet the more the food is needed, the more rapidly the sparse reserves dwindle. In our own well-fed world these same phenomena existed as recently as a generation ago in the shape of what was called "spring fatigue" caused by shortage of vitamin-carrying fruits and vegetables. Only when transcontinental railroads and transoceanic shipping entered the scene did hunger actually vanish from the North American prairies and continental Europe. In principle, mankind thus possesses two devices to make food and feed available until the next crop becomes ready: (1) preservation combined with storage; (2) long-distance hauling of food by sea and land.

FOOD STORAGE

Historic practices

A considerable portion of the world's food is stored, either as harvested or after processing. Obviously the quantities stored depend mainly on the volume of production. The storage of nonprocessed products is the most important to the world's feeding. The key issue, frequently overlooked, is how cereals (grains), pulses (peas, beans, lentils), and tubers (potato, yams, and cassava) are handled and protected.

The long-time storing of grain and beans was always a prime concern to mankind but did not become a life-and-death issue until modern times when the population pressure forced man to expand such crops beyond semiarid regions into humid areas with heavy rainfall and furthermore forced him to move large quantities of grain through trade.

To keep well, grains must be harvested dry after ripening in the field. Wind and sun may aid at the time of harvest, but man must then shelter his stored grain, as he learned very early in history. The Sumerians and the Egyptians used large airtight containers as sealed granaries more than three thousand years ago and, as far as is known, these were highly efficient. This practice was in principle identical to what today is termed controlled-atmosphere storage and is based on reducing the amount of oxygen in the storage air and elevating the carbon dioxide level. In these early practices this was accomplished by the ongoing respiration of the stored products in the closed container, thereby using up oxygen and emitting carbon dioxide. Today this principle is employed also in the storage of fruits, in particular apples.

Ceramic development, proceeding simultaneously, facilitated such refinements in storage techniques. In the end it became possible to make the containers sufficiently liquid-tight to store food oil. The walls of storage buildings or subterranean storage facilities were made air-tight through similar advances. Hermetic sealing also diminished the risk of attacks by rodents and other pests, besides reducing thievery. Insects and rodents are the two major pests that spoil grain in storage. Despite modern technology and fumigation of grain and bins, it is estimated that these marauders destroy more grain than is presently distributed through world trade. Such losses are by no means limited to developing countries.

Another serious and long-known difficulty with grain storage is the appearance of mold. In Scandinavia and Russia, where rye was the special grain crop, wet conditions often prevailed during harvest. Molds then develop on the grain, producing deleterious substances which affect both men and animals. These toxic compounds, mycotoxins as they have been called, were not identified until recently. The world's rice cultivators are still battling similar difficulties. During rainy seasons it is very difficult to protect rice stores against excessive moisture. Fungal damages are therefore quite common. The harmful compounds are in this case two: islanditoxin, and a yellow pigment named luteoskyrin.

Current practices

Today, most grains in developed countries are harvested by combine, a single machine for all the harvesting and associated operations such as cutting, threshing, winnowing, and cleaning the kernels. Corn requires a specialized harvester, the corn picker.

Little grain is stored on the farm. Most is carried by trucks to elevators, towering cylindrical bins made of concrete. Such elevators are located in farm areas, around cities, and at shipping ports. A distinction is therefore made between country elevators and terminal ones. The name "elevator" applies because the grain is carried to the top by an endless moving belt, then dumped into the huge ventilated storage pit. At intervals the grain may be reshuffled. When needed it is moved through a chute at the bottom of the elevator directly into railway cars, trucks, and shipping vessels. At some stage the grain is generally graded as to kernel size, volume and weight, moisture content, degree of damage, and other qualities.

Soybeans, peanuts, other beans and nuts are handled and stored in a similar way in ventilated bins of appropriate sizes.

The most widely used farm method for storing potatoes, other root crops, onions, cabbage, and apples is an insulated above-ground building equipped with storage bins and cooled by air. Fans circulate the air but, more importantly, remove the heat generated by the respiring commodities. The fans also cool them by introducing outside air (above the damaging freezing mark) when it is at a lower temperature than that in the store, as during the night.

Cold storage

A major improvement was refrigerated warehouses adapted for the storage of all kinds of perishable commodities. Besides fruits and vegetables, they receive meat, eggs, dairy products, fish, and other perishables. This kind of storage now utilizes mechanical refrigeration; in its early history the cooling medium was ice. A complete cold chain has gradually become a reality in the United States, providing cooling from the point of harvest through the holding (storing) of commodities and also manufactured products; during transportation at all stages, and in wholesale and retail markets. Meat, butter, eggs, bananas, and other fruits are carried in refrigerated vessels, trucks, railway cars, and more recently in cargo planes. Supermarkets and other retail outlets have refrigerated display cabinets. Homes and institutions are equipped with refrigerators. Frequently general cooling is extended into preserving the foods through freezing.

FOOD PROCESSING

How plant products are made digestible

Man either cannot use, or at best can only inefficiently use, his food-plant products in their natural state. He can indeed chew and swallow grains, seeds, and tubers (for example carrots) but any such consumption yields extremely little nourishment. Juicy, mature fruit may render a little more. Only when man breaks through the plant cell wall in a more effective manner do the gastric juices really gain access to the nutrients encased within these cell walls. This requires quite drastic processing, such as popping, milling (extended, repeated crushing), fermenting, long-time cooking, or comminuting. The milling of grains—crushing them and separating their inedible parts—is an ancient kind of processing, older perhaps than any save cooking. Fermentation is almost as old. Both presumably antedate plant cropping, since they can be applied to wild seeds as well as to cultivated grains. Other plants require various kinds of processing.

Fermentation is in particular the basis of the utilization of soybeans, peanuts, and similar seeds by Asians and Africans, through which they produce cheeselike curds. A milk is further made through the cooking of oilseeds (like soybeans and peanuts). Whether it was a chance happening or the fortunate outcome of trying different fermentation processes, the further result was to remove numerous deleterious or even toxic ingredients in the original raw material. Certain leguminous seeds in India cause leg paralysis. Others contain antivitamins, directly counteracting vitamins such as thiamine and pyridoxine. A surprising number of the leguminous seeds contain so-called trypsin inhibitors, which in a negative way affect protein utilization. Recent findings have detected such compounds also in certain cereals, even in wheat. Many nuts contain bitter compounds, several of which are harmful to man. Prominent among these are the cyanogenetic glucosides which in their metabolic breakdown release hydrocyanic acid. This is the specific ingredient appearing when bitter almonds are crushed. This particular chain of reactions takes place in a great many other foods, one important example being the cassava—manioc—of Brazil and Africa. Naturally such foods need to be detoxified prior to consumption.

Preservation methods

Perishable foods need to be preserved to make possible their long-time storage, whereby man accomplishes a year-round availability and a reduced dependence on growing and harvesting seasons. The methods used have to control intrinsic chemical changes and check microbial spoilage.

The following methods have been contrived for this dual purpose:

Drying (dehydration)	Fermentation
Salting	Freezing
Smoking	Cooling
Pickling (marinating)	Canning

The simplest means of preservation is offered by the cold winter-season temperatures which permit safe holding of most commodities like grain, beans, nuts, and especially tubers and root crops.

Drying is Nature's own device to save the ripened seeds, and in early days sun and wind were man's principal agents for removing water from food. Modern techniques have extended this preserving method into what is called dehydration by speeding up the water removal through heating, vacuum treatment, and other means. Sometimes drying is supplemented by smoking, especially of meat, fish, and cheese.

The preserving qualities of ordinary salt created the basis for another invaluable procedure with a long history. As late as 1900 most bulk foods in the United States were preserved with salt: meat, butter, cheese, fish, and even vegetables. Now salt is less used as a preservative than as a flavoring. Sugar is another important preservative in the making of jams, jellies, fruit syrups, and fruits.

Bacterial cultures initiate fermentation in many foods, enhancing their digestibility and making them less perishable by the formation of acids, in particular lactic and acetic acids, formed during fermentation. Cheeses, fish sauces, and sauerkraut are three key items in this category. The Chinese and Japanese have developed similar products based on soybeans, peanuts, coconut and the like. Fermentation also led to pickling, sometimes termed marinating, which accomplishes preservation by directly adding vinegar (acetic acid).

Freezing has almost as long a history as drying and goes back nearly to the dawn of man. It has evolved into a highly sophisticated technical procedure. By moving far below the freezing point of most foods (30° to 25°F) into the range of 0° to −20°F, it is possible to preserve flavor, appearance, nutritive value, and in many instances also structure. Most foods, even elaborate dishes such as complete TV dinners, change little when held at these low temperatures for weeks and months. Microbial spoilage is then under control.

In canning the destruction of microorganisms and prevention of renewed contamination is achieved through heating food in hermetically sealed containers.

Among commonly used foods *a few examples* are given below within each category as a reminder of the tremendous role preservation plays in modern living.

Dehydrated

Fruits (apricots, dates, apples, peaches, raisins)

Potato (chips, flakes, flour)

Nonfat milk solids

Beef

Cod

Canned

Tomato juice

Fruits (apple sauce, pineapple)

Fruit juices (pineapple, apple, cranberry)

Corned beef

Luncheon meat (Spam, Treat, Mor)

Fish (salmon, tuna, sardine)

Soups

Frozen

Fruits (berries, peaches)

Vegetables (peas, spinach, broccoli)

Fruit-juice concentrates (orange, lemon)

Fish fillets (cod, sole, haddock

Shrimp

Pies and pizza

TV dinners

Salted

Ham, bacon

Sausages

Herring

Fermented and canned

Cucumber pickles

Sauerkraut

Historic practices

With the exception of canning, current methods of preservation have a very long history. Drying, salting, fermentation, and freezing are all based on thousands of years of experience. Most of them have been improved technically through scientific advances, especially during this century.

Canning is the only preservation method new for modern times. It was invented in France in the beginning of the nineteenth century, but made its triumphant breakthrough in the past hundred years. There are few foods which are not generally canned in one kind of pack or another, cereals being the chief exception. But canning also had its precursors in such procedures as the cooking of jams, the embedding of meats in fat, and boiling in general, sometimes with the addition of vinegar. Perishable foods such as animal products, fruits, and vegetables are still preserved in many regions through such less sophisticated methods.

Salting and drying have lost ground in the affluent West to canning and freezing, yet these old-time methods are highly important to hundreds of millions of people. In medieval Europe most fish and meat were salted. Herring and cod were salted and dried. For centuries, historic long-distance sea voyages and even land journeys by explorers and traders depended on salted and dried food. Scurvy, a serious form of vitamin-C deficiency, was orginally attributed to the high amount of salt in such diets.

Silaging

Old-time haymaking in the field has been replaced by modern mechanical devices for cutting, crushing, drying, and compressing hay into bales, wafers, or pellets. Old-fashioned hay is increasingly being replaced with other forage crops handled the same way. Such forage, whether corn, sorghum, legumes, or others, is also preserved in silos for off seasons by employing controlled fermentation or by adding acids to check microbial spoilage. Sometimes low-grade molasses, a waste product from the manufacture of sugar, is added to nurture acid-producing microorganisms, thereby attaining a preserving effect. The end product of these processes is called silage, a feed with high nutritive value.

Milling

Milling is undisputedly the largest and most important branch of the food industry. Nearly all grain must be milled to be usable as human food, primarily to make flour for baking and cooking, rice being an exception. Seed coats (hulls) and seed germs are in most instances removed; the germs contain oils that oxidize and severely limit the "keeping" quality of flour during storage. The kernel itself is crushed and milled and the flour sifted according to particle size. The degree of extraction in the production of fine flour from wheat is about three-fourths. The residue is middlings and bran, used chiefly as animal feed. Even primitive milling yields some bran residues. This is a price that has to be paid in order to make the nutritive content of grain seeds available to man. The inevitable loss of some B-vitamins and calcium in the milling is often compensated by so-called fortification, that is, by adding these ingredients to the final flour.

FLOW OF CEREAL GRAIN

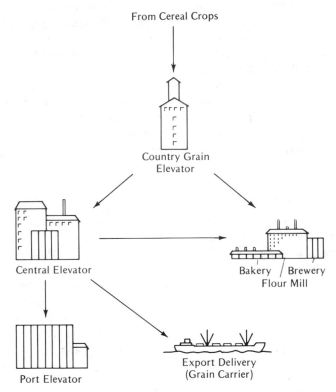

From Cereal Crops

Country Grain
Elevator

Central Elevator

Bakery / Brewery
Flour Mill

Port Elevator

Export Delivery
(Grain Carrier)

Initial steps in the marketing of cereal grains. Grain moves via elevators to flour mills, bakeries, breweries, and the like, or to exporting ports for storage and dispatch.

In the milling of rice, about half the volume comes out as whole kernels, a sixth as fragmented kernels, and an eighth as bran. The remaining fifth is husks, which are discarded or used as fuel. The silvery seed coat removed in the final polishing of rice is rich in vitamins, especially B_1, B_2, and B_6. Paradoxically, rice bran therefore has a higher nutritive value than the rice itself, but unfortunately these nutritive riches are not directly accessible to the human gastric system. The bran is therefore utilized as animal feed. It could yield first-rate edible oil and thus furnish the rice-eating people an important source of fat, as yet only partially recovered in Japan and the United States. Food research here has a vital task, since eight times the oil produced from olives could be extracted from this source. Rice could actually contribute 13 pounds of edible oil annually to each of the world's rice eaters.

Parboiling

A processing practice of central importance is the parboiling of rice. Most rice eaten in the Western world is now preprocessed through boiling prior to the milling, which facilitates rapid cooking later. The East Indians developed this method two thousand years ago, but little realized that in this way their entire subcontinent was saved from various vitamin-deficiency diseases that hit other parts of Asia when these countries introduced polishing of the rice. During this parboiling process the vitamins in the seed coat penetrate into the seed kernel proper, which is otherwise almost void of vitamins. The vitamin losses through the subsequent polishing are in this way reduced. Furthermore the seeds become less brittle and do not crack as much during the milling, bringing down by half or better the losses inflicted by broken kernels.

Special processing of plant products

The first large-scale food industries were the bakeries in ancient Egypt and Rome. They were the precursors of the modern development where not only processing and preservation, but also cooking and other preparations are transferred from the home to the factory, which produces semiprepared or ready-to-eat foods, often called "convenience foods." Even older than the bakeries were the presses which extracted oil from olives. These were the forerunners of the fat and edible oil industries which press or extract fat from a number of oilseeds. The margarine industry is the largest among the food-fat manufacturers. This product is chiefly based on vegetable oils from soybeans, peanuts, and sunflower.

Other major cereal products manufactured industrially are macaroni and breakfast cereals. Macaroni is made by extruding dough through dies to create a multitude of shapes. Eggs or special nutrients may be added to the macaroni dough. The manufacture ends with a drying process. Breakfast cereals are made into many types such as flakes, granules, or nuggets, generally ready-to-eat. Wheat and oats are milled to make breakfast cereals that require cooking before eating.

Akin to bread as a processed cereal product is beer. Both involve the same biochemical processes. Most beers are made from barley but wheat, millet, and rice beers are made in some countries. Corn and rice are frequent adjuncts in current commercial brewing. The first step is the germination of the kernels (malting) to produce enzymes for the conversion of starch into sugars. Malting is followed by mashing the malt and added ingredients. The mash is filtered to give wort, which is then boiled. At this stage yeasts are added and a controlled fermentation carried through, in which the sugars ultimately break down into alcohol and carbon dioxide, giving the final beer, which is stored in kegs or tanks or bottled. Hops are added to keep out undesirable interference from microoorganisms other than yeast.

Corn is the base for the making of syrups (concentrated sugar solutions) and starch. Starch is also made from potato, in particular in Europe.

The manufacturing of sugar is chiefly based on cane and beets. It has increasingly been geared to the making of an end product free from minerals and protein. Under primitive conditions, as in rural parts of Central and South America and India, less refined sugar products are marketed that have the advantage for the consumer of containing nutritionally significant minerals and trace elements, such as calcium and iron. However, there is a risk that these sugar products will be contaminated.

Potato is made edible and digestible mainly through cooking but it may also be grated for preparation as pancakes or related dishes. During this century industries making special potato products have emerged, such as flakes or powder for mashed potato, French-fried potato, chips, and others. Similar flour, flakes, grits, and other products are offered by budding banana industries.

In tropical Africa and Brazil related industries exist to make tapioca flour from cassava tubers. The tubers are grated, and the pulp washed in water to eliminate poisonous hydrocyanic acid. The pulp is then pressed and dried into flour. From the root of the taro (*Colocasia esculenta* L.) another product is made. The cleaned, chopped roots are strained into a paste called poi, which used to be a bulk food on many Polynesian islands. On some of them there are still special factories for this purpose. The authentic menu for a Hawaiian banquet, the luau, includes poi.

Products that are similar to cheese curds are manufactured through fermentation from many kinds of beans, nuts, and other seeds. Such products are encountered in many variants all around the globe. Several microorganisms are usually involved in the fermentation, but the prime role is held by bacteria yielding lactic acid, which has a preserving effect. Several molds are active but in particular those belonging to the *Mucorales* group. Such products rarely cause poisonings. Empirically man learned under which conditions such fermentation may be hazardous.

Most fruits and vegetables are both canned and frozen; some are dried. A trend since World War II has been to drink fruits rather than eat them. This has created a major new industry in both Europe and North America. Europe is dominated by juices of apple and black currant. The United States has favored citrus juices also made into concentrates, chiefly orange, but also grapefruit and lemon. Tomato juice has become a standard food item in many countries.

The demand for convenience has pushed on to the food market an avalanche of new processed foods, ready-to-eat, semiprepared, or in other degrees of preparedness for eating. Traditional commodities, such as potatoes and carrots, appear each in ten to twenty alternative preparations—cut in different ways, prepeeled, tailored for French-frying, and many more. This development is termed fractionation and has vastly expanded the inventories of supermarkets. In the United States the listed market items now reach 6,000 to 8,000 in the average store. In the wake of this new trend traditional beverages have emerged as dehydrated items, especially soluble coffee and tea. Newer types are freeze-dried.

Processing of animal foods

In contrast to plant products, which as a general practice must be treated to become nutritionally accessible and digestible as human food, animal products—milk, meat, and eggs—can be eaten with full benefit even in the raw form. For these, processing serves another function, namely that of preserving, making them less perishable. Nonetheless the processing industries manufacture a great many special food products, some of which are listed here:

Milk	Meat	Eggs	Fish
Fresh (market) milk	Sausages	Packaged, fresh eggs	Fish fillets, also frozen
Skim milk	Preserves	Egg solids	Canned fish
Dried milk	Cold cuts		Grated fish
Cheese	Meat balls		Fish dumplings
Butter	Meat stews		Pickled fish
Ice cream	Meat pies		Fish sauces
			Caviar
			Protein concentrates

The harvests from the waters are preserved with the same methods as agricultural products—through salting, drying, fermentation, pickling, freezing, and canning. They have given rise to large-scale processing industries in most major fishing nations. Many prepared specialties are also made commer-

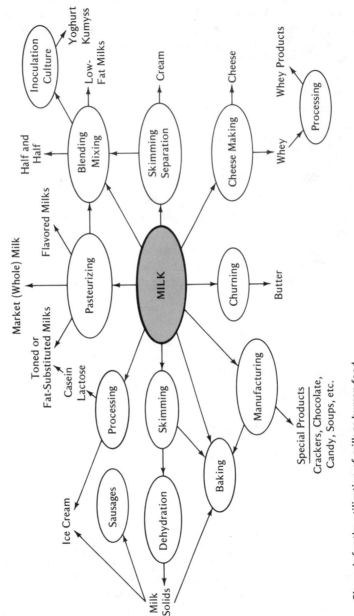

Channels for the utilization of milk as human food.

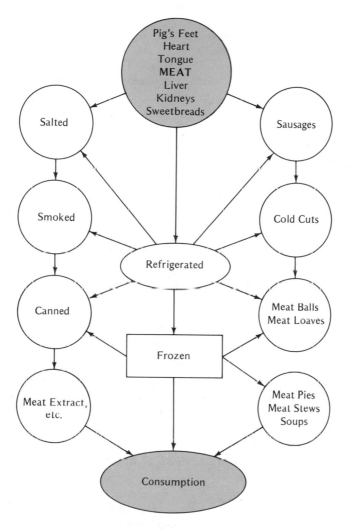

Channels for the utilization of meat as human food.

cially, such as fish balls, soups, and jellies and in later years also fish sausages, a Japanese innovation launched in the 1950's and gaining a major market in Japan in the 1960's. The fisheries revolution since World War II, described in Chapter 6, has entailed the transfer of a considerable portion of this handling and preparation to especially equipped vessels operating at the fishing grounds, floating processing plants.

Chemical additives

Since World War II, much of the food debate in well-fed countries has focused on the use of chemical additives. The matter has been greatly confused by a lack of clear distinction between chemicals: on the one hand, those used in manufacturing with specific technical and nutritional aims in mind; on the other hand, certain chemicals that have appeared as contaminants. This latter group includes especially the residues of pesticides and fungicides used on crops in the field. Such compounds are obviously not food additives in a strict sense but rather are troublesome pollutants.

Chemicals used as true food additives may be categorized in the following manner:

Nutrients	Emulsifiers
Preservatives	Desiccating substances
Antioxidants	Flavor substances
Thickening agents	Coloring matter

Four factors are in this context of particular importance:

1. Despite the intense debate the development, above all in the satisfied world, has largely gone in the opposite direction, namely less dependence on chemicals in the preservation of food. Since the turn of the century freezing, canning, and modern dehydration have created a large nonchemicalized sector as regards daily food. Until about 1900, the preservation of meat, fish, butter, cheese, and vegetables, was still dominated by salt. The human body had to remove annually, mostly via the kidneys, at least 200 pounds of salt (sodium chloride), often more. Most of this big chemical load has been eliminated.

2. This major breakthrough for nonchemical procedures has removed from the public-health scene a great number of very hazardous compounds resulting from molding, putrefaction, and other spoilage. Nowadays we know far more about the toxic nature of many of these compounds and, in particular those resulting from molds, the mycotoxins that constitute hazards to grains and oilseeds, and, via feedstuffs, to animal products.

3. The volume of technical aid to developing countries has not included minimal efforts to mobilize refrigeration technology for the benefit of the hungry, warm world where it is actually more crucially needed than in the satisfied world. Likewise, little attention has been devoted to their need for packaging.

4. Sun, wind, and salt are still the prevalent food-preserving resources and they can be made much more efficient. Chemical preservatives may very well maintain their position as an efficient and cheap method for the hungry world. Radiation preservation and freeze-drying have very little to offer to a world in misery. It is deplorable that the study of these particular methods has dominated to such a high degree the food research since World War II.

Fabricated foods

"Synthetic food" is a misnomer commonly encountered. Outside of food additives, very few chemical compounds used as food are manufactured through chemical synthesis; even fewer have turned out to be amenable to the metabolism of the human body. Furthermore, they are far from competitive in price.

The term "synthetic food" generally covers fat, protein, and vitamins produced through the growth of microorganisms (yeast, other fungi, or bacteria) on special substrates. An alternative way of making "synthetics" is the chemical conversion of cellulose, starch, or carbohydrates into sugars. A third category is the making of imitation foods. An example is the tailoring of soybean protein, spun into fibers, to simulate beef, bacon, or poultry; the milk protein casein is in this instance used as a binder and flavor substances are added to enhance the resemblance. Imitation milk may be made using soybean protein and various vegetable fats. The most successful item in this category is coffee whiteners. Efforts are currently being made to establish the term "fabricated foods" for these products largely based on ingredients manufactured from plant crops, livestock, or microorganisms.

Making food strictly through chemical synthesis is an old dream but one quite removed from any economic reality. This kind of food would not, in fact, free man from his bondage to nature. Such synthetic foods, when eaten, would ultimately break down into carbon dioxide and ammonia and return to the carbon and nitrogen cycles of nature, to be recaptured only by photosynthesis and nitrogen-fixing organisms.

The best, perhaps the only reasonable, way to improve on man's food base would be to accelerate this natural cycling or, still better, short-cut it. This will presumably be an inevitable outcome of urbanization, currently coupled with a mounting accumulation of sewage, which is overloading natural waters with excessive pollution. In the future, as a result, sewage plants will have to be transformed into food-producing centers. Various final products emerging from these new cyclings will be such foods as yeast, insects, fish, rabbits, squab, quail, or other small birds.

Waste and waste disposal

Food animals and poultry in the past often came to retail markets with hides, feathers, hoofs, and claws still on—sometimes even live. In recent decades this has become less common in our Western world, where such inedible parts are now largely removed in early processing. Most animals and poultry are slaughtered, eviscerated, skinned, boned, reduced to wholesale or even retail cuts in central plants; fish are eviscerated, their heads and fins and tails removed, and even filleted. Plant products also may have stems, peel, outer leaves, and seed pods removed. Grain milling has always removed the chaff (bran) and middlings. All this diminishes the volume of household waste and communal garbage, but concentrates and enlarges the volume from the food processing industry, which has as a result become an important factor in water pollution. It has increasingly been necessary to convert such waste into feed or to salvage certain food ingredients. This applies to waste from slaughterhouses, poultry establishments, dairies, and other processing plants. Some waste is spread as fertilizer in combination with irrigation. Algae, yeast, or bacteria are raised on such waste. These products have so far mostly been utilized as livestock feed, but also as feed for fish and other aquatic animals in cultivation ponds, the last especially in Asia. In the Soviet Union and Eastern Europe pond cultivation is often combined with raising of ducks.

The developing countries and food processing

Most developing countries lack an adequate infrastructure in the form of storage facilities, food industries, and other processing plants. In rich nations we take all this for granted. This third dimension of the food issue has been grossly neglected. The tragic result is that at least half of what the soils produce is never consumed by either man or livestock. Both foodstuffs and feedstuffs require storage, preservation, and in many cases special processing. It is therefore safe to say that an enlarged production of food and feed does not necessarily mean that more people are being provided.

Equally valid is the assertion that many hundred millions more people could be fed without producing one ton more of food, merely by a vigorous campaign against waste, losses, and spoilage. Construction of more storage facilities and food-processing plants may therefore be the more effective toward providing for more people. In addition these facilities are cheaper and easier to build than fertilizer plants and expensive irrigation dams.

We who belong to the well-fed world have great difficulty in grasping the complexities that confront the food industry in the hungry countries. In many instances such unheeded obstacles have jeopardized the operation of already constructed plants and in other cases prevented the creation of new ones. The most critical factor in this context is water; water in adequate quantity and quality is a prerequisite for even a minimal degree of sanitation. Only a few additional such complications will be referred to here:

Large fluctuations in the availability of raw products occur from season to season and from day to day as well as from year to year. Volumes of raw products for processing on a scale that is economically feasible are therefore often inadequate.

Raw products must frequently be purchased in small quantities. As a result the quality varies with seasons and place of origin.

Losses are large, especially of animal products, because of attacks by parasites and numerous animal diseases.

Lack of refrigeration facilities, especially for the handling of raw products, may jeopardize the entire production.

Large losses take place in all the links of the food chain; in agriculture due to poor pest control, in storage, and during transportation and processing.

DISTRIBUTION AND MARKETING

Refrigeration, transportation, and packaging

In the developed world man has moved far away from sustenance farming toward a market economy, involving in some cases entire continents as in the United States, the Soviet Union, and Australia. With increased urbanization and industrialization as well as intensified mechanization of agriculture it has become imperative to improve transportation in order to secure a satisfactory distribution of food. The use of refrigeration in ships, railroad cars, and highway trucks has created transport chains that protect perishable food from rapid spoilage during the summer season and from frost damage in the winter. Airplanes have of late gained importance in this long-distance hauling of food; troublesome port transfers have thus been eliminated. An example of such air transport of a major commodity is meat deliveries from Chicago to Hawaii.

Food transportation costs show a steeply mounting trend comparable to the population growth and the ever larger distances between producing regions and consumer centers. These costs interact with the demand for improved packaging and the desire to lower package weight in relation to contents. Transportation and packaging present particularly conspicuous differences between the rich world and the hungry nations. Even within the affluent world, privileged top strata of society are often the prime beneficiaries of the impressive technological advances of our time: refrigeration, food processing, transportation, and packaging.

Large-scale changes in retail trade

During this century changes in retailing of food in the Western world have been revolutionary to say the least. Two developments have chiefly contributed to this: (1) the automobile has become almost every man's property, allowing long-distance pick-up of daily food, and (2) packaging technology has advanced at a rapid pace, in regard to machinery and materials. There are closing machines with the almost unbelievable capacity of sealing 600 to 1,000 cans a minute; these are on stream with equally fast machines that fill the containers and weigh the contents. The collectivization of society and the great influx of women into gainful employment have brought about a movement of cooking away from the home to processing plants. Schools, hospitals, and other institutions, plant cafeterias, and innumerable eating places are increasingly assuming the function of supplying food at the point of consumption. Currently in the United States these account for 25 to 30 percent of the food market. This vast stream of foods thus bypasses the retail trade, which is increasingly dominated by supermarkets.

Food distribution in developing countries

In food distribution the developing countries lag behind their needs at least as much as if not more than in food processing. Local farm markets and home delivery of milk, meat, fruit, and vegetables are still prevalent in many parts of the world. Sophisticated distribution is not compatible with subsistence farms, often less than two acres in size, that are predominant in world agriculture. Approximately 250 million of the world's 350 million farms are thus small.

In the developing countries, the distribution of farm products or even industry-prepared food is confronted with further serious obstacles, above all the following:

—Undersized and deficient road systems

—Shortage of railroad cars and trucks for delivery

—Less suitable location of production in relation to population centers (due to lack of planning or to shortage of agricultural land, which cannot always be remedied)

—Inadequate storage facilities and consequent defective conditions for storage

—Lack of suitable packaging material, hence use of material easily attacked by molds, penetrable by insects, or not moisture-proof

—Less effective food control (permitting adulteration such as water in milk), specifically less suitable livestock inspection

These shortcomings are more or less common in large parts of Latin America, Asia, and tropical Africa, and cause considerable losses of food in the distribution chain.

LOSSES TO THE GLOBAL HOUSEHOLD

Even in the developed world—the United States, the United Kingdom, and Australia—the cities are involved in a heavy battle against rodents. According to estimates made in India, rats eat more grain than the large deliveries from abroad bring into the country; their number is indicated as being in the billions. In many parts of tropical Africa and Indonesia, rats and insects—chiefly locusts—are themselves eaten as an indispensable supplement to nearly unavailable meat. It would take forceful measures to break the sway of rats and insects.

The third dimension of the food issue—storage, processing, and handling of the foods produced—could very well become the most important factor in the battle against world hunger. As it now is, the losses are staggering, and there is no doubt that hundreds of millions more people could be fed if these matters were properly taken care of. The big losses occur during storage of raw products such as grain, beans, and tubers. Even in temperate countries losses may reach one-tenth, in critical years twice as much. In warm latitudes the losses often are as high as one-half. Thus, for instance, half the sorghum crop in tropical Africa is eaten by insects during a single year's storage. Birds also take a toll—not only in the fields; by pecking holes in grain bags they ruin considerable amounts of grain.

All this together with the enormous losses in crop and animal production discussed in previous chapters, is part of the GROSS NATIONAL WASTE on the food account. It is rarely calculated but should be established as an item on the debit side of the ledger to be balanced out against the GROSS NATIONAL PRODUCT on the credit side.

REFERENCES AND RECOMMENDATIONS
FOR FURTHER READING

Benjamin, E. W., J. M. Gwin, F. L. Faber, and W. D. Termohlen. *Marketing Poultry Products.* New York: Wiley, 1960. 328 pp.

Borgstrom, G., *Principles of Food Science.* New York, Macmillan, 1968. 2 vols., 397 and 473 pp.

Duddington, C. L., *Microorganisms as Allies.* London: Faber, 1961. 256 pp.

FAO. *Meat Hygiene.* Rome: FAO Agricultural Studies, No. 34, 1957. 527 pp.

Kent, N. L., *Technology of Cereals.* Oxford and New York: Pergamon Press, 1966. 262 pp.

Kon, G. K., *Milk and Milk Products in Human Nutrition.* Rome: FAO Nutritional Study No. 17, 1959. 76 pp.

Lawrie, R. A., *Meat Science.* London and New York: Pergamon Press, 1966. 368 pp.

Moore, J. R., and R. G. Walsh. *Market Structure of the Agricultural Industries.* Ames: Iowa State University Press, 1966. 412 pp.

Munro, J. W., *Pests of Stored Products.* London: Hutchinson, 1966. 234 pp.

Price, J. F., and B. S. Schweigert (eds.) *The Science of Meat and Meat Products,* 2nd ed. San Francisco: Freeman, 1971. 420 pp.

Pyke, M., *Food Science and Technology*, 2nd ed. London: Murray, 1968. 219 pp.

Topel, D. G., *The Pork Industry.* Ames: Iowa State University Press, 1968. 236 pp.

REVIEW AND RESEARCH QUESTIONS

1. What causes spoilage of food or its raw products?

2. Why must man arrange storage for part of his crops and animal production?

3. List the most important methods for holding food in storage or preserving it through processing.

4. Through which channels do cereal grains move before ending up as bread on the consumer's table?

5. Why are harvested but unprocessed plant products less digestible to man than animal products at the same stage?

6. Discuss the relative significance of salted and dried foods to the hungry world and to our technically more advanced world.

7. Describe the process of grain milling.

8. What does a bakery do?

9. What different kinds of products (food and feed) are made from corn (*or* from potato)?

10. List different ways to preserve and process juicing fruits such as oranges or pineapples.

11. What meat (*or* dairy) products do you regularly eat? List them and outline briefly how they are prepared.

12. What is meant by food additives? Discuss the present controversy as to their use.

13. What is meant by "synthetic" foods as contrasted to "fabricated" foods?

14. Why has waste from food-processing plants become such a grave issue?

15. What advantages do we in the satisfied world gain through possessing a food industry, which by and large the poor world lacks?

16. Review how the bulk of your daily food reaches your home or supermarket—starting in the field, on the seas, or in the barn.

17. What is the global role of food waste and spoilage and what needs to be done to remedy this?

International Trade 9
in Food and Feed

World trade in food and feeds fills the function of long-distance feeding and supplementation, in particular to regions that do not raise adequate quantities to provide for their population. However, and contrary to the traditional attitude, national self-sufficiency in these commodities remains desirable in a rational, well-organized world. It is most unfortunate that we have allowed world population to grow to such dimensions that the world food trade is imperative, for it can only serve as a stopgap, a device for temporary relief, or as an expedient when catastrophe hits.

In past times food played a subordinate role in the world exchange of goods. Salt for preservation was, however, an important commodity. The early food trade was essentially regional and limited: camel routes in the Middle East, ship traffic on the Mediterranean and the Black Sea (Rome received one-third of its grain from its protectorates Egypt and Carthage), coastal traffic in the Far East such as that between Indonesia and China. From the seventeenth century onward, fast sailing ships brought tea and spices from the Far East to Europe. In the early nineteenth century, limited quantities of grain were shipped, also by sailing ships, from Australia and Argentina to Europe.

Long-distance delivery of any magnitude did not become feasible until modern transportation could offer steamships, motor ships, and trains. During the latter part of the nineteenth century, mechanical refrigeration came into use and made into reality the transoceanic deliveries of perishables such as meat, butter, and fresh fruit. Europe became the main recipient of large quantities of food from practically all continents. World trade in food reached its peak in relative terms during the 1930's but now rarely exceeds one-tenth of the world consumption.

In volume transported, grain has the lead, followed by sugar. Next come oilseeds, primarily soybeans. Fruit takes fourth place, dominated by bananas, oranges, and apples. Oilseed cake is the next item, and finally coffee, cocoa, tea, and spices. Due to the distribution of purchasing power in the world, the lion's share of food and feed commodities moves to and between the well-fed and affluent nations. Naturally, any country's true surpluses for sale on the world market have as a prerequisite adequate soil and water resources which enable the country to produce more than is needed to feed its people. This point of view has not been sufficiently considered in the discussion about the exchange of goods between countries and about the structuring of international food trade. In far too many instances food exports are maintained at the cost of critical domestic malnutrition. The cash crops exported may include food and/or other plantation commodities. The exporting countries, however, have been forced to devote a growing share of their earnings in foreign exchange to the purchase of direly needed food. This development is an immediate result of the population explosion and is further compounded by declining prices for basic commodities coupled with mounting prices for industrial hardware. The hungry, poor world has since 1952 made a notable gain in volume of deliveries, exceeding 35 percent, but its net gain in foreign currency is a petty 4 percent. This dilemma stimulated the convening of the United Nations Commission on Trade and Development (UNCTAD). Three major conferences (in Geneva, 1964, in New Delhi, 1968, and in Santiago, Chile, in 1972), however, made little advance toward coming to grips with this crucial obstacle to world development.

CHANGED PATTERNS
IN TRADE AND PROCESSING

At the turn of the century there was a great deal of talk about the benefits of producing food and feed in those countries where doing this would be cheapest and most advantageous from the climatic point of view. In this way commodities would become cheap in price and such trade would lead to increased prosperity, it was maintained. This line of thought, in combination with the idea about industrial countries and raw-material countries as two distinct categories, came to dominate trade policies. This thought pattern has survived in the present economic debate despite the fact that mankind long ago passed the point in time when such an ideal arrangement was workable.

Man has now become too numerous and is forced to produce food and feed even under conditions which are obviously unfavorable or demand uneconomical capital investments. The truly needy possess too little purchasing power to import food. World trade in food has therefore constantly been shrinking in relative volume. Less and less of the soil's total yield is being carried from one continent to another. Not until the 1960's did an opposite trend toward expanded international trade become prevalent as the result of large aid deliveries and bigger purchases by the developed world both from rich and poor nations; but this trend is once again waning.

Some of the reduction is in waste and tare tonnage; some of the waste is usable. World trade already is receiving more than 70,000 metric tons of banana flakes, originating in the many plants operating in Brazil and Central America. Peel and stalk are converted into cattle feed. Losses through spoilage are almost entirely eliminated.

Coffee is another important article in world trade of which North America and Western Europe take five-sixths. Here also a new economic order is shaping up. Plants for making coffee concentrates or dried solubles are gradually being built in the producing countries. The coffee grounds become valuable cattle feed.

A similar development has taken place as to oranges, in this case with the United States in the lead. The foremost industrial orange product is juice concentrate. Peels and other residues are silaged or mixed with molasses for use as cattle feed. Florida once sent her cattle north to fatten on the rich pastures of the prairie rangelands, but now has no less than twelve slaughter-houses mainly based on the waste from juice-concentrate plants. In the future we will not be able to afford peeling and eating oranges or bananas and thus discarding as garbage what is too precious in a world forced to economize.

THE COMMODITIES IN THE TRADE

Grain

Rice, despite the fact that it is second only to wheat as the dominant world grain, holds a very modest rank in the international food trade. Few rice-producing countries have a surplus to offer, in fact only Thailand, Burma, and Cambodia. The United Arab Republic (Egypt), Pakistan, and China export rice despite considerable grain shortages of their own. The United States, although a minor producer, accounts for one-third of the world trade, another evidence of the limited over-all trade in rice.

The world grain trade is dominated by feed cereals. Three-fourths thereof is brought from North America to Western Europe, chiefly corn but also considerable quantities of wheat. In addition Europe buys wheat from the River Plate countries and millet from tropical Africa.

Relief deliveries since World War II to mitigate famine and undernourishment have consisted chiefly of wheat. This flow actually started after World War I with shipments from North and South America to war-devastated Europe. Emergency deliveries to hungry nations were resumed after World War II and have since been a permanent feature in the international transfer of food. Despite this, little has been done to normalize these shipments as a continuing feature of the global exchange of commodities. Most United States deliveries have taken place within the framework of special assistance programs such as those under Public Law No. 480, Food for Peace, and similar aid programs.

Oilseeds

Oilseeds, above all peanuts and soybeans, constitute another important category in world trade. The export of peanuts has shrunk substantially since the 1930's, but Africa (Nigeria, the Ivory Coast, and other countries) is still shipping two-thirds of its peanut production to Europe. From the Philippines, Indonesia, and the Fiji Islands dried coconut (copra) goes to Europe and North America. The international trade in palm nuts and kernels as well as in cottonseed is also significant.

The common name for this kind of commodity is *oilseed crops.* By and large they serve as raw material for the margarine industry and for the manufacturing of other fats and oils. The press residues, high in protein, are utilized in the form of cakes or meal.

Though many oil-extracting industries have been created in the crop-raising countries themselves, the world economy has not adjusted to the realities of protein needs. Almost all oilseed cakes and meal reaching the world market are absorbed by Europe, which in this way is receiving no less than 2 million tons of protein. Even hungry India has gone back to the pattern of colonial days and is providing peanut cake to feed the cattle of the United Kingdom and other European countries. In effect, India has become the biggest exporter of this item on the world market, though she needs every ounce of this valuable protein for her own undernourished millions.

The large soybean acreage of the United States, much of it created since World War II and now exceeding 2.5 million acres, provides first of all the basis for the United States margarine industry. The press residues are utilized as cattle and hog feed. A mere one-tenth is used directly as human food. Of the exported soybeans about three-fifths go to Western Europe and one-third to Japan; Canada, Israel, and Taiwan share around 8 percent (see table on page 222). Only a pittance reaches the needy world.

By contrast, in the overpopulated and poor countries of the East, soybeans are almost exclusively human food; they are too expensive to use otherwise. World trade in soybeans is entirely controlled by the industrial and market interests of the West. Thus it is not the nutritive needs that dictate where the soybean deliveries go, nor those of oilseeds in general. Europe and the United States do, however, ship minor quantities of soybean products to hungry countries where they are distributed, to a large extent in cooperation with UNESCO, through child-feeding programs and in clinical work on malnutrition. Some are used in the manufacturing of soybean milk, but the quantities are small in relation to actual needs.

Sugar

As was discussed in Chapter I, the Soviet and European beet-sugar production has dethroned the once almighty cane-sugar production and brought down the relative dimensions of the world's sugar trade. The United States is recipient of almost one-fourth of the sugar in world trade, followed by one-tenth each for the United Kingdom and Japan (see page 218). Despite its own high sugar production, the U.S.S.R. has, however, taken over the United States role of chief buyer of Cuba's sugar. Much of that sugar is resold by the Soviet Union. Sugar attracts a disproportionate attention in world affairs and is more than most other commodities competing for the markets of the well-to-do. The time when the Caribbean upheld a sound trade and could buy dried fish and salted meat through sugar and rum, thus exchanging calories for protein, is coming to an end as the population upsurge already forces most of these countries to buy grain, beans, and other bulk food for major portions of their people.

Luxuries and abundance

Meat, eggs, cheese, and butter moving in world trade are transported in modern vessels, equipped with refrigeration or freezing installations—and largely to North America and Europe. This is essentially also the case with fruits and vegetables. The table on page 226 and the illustration on page 138 show how little the more than 2.5 billion people on the other side of the hunger gap actually do receive. Upwards toward 70 percent of the world's refrigerated fleet is engaged in shipping bananas to Western Europe and North America. This is the more remarkable since almost half the transported weight (around 4.7 million metric tons) until recently was made up of the stalk and the peel, which end up in the garbage cans of the West. The fresh bananas are now cut from the stalk and shipped in cardboard containers. The discarded weight is still close to half. The rest of the international fruit and vegetable trade is dominated by shipments to Western Europe from practically all continents.

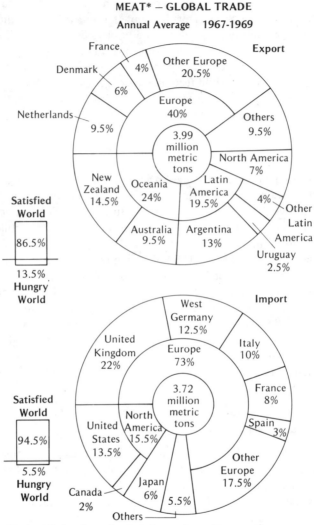

MEAT* — GLOBAL TRADE
Annual Average   1967-1969

Export

France
Denmark
4%
Other Europe
20.5%
6%
Europe
40%
Netherlands
9.5%
3.99 million metric tons
Others
9.5%
North America
7%
New Zealand
14.5%
Oceania
24%
Latin America
19.5%
4%
Other Latin America
Australia
9.5%
Argentina
13%
Uruguay
2.5%

Satisfied World
86.5%
13.5%
Hungry World

Import

West Germany
12.5%
United Kingdom
22%
Europe
73%
Italy
10%
3.72 million metric tons
France
8%
United States
13.5%
North America
15.5%
Spain
3%
Canada
2%
Japan
6%
5.5%
Other Europe
17.5%
Others

Satisfied World
94.5%
5.5%
Hungry World

*Fresh, chilled, or frozen (not including poultry and horsemeat)

Note that only 5.5 percent of the meat in the global trade moves to recipients other than North America, Europe, and Japan.

The second biggest food item in transoceanic refrigerated hauling is meat, around 1.6 million tons. The vast cattle herds of the Argentine pampas were tapped to feed Europe as early as the end of the eighteenth century, when salting was used for preservation. Most meat now hauled over long distances is either refrigerated or frozen. Such shipping became the rule at the turn of the century for bringing meat to England and the European continent from South America, Australia, and New Zealand. Most corned beef is still sold to the United States, with the United Kingdom a distant second, as in the infancy (end of the 1800's) of this South American industry.

Excess purchasing power among the affluent is largely dictating the flow of food items in the world market. Hams from Canada, Poland, Denmark, and the Netherlands weigh the shelves of United States food markets. No less than 500 kinds of cheese are also found there. Beer is moving back and forth across the world despite variations in types being only minor; no fewer than forty foreign beers enter the United States market. A lively flow of delicatessen items to, from and between nations goes on, despite hunger and poverty being the lot of the majority or sizable minorities in most countries. Another glaring example of opulent preemption in food is shrimp, collected for the United States market from seventy countries, many of which are seriously malnourished. In this luxury category we also find strawberries flown from California to Scandinavia, king crab from Alaska to New York and France, Canadian lobster to West European countries. These are only a few random examples.

During a couple of years in the 1960's Holland was the leading importer of dried skim milk and alone purchased more than the hungry world got through UNICEF and other aid programs. The dried skim milk (nonfat milk solids) was used to produce veal, which Holland in turn exported to Italy. This trade still goes on but on a smaller scale. The top-ranking agriculture of Denmark received in the latter half of the 1960's an amount of protein exceeding 250 lbs. per person annually, six times what the average Dane got through his high-quality diet during the same period. Peanuts from tropical Africa and feed grain and soybeans from the United States thus make significant contributions to the food production of Denmark. The same quaint conditions prevail in several Western nations, even though the proportions may not be as exaggerated.

Thus a picture emerges of a world where, despite all the rhetoric about battling world hunger, the lion's share of the food and feed moving in world trade is streaming into the well-fed Western world:

     —One-half of all beans and peas

     —More than one-half of the wheat

     —Three-fourths of the corn

     —Three-fifths of the soybeans

     —Nine-tenths of the peanuts (groundnuts)

     —Three-fourths of the oilseed cake

PROTEIN PURCHASES AND CONSUMPTION   1967-1968
(kilograms per person per year)

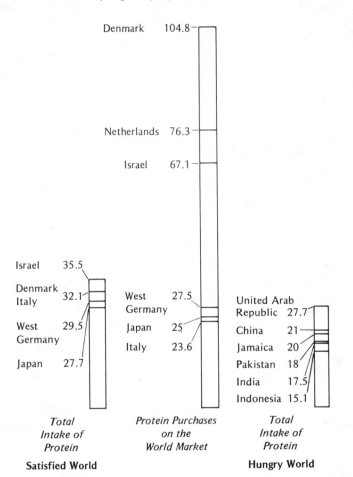

Protein purchases in the world market (central portion) compared to total annual protein intake (both plant and animal protein) in the satisfied world (left) and the hungry world (right).

Nevertheless we Westerners maintain the illusion that Europe is self-sustaining. Despite the hard-pressed food situation for two-thirds of mankind, Western Europe is the receiver of more than half of the United States wheat deliveries to the world household and gets considerably more than India. England alone gets twelve times as much grain per person as India.

On top of this, a large part of this import is used in the United Kingdom for the number one position as beef importer in the world and is the biggest importer of fish and shellfish, far outdistancing all other nations. One-tenth of the protein in the ocean catch is absorbed by the United States.

The ocean harvests

The harvests of the sea are particularly perishable. Yet close to half the ocean catches move into world trade, considerably more than for any other food category. The chief reason is that almost half of the catches are utilized for the same purpose as oilseeds. Oil is pressed for the margarine industry, chiefly of the West, and the remainder is dried into fishmeal to make high-quality protein feed for livestock production (chiefly broilers, egg layers, and hogs) in Europe and North America.

Of the fish and shellfish in world trade directly utilized as human food, two-thirds, calculated in weight, goes to the well-fed world. The chief products are canned salmon, tuna, and crab, and various kinds of frozen products, mainly fish fillets and shrimp. The remaining one-third comprises the dried and salted fish that now as formerly serves as cheap food for needy peoples, above all in Central America, the Caribbean Islands, Brazil and tropical Africa. If we look to protein, the chief ingredient, salted and dried fish contributed until the 1960's more than half the food-fish protein in world trade. The ratio is distorted by the fact that the other products weigh more, chiefly because of their higher content of water.

Production inputs

A prerequisite to food production is a considerable transfer of goods needed for inputs into modern agriculture, such as farm equipment, fuel, fertilizers, and spray chemicals. The equipment includes aircraft for spreading fertilizers and spraying crops and animals against pests and diseases. This trade also takes place primarily between the well-to-do countries. The goods of this kind that find their way to the agriculture of the developing countries have until quite recently been almost exclusively used to increase the harvests of export crops and to improve their profitability. Very little is reserved for producing food for the people themselves. A mere one-eighth of the fertilizers of the world is used by the developing countries and both in Africa and Latin America most of this is applied to plantation crops. The hunger crises of India in the 1950's and 1960's have illuminated the urgent necessity for the hungry countries to expand the use of fertilizers, this to stop the further mineral depletion of their soils.

SHIPPING RESOURCES
AND THE WORLD HUNGER

The circumstances discussed above must not obscure the indisputable fact that food trade during the period after World War II became a distinctive new feature in alleviating world hunger. The United States wheat deliveries to India are without parallel in history. For several years during the 1960's they reached a half million tons per month and sometimes even exceeded that quantity. This volume involved transportation difficulties: more than 400 vessels were employed in this conveyor-belt operation over the oceans. The ports of India were not equipped to handle such huge shipments and provisional receiving stations had to be arranged or the ships were forced to anchor offshore while being unloaded. Canada also aided in providing India with much-needed grain and furthermore sold large quantities to China. Australia participated also in selling to China. During the 3-year period from 1965 to 1967, China received no less than one million tons monthly, still a mere 3 percent of its total annual grain consumption. The purchased quantities went primarily to feed the inhabitants of the recipient port cities.

These figures serve to underline the fact that the total world trade in food and feed, as well as the food surpluses accumulated in various parts of the globe, is inadequate to banish world hunger. The shortage of food will become still more acute in the decade of the 1970's. Before 1980 the hungry countries will need 300 million metric tons more grain annually than they now consume. Even if the unbelievable were to happen and half thereof could be produced in these countries themselves, world trade would still be forced to handle five times the grain it handles presently. This volume would not only overtax the ports of recipient countries and demand enormously enlarged capacities; it would in addition cause almost unmanageable strain on the facilities of the supplying countries, primarily the United States and Canada. Not even the transport routes for delivery from the prairies via the St. Lawrence Seaway or down the Mississippi River would be adequate. Besides, the chances for a production increase of this magnitude in the poor countries seems dubious, to say the least. The so-called "green revolution" has changed nothing in this regard (see p. 176).

CARDINAL FEATURES OF THE FLOW
OF FOOD AND FEED

In summary it may be stated that grain has involved more shipping tonnage than any other dry commodity. (In single years the deliveries of coal and coke have been larger.)

Among the many anomalies in present-day world food trade, four deserve special attention:

1. Nine-tenths of the exportation of the developing countries consists of food, feed, and other agricultural products while the volume of industrial goods is negligible.
2. The United States ranks next to England as the largest importer of protein.
3. The United States is the leading buyer of fish protein (tuna, fish fillets, shrimp, lobster, and fishmeal) on the world market.
4. The developing countries stand alone as suppliers of sugar, coffee, tea, cocoa, and bananas, and are major suppliers of oilseeds to the fats-and-oils industry of the Western world and oilseed cake and meal to the feed industry of the rich nations.

For certain commodities, such as wheat, sugar, coffee, and cocoa, long-range international trade agreements exist as to production, quantity, and quality. Their primary aim is to avert trade disturbances through temporary surpluses and to dampen price fluctuations, equally damaging to exporters and importers.

The total exportation of the developing countries during the first half of the 1960's exceeded their importation. This state of matters is partly due to their heavy burden of debts through international loans. They are about to drown in debts and are forced to use 40 percent of new loans for the servicing of previous loans. Latin America, where this burden is the heaviest, used in the mid-1960's no less than 15 percent of the export receipts for these purposes, that is, for interest and principal payments on foreign loans.

REFERENCES AND RECOMMENDATIONS
FOR FURTHER READING

Cutajar, M. L., and A. Franks, *The Less Developed Countries in World Trade.* London: Overseas Development Institute, 1967. 210. pp.

Pincus, J., *Trade, Aid, and Development.* New York: McGraw-Hill, 1967. 400 pp.

Thomas, R. S. and E. C. Conkling. *Geography of International Trade.* New York: McGraw-Hill, 1967. 190 pp.

REVIEW AND RESEARCH QUESTIONS

1. Which are in tonnage the biggest items of world trade in agricultural products?

2. How do Public Law 480 deliveries to the hungry world compare in volume with United States sale deliveries to Europe?

3. Oilseeds are grown for the purpose of obtaining fats and oils. What happens with the press residues (oilseed cake and meal)?

4. Describe the sales of soybeans from the United States on the world market, and the main recipient countries.

5. How are fishmeal and fish oil traded on the world market? Who are the chief buyers?

6. Discuss the merits of the banana trade.

7. What is the function of UNCTAD?

8. Review what world trade does to alleviate world hunger.

Section III

Consumption

Man's Needs   10

Man's body has frequently been compared to a motor, requiring fuel (food) in order to run. For quite some time the notion was prevalent that when a person reached adult age fuel was the only thing needed to keep the body machinery running. As knowledge expanded and the science of nutrition evolved, this general concept was profoundly adjusted. The daily tear and wear of the body is considerable, and constant repair and renewal are taking place. In this sense the Roman adage, "Man is what he eats," conveys a basic truth. Within six to seven years most parts of the body are renewed. Blood has an overturn rate of only 10 to 15 days, while other tissues are restructured at a slower rate. Brain and nerve tissues constitute a notable exception and carry no regenerating capacity. As does all machinery, the body also needs lubrication.

THE MAIN NEEDS

Pursuing the analogy of a motor, a man's nutritional needs can be categorized in the following manner:

1. Energy-supplying ingredients, that is, fuel: mainly fat and carbohydrates.
2. Body-building substances, for growth, repair and maintenance in general: chiefly protein.
3. A number of special molecules which the human body cannot synthesize, which have key functions in vital body processes: mainly vitamins and minerals. These compounds could be called functional and play the above-mentioned role of "lubricants."

The human body contains twenty to thirty basic elements, all of which have their source in the air we breathe and in the food and water we ingest. From this food our gastric system selects ingredients vital to the function of our body. In the digestion the array of available nutrients is expanded through biochemical reactions and regroupings. Food is man's only source of nutrients. Any shortages or deficiencies in his intake affect health, bodily efficiency, and mental alertness. Resistance to infections and other diseases hinges upon the adequacy of the food intake, as does recovery from damages (broken limbs, wounds, abrasions). Currently, we believe we know how to compose an adequate diet, yet at no time in history have so many hundreds of millions of people suffered from shortages and deficiencies, from undernutrition and malnutrition.

A true understanding of the world's hunger crisis depends on recognition of the basic nutritional needs. They will be briefly summarized.

ENERGY-SUPPLYING FOODS

Calories and calorie requirements

The potential energy contained in foods is measured in calories. By definition, 1 Calorie is the amount of energy (heat) required to raise the temperature of 1 kilogram of water by 1 degree centigrade.*

One hundred grams of sugar may release 400 Calories, as against 900 Calories from the same amount of fat. Meat is 60 percent water; thus, in 100 grams of meat, 40 grams constitutes "food" in a strict sense, and is a mixture of 45 percent protein and 55 percent fat with a Calorie potential of 250. One hundred grams of cod fillets contain only 20 grams of food (98 percent protein, 2 percent fat) and a modest 68 Calories.

A great number of factors determine a person's actual needs of calories, among them age, sex, body weight, occupation, type of personality, and activity level. There are as a result many individual deviations from standard values listed in tables. Yet international organizations have through nutritional studies tried to formulate general guidelines for desirable average intake of nutrients. These nutrients may, however, originate from a broad spectrum of different kinds of food.

Practical experiences have by and large substantiated the validity of

---

*This is the nutritionists' Calorie, the "large calorie" or "kilogram calorie" or "kilocalorie"; the calorie of the physicists is the "small calorie," defined as the amount of energy required to raise the temperature of 1 gram of water by 1 degree centigrade. Thus the nutritionists' Calorie is 1,000 of the physicists' calorie. The notation distinction (C versus c) is disregarded in many popular publications.

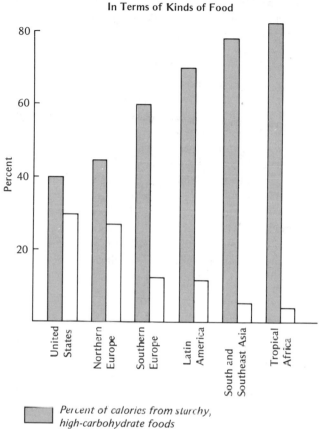

NUTRITIONAL STANDARD   1965-1968

In Terms of Kinds of Food

Percent of calories from starchy,
high-carbohydrate foods

Percent of calories from animal
products

Poor nutritional standard is reflected in the relative amount of bread and
tubers (potato, sweet potato, cassava) in the diet, indicated above in the
left-hand bars; better standards, in the amount of calories taken in through
animal products (meat, milk, fish, eggs, and the like), shown by the
right-hand bars.

such norms or standards. An average Western man with a body weight of 70
kilograms (154 lbs.) requires 3,000 Calories per day when exerting normal
physical activity. Heavy work increases the calorie demands considerably. A
lumberman or road builder may need 5,000 Calories or more. Sedentary
office work, on the other hand, reduces Calorie requirements down toward
2,000.

The Calorie expenditures required to sustain minimum body activity (Calorie needs at complete rest, also called the basal metabolism) for a 154-lb. male is 1,500 to 1,600 per day. Children require more calories than adults per unit of body weight. With increased age, the general activity and mobility are as a rule reduced—the metabolism proceeds at a slower rate—and after age 30, fewer calories are required. At age 70 the calorie intake normally is one-third less than at age 25. These are merely a few examples to give a general idea of the relationship between calorie requirements and age. Such data are readily available in detailed calorie tables, carefully computed and studied.

Any excess intake of calories is stored as glycogen in the liver or as fat in various body tissues. When a person is ingesting less than the actual energy expenditure of the body, calorie resources within the body, primarily fats, are consumed. The consequence is "reducing," decrease in body weight. There is, however, a limit for how far one can go in reducing without jeopardizing health and survival. In extreme cases starvation sets in. When all deposited fat is used up, protein is next used as fuel. A main source of protein fuel is the muscle tissue. As the depletion progresses, these tissues become increasingly watery. This change results in swellings—so-called hunger edemas. They are unmistakable signs of critical food shortage.

Calorie providers

Foods when digested supply animals, including man, with energy and body-building substances. The fats release energy in the ratio of about 9 Calories per gram, the carbohydrates and proteins about 4 Calories per gram. Proteins, important as body-building substances, are discussed later in this chapter; carbohydrates and fats, as was mentioned earlier, are consumed especially for their energy-supplying qualities; they are the fuel foods for the body-motor. Foods rich in carbohydrates (starches and sugars) are in general more plentiful and less expensive than high-protein foods. Fat-rich foods tend to be more expensive than carbohydrates but less so than proteins.

Since most of the people in the world, even in the well-fed countries, are forced to economize in their food purchases and food habits, they select for energy purposes foods which are rich in carbohydrates or fats. Starch which, when digested, is split into different kinds of sugars, is the major ingredient in bread, and in other flour products commonly called cereals. In addition, starch is found in potatoes and most other tuberous foods. Refined sugar and fat such as butter and vegetable oils are other important sources for body fuel.

A distinction is commonly made between visible and invisible fat. Visible fats are used as spreads and for cooking—primarily butter, margarine, and oil. Since ancient days oil has been pressed for this purpose from olives and it remains an important food oil alongside many new types manufactured from oil-rich seeds such as soybean, peanut, and sunflower; land and marine animals also furnish oil. After industrial treatment, these fats and oils become important ingredients in margarine.

Invisible fats are present in most foods, even in berries. But in quantities sufficiently large to be important in the energy metabolism of the body, they are found as major components in milk, in certain meats such as bacon, and in some fatty fishes such as herring, mackerel, and salmon. Nuts in general constitute a rich source of fat, chestnuts being exceptional in carrying more carbohydrates, chiefly starch.

Carbohydrates and fats are metabolized in the body through oxidation, somewhat as is the fuel in a motor. The resemblance can be taken one step further, since it has been discovered that the body also possesses "spark plugs," consisting of a series of chain reactions induced by special organic phosphorus compounds. They release the initial energy, which in turn frees other energy bound in fats and carbohydrates. It is particularly noteworthy that these energy-producing metabolic processes take place at body temperature levels, far below what any modern chemical factory employs or needs in order to carry through corresponding processes on an industrial scale. These energy-transferring processes are the basis for the maintenance of body temperature as well as for the life functions in general; most of these are directly dependent on energy. In heavy physical work, the muscles use the most energy, but normally the secretory activities of the kidneys require the most, in relative terms.

There are major differences between various kinds of fats. Almost anyone recognizes that butter differs in composition from olive oil. Fats are built up of lengthy chains of fatty acids, the composition of which varies a great deal. Modern fat research has made great progress in recent years: witness the public familiarity with terms such as unsaturated and polyunsaturated fatty acids, cholesterol, hardened fats, and essential fatty acids. It is not possible within the compass of a small book like this one to give a full orientation about all these matters and the important research findings related to them. Basically, however, fats present three fundamental aspects which are essential with regard to world feeding.

First, even though fat is an important source of calories and attractive in terms of flavor and aroma, it is easy to get too much. The total intake of fat should never exceed one-third of the calorie intake. If this rule is heeded, the question of the composition of the fat becomes a secondary matter.

Second, some essential fatty acids, vital to life, carry almost the characteristic features of vitamins and are required in very small quantities.

TOTAL FAT CONSUMPTION   1965-1968

(grams per day per person)

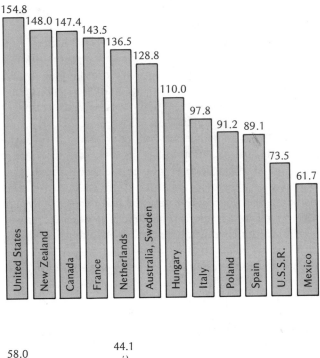

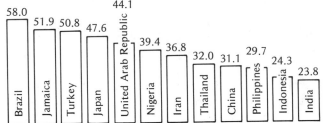

On our side of the hunger gap, the only country in the category of low fat intake is Japan.

They are requisite to the health of the skin as well as to the normal metabolism of the body.

Third, fat is a carrier of so-called fat-soluble vitamins, primarily A, D, and E, all of which are essential to the well-being of the human body.

We in the well-fed world, who battle obesity and overconsumption of fat, have great difficulty realizing that there are many more millions around the globe who are desperately short of fat. Shortage, even gross deficit, is extremely common in less developed countries. This has serious repercussions. By resorting to fat, we in the rich world save in weight and volume of food we eat. As a result, we make considerable economic gains by reducing storage space and expenditures for storage and marketing. If one is forced to eat carbohydrates instead of fat, the necessary quantities of food become much larger in volume, frequently two to three times. This in turn makes the food more expensive and complicates the economy. Much more important, however, is the fact that when all calorie needs are not satisfied, as frequently happens in the undernourished world due to the shortage of fat, the body instead uses valuable and more expensive proteins for fuel instead of for maintenance and growth. Only when the body's energy needs are filled, that is, its calorie requirements, does it use food for purposes other than fuel. In case of fuel deficit, the body machinery is run with anything available, including protein.

This shortage of fats within the hungry world is reflected not only in swollen tissues and edemas. These may also be induced through shortage of protein. Lack of fat is further reflected in the common occurrence of damages and infections on skin and mucous membranes. Moreover, a whole series of diseases are caused by deficiencies in fat-soluble vitamins.

Calories and hunger

Many people in the less well-fed world, the Asians for example, are short in stature; even adults may weigh less than 120 pounds. Since metabolic rates are similar for all people, such small people might be expected to require fewer calories. But, generally, they have fewer machines and technical devices, hence need far more calories than do people in the affluent countries. They work harder in the soil, they often have to walk many miles to pick up water, to deliver what they produce, or bring home needed items. They walk as much or more than we Westerners did as farmers a hundred years ago. They further grind their own grain, often by manpower, and in other ways prepare their food without help of machines. In other words, they have much more heavy physical work, demanding more calories.

Against this demand stands the fact that most of these people live in the warm regions of the world. Consequently, they do not need to produce as much energy as we in the north to maintain body temperature, in order not to feel cold. In recent years, however, military studies have shown that the work of the kidneys represents a highly energy-demanding activity of the body, and in warm areas, these internal organs must work much harder to compensate for the greater water losses through perspiration and evaporation. Energy for these vital processes must be taken from the food. The quantity difference in needs for calories between north and south, rich and poor, is therefore not as large as one might have imagined.

The calorie illusion

Hundreds of millions of people in the world do not get adequate amounts of calories. In principle it should be easy to provide everyone with sufficient food energy. A simple calculation shows that the United States, by growing sugar beets on the tilled land in the north and sugar cane in the south, could easily on its own produce more calories than the entire world population would need. But both common sense and our present knowledge of nutrition tell us that no one can live or even survive on sugar or fat alone. Food must contain a number of additional compounds, the most important of which being cell-building proteins.

The early discussion about global food supplies was highly distorted by alleged experts among economists, politicians, and others, who limited themselves to considering calorie needs and attempted to show how easily these could be filled. This confusion is still prevalent but less commonly so, as there is a better understanding of nutritional needs. There is also increased awareness of the complexities of the food and nutrition issue.

BODY-BUILDING FOODS

The biblical metaphor that man does not live by bread alone can also be accepted as a literal statement and refer to our entire diet. Energy is not sufficient for the growth and maintenance of the body. Body-building substances are required in addition. Next to water, protein is the most important ingredient of the body and in effect constitutes the basic substance of each cell. As a result, some of our food intake must consist of protein-rich foods, such as animal products: meat, fish, eggs, milk, and cheese. Many plant products contain protein but, as a rule, the amount is less than in animal products. Among vegetable products, peas, beans, and nuts are those richest in protein. Grain products—cereals—contain much less protein, but as they are eaten in relatively large quantities, most people in the world get most of their basic protein need filled through cereals, often two-thirds. Starch-rich tubers, such as potatoes, are low in content of protein, but since they too are eaten in relatively large quantities, they likewise make essential contributions to the protein balance.

The complexities of the proteins

The percent of protein in any food does not always accurately mirror its value as a protein source. A conspicuous example is white potato. Its tubers contain five times as much water as do the cereal grains. The dry matter is 10 to 12 percent; in this dry matter most potato varieties contain almost as much protein as do cereals. This relative composition is not changed either by drinking additional water with the cereals or by eating the water in the potatoes.

Not only does the amount of protein vary from food to food but so does the quality of the protein. The nutritional value of proteins is, as a rule, lower in plant than in animal products. Protein consists of lengthy chains of "building stones" called amino acids. More than 30 such amino acids are known, of which 22 constitute essential ingredients in the proteins of human foods. Man must obtain eight of these through his food, as the body is unable to synthesize these essential amino acids (EAA), either in the intestinal system or in the body tissues.

Individual amino acids vary in amount in different kinds of proteins; some of them lack one or more amino acids. They are put together into protein in different sequences and in varying relative quantities. This is reflected in the aminogram, indicating the percentage amount of individual amino acids in each protein. The percentages may vary from food to food and the proportions affect the nutritional value of the protein as human food—its capability to sustain growth, maintenance, or repair of the body tissues.

Proteins are broken apart in the digestive process into amino acids, or into groups of three or four amino acids called *peptides*. Further enzyme action breaks the peptides into individual amino acids. The blood transports the amino acids to various parts of the body. In the wear and tear of the body tissues amino acids are being consumed or used up and must be replenished. This the body does figuratively speaking, by picking for repair purposes from the blood stream the needed building stones in the form of amino acids. If this repair is not done, disturbances occur in the metabolism and in the functioning of the tissues. One could compare the blood stream with the conveyor belt in a repair shop: each tissue or organ picks up from the blood—the belt—what it happens momentarily to need for replacement.

Sources of proteins

As was indicated, most people obtain their basic protein requirements from plant products, primarily cereals. This is not adequate. A person must

PROTEIN IN SELECTED FOODS

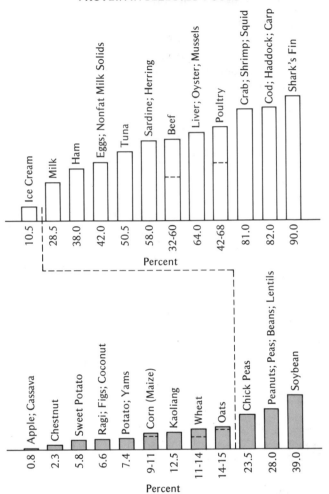

The figures indicate grams of protein per hundred grams of dry matter (the dotted lines in certain bars indicate degrees of variability). Only foods to the right of the angled dash line have sufficient protein to permit their use for protein supplementation in human food.

theoretically receive at least 12 percent of his calories in the form of protein. Wheat, rice, and other modern grains seldom reach this level, although older varieties did. Subconsciously early man presumably stayed with the food products which gave him a greater sense of repleteness. Thus he was led to the discovery of plants like buckwheat, quinoa, and amaranthus (related to pigweed), all of which carried better aminograms than common cereals. American Indian civilizations in the Andes cultivated *dent* corn, which was superior in this respect to the *flint* corn grown by the North American prairie Indians. Modern genetics has bred this superior trait into new varieties with a high amount of lysine, an essential amino acid, and in this way managed to improve the corn commonly grown today.

Another alternative is to supplement the diet with protein-rich foods. This was discovered early in history by several civilizations. South American Indians who largely subsisted on maize (corn) raised the protein level of the diet by growing beans with a protein content of 22 to 30 percent. The Chinese and Japanese used the soybean for the same purpose long before anything was known of its particular nutritive merits. Animal products, such as meat, milk, eggs, and fish, are the safest nutritional supplementation to cereal products, primarily because they contain high relative levels of proteins (50 to 85 percent) and also fill needs for specific amino acids that are short in tubers and cereals.

Critical minima

The protein issue is complicated because man must have certain minimal quantities of essential amino acids. Those amino acids that man cannot synthesize himself consequently must be provided from external sources. Unfortunately, few plant proteins contain all these supplementary needs. A relative shortage of a single one of these crucial amino acids, prevents the body from fully utilizing the other amino acids. One could picture this situation by imagining a tub with one of the staves too short; the tub cannot be filled above the top of this particular short stave. When such relative shortage in one or more amino acids occurs, a considerable portion of the intake of protein and amino acids is simply not utilizable and thus wasted.

For example, a person subsisting exclusively on corn must, in order to provide adequately for the minimum requirements of the body with regard to all amino acids, eat a quantity double what is required to fulfill the calorie needs. This presumably explains the paradox that protein shortage is often associated with sustained hunger even though it may promote the intake of far too large quantities of calories.

Modern food science and nutritional research have developed the practice of supplementing any food with amino acids which are in relative shortage. This is done in modern poultry feeding. Studies of conditions in many parts of the world show that, often empirically, such supplementation has been introduced. A good example of this is the rice-eating Chinese. For centuries, or even millenia, they have eaten a special type of cabbage, the

FOOD QUANTITIES REQUIRED FOR
HALF OF DAILY HUMAN PROTEIN REQUIREMENT

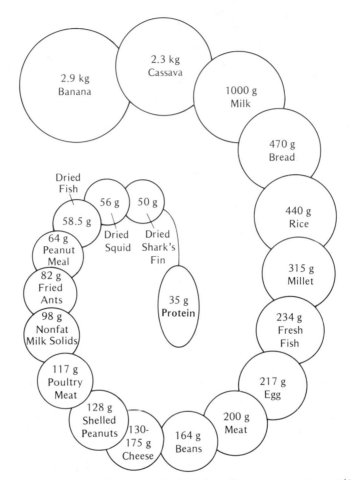

Amounts of various foods providing half the daily protein requirement (35 g/day) of a 70-kg man (154 lbs.). Note: weight of egg is without shell.

protein of which complements the rice protein and thus provides those amino acids lacking in rice. Likewise the soybean had an interesting supplementary assortment of amino acids in relation to cereal protein.

The illustration on p. 159 shows how amounts of essential amino acids, such as lysine, methionine, and tryptophan, are all relatively low in cereal proteins, while methionine and tryptophan are not adequate in legumes. All

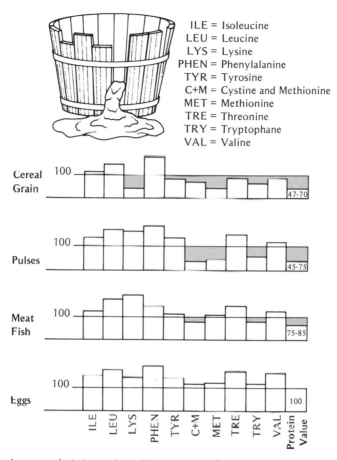

ILE = Isoleucine
LEU = Leucine
LYS = Lysine
PHEN = Phenylalanine
TYR = Tyrosine
C+M = Cystine and Methionine
MET = Methionine
TRE = Threonine
TRY = Tryptophane
VAL = Valine

Aminograms (relative amino-acid composition) in key food commodities. Only eggs satisfy man's minimum requirements (indicated by the 100 level) of all amino acids.

three of these amino acids exist, however, in fair amounts in most animal products. But chicken eggs provide all eight essential amino acids and, furthermore, these are in proportions which correspond to the specific needs of the human body. Egg protein thus fulfills all reasonable requirements. The same is true with two of the proteins in milk (lactoglobulin, lactalbumin), but not with the chief milk protein, casein; nature obviously did not make cow's milk merely to feed man. Incidentally and ironically, it is the whey, often discarded in making milk products, that contains the best and most perfect of all the proteins in cow's milk.

In the well-fed world we are in the fortunate position of being able to compensate for such relative shortage simply by eating more protein.

An inadequate calorie content in the diet means that proteins in the food are not used for the primary function of growth and maintenance but rather to fill in the calorie void by supplementing minimum needs for energy. As was pointed out earlier in this chapter, it is poor economy to use expensive protein merely as an energy source. In tackling the grim shortage of protein in the undernourished world, it is therefore most important to ensure that minimum requirements of energy are provided through less expensive fat and carbohydrates. Only when this is done, is the body in a position to rebuild its destroyed cells or create cells for its growth out of protein and amino acids.

BALANCING NUTRIENTS

As discussed previously, our foods vary considerably with regard to their calorie content, the amount of heat energy released per gram of ingredients as they undergo combustion through the metabolic processes of the body. But they differ still more as to the relative amount of various nutrients. Dominating are three major categories: proteins, fats, and carbohydrates. All are in general carbon compounds.

Carbohydrates are chiefly the sugars and starches. Many carbohydrate foods contain certain bulk substances, such as cellulose, lignin, several pectins, and other polysaccharides. These do not contain anything of nutritional value but, as they pass through the body, they function as filling agents in the intestinal system. Some foods, such as refined sugar or food fats and oils, consist of one single nutrient. Finally, our foods convey vitamins and minerals to a varying degree and quantity. The nutritional composition of most foods has been analyzed in detail and such data are published in nutritional tables.

To the layman it is far too complicated to plan the weekly or daily diet on the basis of such tables. It suffices to have some general idea of the role of various foods in the diet. For practical nutritional purposes, foods are generally placed into four major categories:

1. Bread and other cereal products
2. Fruits and vegetables
3. Meat, fish, eggs, beans, peas, and nuts
4. Milk and other dairy products

DAILY FOOD: U.S.D.A. SCHEME

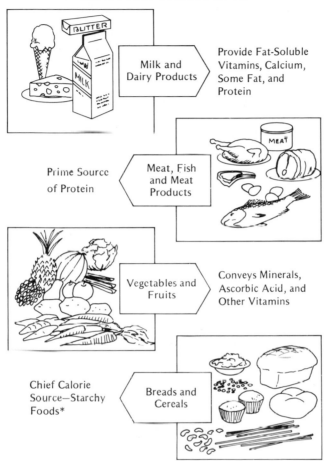

Milk and Dairy Products — Provide Fat-Soluble Vitamins, Calcium, Some Fat, and Protein

Prime Source of Protein — Meat, Fish and Meat Products

Vegetables and Fruits — Conveys Minerals, Ascorbic Acid, and Other Vitamins

Chief Calorie Source—Starchy Foods* — Breads and Cereals

*Sugar and fats supply additional calories.

Preferably each meal should contain items from each of these four categories, in order to ensure that a meal conveys adequate quantities of the many nutrients required by the body.

The hungry world can rarely afford the luxury of selecting daily food to contain both dairy and meat products. The scheme shown in the chart on page 162 is better adapted to these conditions as a yardstick for the adequacy

DAILY FOOD: WORLD SCHEME

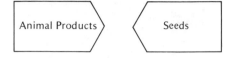

A. Protein Group

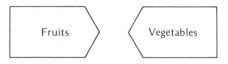

B. Vitamin-Mineral Group

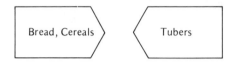

C. Carbohydrate Group

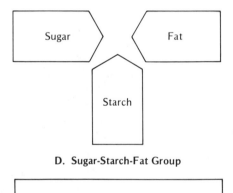

D. Sugar-Starch-Fat Group

World scheme for daily food (designed by the author).

of a daily diet. Each meal should include foods from each of the four groups.

VITAMINS AND RELATED COMPOUNDS

Nutritional science has gradually, step by step, expanded into a very long list those known special compounds that the human body requires to function

Food groups for the hungry world

Group A. Protein Foods

Animal products	Seeds
Milk and dairy products	Pulses: beans, peas, lentils, etc
Eggs	Oilseeds: peanuts, soybeans, sun-
Meat and meat products	flower seeds, etc.
Fish	Nuts: walnuts, almonds, pecans,
Shellfish	chestnuts, filberts, acorns,
Game	etc.

Group B. Vitamin-Mineral Foods

Fruits	Vegetables
Pomaceous fruits: apples,	Carrots
pears, etc.	Radishes
Stone fruits: plums,	Cabbage
cherries, etc.	Leafy vegetables
Citrus fruits: oranges,	Shoots: palm, bamboo, etc.
lemons, etc.	Seaweeds
Mangoes, etc.	

Group C. Carbohydrate Foods

Breads and cereals	Tubers
Flour	Potatoes
Grits	Sweet Potatoes
Flakes	Yams
Macaroni	Cassava
	Plantain
	Banana

Group D. Fats, Oils, Sugar, Starch, Alcohol, etc.

Starch	Butter
Sugar	Lard
Honey	Shortenings
Alcohol	Margarine
Salt	Vanaspati
Spices	Oils: olive, sesame, etc.

E. Water

smoothly. In consequence, the vitamin concept has lost its original clear definition. Vitamins are basically nothing other than particular chemical compounds man needs to acquire through his food.

The original list of vitamins carried eleven items known now to be essential to man's metabolism and thus to his health. In addition, there are many substances, at least ten, which, like the original vitamins, must be provided through the food and are active in very small quantities; these include biotin and folic acid. Certain essential fatty acids (EFA), are also indispensable in the diet; examples are, linolenic and arachidonic acid, of which only micro quantities are required. Each such compound has, like each individual vitamin, its particular function in the body.

Earlier it was believed that all vitamins must be provided with the food and that most of them had to be procured through plant products. Gradually, it has been established that under certain circumstances several of them can be made by the human body, directly or with the aid of the intestinal flora. Only with regard to vitamin C (ascorbic acid) and vitamin E (tocopherol) is man entirely dependent on dietary sources.

Several of these functional compounds have been synthesized chemically, or extracted, and can be made available in tablets. These are almost exclusively used in the well-fed world, often in animal feeding.

A compound apart is vitamin B_{12}, sometimes called the microbial vitamin. This is essential to the body and in particular for the utilization of proteins. It seems that only microorganisms are capable of putting together this peculiar molecule, which uses cobalt as an activator. As microorganisms are active in all animal bodies, we find that milk, eggs, and meat contain B_{12} most likely originating from the microbial activity in the animals' intestinal system. This is one key factor in the higher ranking of animal proteins as compared to plant proteins in basic human nutrition. In an extreme vegetarian diet man runs the risk of utilizing protein poorly even though sufficient quantities are consumed. If the blood gets too little B_{12}, the result in extreme cases may be death. The role of B_{12} is one factor in the not uncommon occurrence of eating soil (geophagy), or even of eating excrements (copro-

---

Partial list of vitamins

Water Soluble

B-complex

Thiamine (B_1)	Pantothenic acid
Riboflavin (B_2)	Cobalamin (B_{12})
Niacin	Biotin
Pyridoxine (B_6)	Inositol
Folic acid	

Ascorbic acid (Vitamin C)

Fat Soluble

Vitamin A	Tocopherols (Vitamin E)
Vitamin D	Vitamin K

Related Compounds

Lipoic acid
Choline
Ubiquinone

---

phagy) among primitive groups. They acquire in this way an indispensable nutritive factor. The microbial flora of soils produces a great deal of B_{12}. Coastal Asians receive this vitamin through the microbial slime on the surface of major seaweeds.

Most vitamins are conveyed by plant products—with B_{12} as an exception. Milk carries, in its fat, vitamins A and E, originating with the feed, not the least in the grass of the rangelands. Milk when udder-warm carries vitamin C (ascorbic acid); most of this is lost in subsequent holding and handling. Fish also pick up this vitamin via their feed, originating in phytoplankton at the start of the lengthy food chains of waters.

Highly refined foods, such as sugar, fats, and starch carry no vitamins or small amounts of vitamins. In the manufacture of margarine, vitamin A and E (tocopherol) are added.

Minerals

The list of minerals known to be indispensable to man has also constantly been lengthened, in particular with regard to a great number of elements needed only in traces. The most important mineral substances in our food are calcium, phosphorus, and iron. If the diet is properly composed, man gets sufficient of all three; as a rule, other mineral ingredients, such as potassium, magnesium, and manganese are then also adequate.

Man needs at least 14 mineral substances, in larger or smaller quantities. The body of a 70-kilogram (154-lb.) standard man carries the following approximate amounts of minerals (in grams):

Calcium	1,000	Sodium	100.0
Phosphorus	700	Magnesium	35.0
Potassium	250	Zinc	2.2

Among new surprises in this area, special mention should be made of the important role of zinc, chromium, vanadium, and selenium. Zinc is a constituent in a great number of enzymes, biocatalyzers which accelerate or facilitate basic metabolic processes in the body. Shortage of zinc induces dwarf growth, not uncommon in several developing countries. Selenium and vanadium are indispensable participants in fat metabolism.

Most foods contain several minerals but in varying amounts. Exceptions are some industrially manufactured foods, such as starch, sugar, and fats, where the residual amount of minerals as a rule is low. This lack has led to a lively debate whether through the refinement of foods our daily diet has not been deprived of minerals, both in kind and quantity. In fertilizing crops three major nutrients (NPK = nitrogen, phosphorus, potassium) have been

List of food minerals

Major	
Calcium	Potassium
Phosphorus	Sodium
Magnesium	Sulfur

Minor	
Iron	Fluorine
Copper	Selenium
Iodine	Cesium
Manganese	Zinc
Molybdenum	Chromium
Cobalt	Vanadium

Contaminants	
Lead	Nickel
Mercury	Tin
Cadmium	Titanium
Ruthenium	

chiefly taken into account. Trace elements and other minerals have been added to the soils only when overt deficiency symptoms have appeared.

The multiple reuse of water with only partial removal of residual minerals in the waterworks and in purification plants constitutes an opposite trend whereby our drinking water is carrying mounting loads of mineral salts. This might compensate for relative reductions through refined foods. This phenomenon is causing concern by reintroducing the heavy work loads to the kidneys, which were common when salt was the predominant food preservative (mentioned in Chapter 8). This chemical threat has been removed from essential parts of our daily diet, in products such as meat, fish, cheese, and butter.

Enrichments

Modern food industry and nutritional science have evolved methods for supplementing the nutrients in key foods by the addition of pure compounds, such as some vitamins, amino acids, fatty acids, and minerals. This practice is called *enrichment* or *fortification* when increasing their relative amount, *supplementation* when they are largely missing or extremely short in the original food; *restoration* when filling in losses incurred during the processing. More significant is the adding to cereals of B vitamins (thiamine, niacin) and minerals (calcium, iron)—a legalized and normalized procedure since World War II in most developed countries. Fruit juices and fruit drinks are commonly given a boost in ascorbic acid. Table salt is frequently iodized. Some countries like the United States add vitamin D regularly to milk; yeast is a common adjunct to soups, stews, and pies—providing B vitamins, amino acids, and protein. Margarine is vitaminized.

WATER

In many ways water is the most critical nutrient; lack of water produces death before starvation does. Seventy percent of man's body consists of water. It is part of all tissues and indispensable to most of the metabolic processes. It is the main transporting agent of the blood and the urine.

Water is consumed as such but is also a major ingredient in many foods. Lettuce carries more water than does milk. The daily water balance of a standard man (70 kg = 154 lbs.) is roughly as shown in the chart.

Daily water balance

Intake	Grams	Output	Grams
Drinking water	400	Perspiration	500
In beverages	580	Breathing (air)	350
In solid foods	720	Urine	1,100
		Feces	150
Total	2,020		2,100

REFERENCES AND RECOMMENDATIONS
FOR FURTHER READING

Crampton, E. N., and L. E. Lloyd. *Fundamentals of Nutrition.* San Francisco: Freeman, 1959. 494 pp.

Fredericks, C., and H. Bailey, *Food Facts and Fallacies.* New York: Julian Press, 1965. 382 pp.

Maynard, L. A., and J. K. Joosli. *Animal Nutrition,* 6th ed. New York: McGraw-Hill, 1969. 613 pp.

Robinson, C. N., *Fundamentals of Normal Nutrition.* New York: Macmillan, 1968. 670 pp.

Tyler, C., *Animal Nutrition,* 2nd ed. London: Chapman and Hall, 1964. 254 pp.

Wilson, E. D., K. N. Fisher, and M. E. Fuqua. *Principles of Nutrition.* New York: Wiley, 1965. 596 pp.

REVIEW AND RESEARCH QUESTIONS

1. Discuss man's requirements for energy-producing and protein foods, respectively.

2. What happens when man gets inadequate amounts of energy through his food?

3. Which are the chief sources of calories in man's food?

4. Review some fat disturbances induced in humans via food.

5. Discuss consequences of shortage in proteins.

6. How do plant proteins compare with animal proteins and what are the criteria for nutritive value of proteins?

7. What is meant by "the calorie illusion"?

8. What significance is attached to the aminogram?

9. For which vitamins must man rely on dietary sources because he is incapable of making those vitamins in his body?

10. What are the unique features of vitamin B_{12}?

11. What is meant by enrichment or fortification of foods?

12. How much water does man need each 24 hours and how is it utilized?

13. What are the complications involved in an exclusively vegetarian diet? Can an acceptable such diet be composed and what are the precautionary measures to be taken?

Food and Population 11

Three overwhelming and highly visible dangers are threatening the future of mankind: nuclear warfare, the population explosion and the hunger gap. They are intimately related. The introduction to this book briefly sketched the trends of the present growth of world population. This chapter will examine the relationships with particular attention to the feeding of the human family.

THE AGE-LONG SLOW GROWTH EXPLODES

The number of humans added to the world in this century is already larger than the total world population in the year 1900. The present 3.7 billion are further expected to almost double and reach around 7 billion by the year 2000. Mankind will, as a result, enter the twenty-first century with a board-and-lodging burden of enormous dimensions.

During the greater part of human history, the number of people was exceedingly small, in particular during the entire period when man fed himself by fishing and hunting and the gathering of wild seeds, berries, and tubers. Not until regular cropping was introduced about ten thousand years ago (probably independently in Mexico, the Middle East, and China) did it become possible to accommodate more people and support greater population densities.

Through various calculations and based on quite detailed censuses, it can safely be stated that the world had about 250 million people at the beginning of the Christian era. Of these, 150 million were living in India and China. Fewer than 80 million were in the Mediterranean region, only 6.5

million in the heartland of the Roman Empire, and 8 to 9 million in the Nile Valley. Wars, crop disasters, and epidemics caused considerable fluctuations from region to region and over time, but the population curve surged unremittingly upward, although the growth was extremely slow until the mid seventeenth century. India's population, estimated at somewhat below 100 million around 300 B.C., increased insignificantly for two thousand years; around 1600 A.D. there were still only a little above 100 million.

Since 1650 (with around 500 million), the world population has multiplied sevenfold. The first billion was reached in 1820, the second in 1930. Then the staggering acceleration set in with a third billion in 1965, and a fourth billion expected during the 1970's. This accelerating trend justifies the term "explosion" and is the most portentous feature of the population development. Currently we are adding some 200,000 people each day or 75 million each year, thus roughly a new United States each third year or more than three Canadas annually. Within less than ten years, moreover, the annual increment will climb above 80 million.

CAUSES OF THE EXPLOSION

With few exceptions the nations of the world in recent years show a reduced *fertility rate** (number of children born annually to 1,000 women in the procreative ages 15-45). But drastically reduced infant mortality in the poor and hungry world has meant survival of more children. As a result the developing world has a larger proportion of young people and thus also of women in childbearing ages than the developed world. Therefore the *birth rate* (number of children born yearly to 1,000 of the the population) has gone up and is as a rule higher than in the rich and well-fed nations. In other words: the hungry world, comprising two-thirds of mankind, grows faster and is in the midst of a population explosion. This was preceded by a similar upsurge in Europe.

Western man actually has increased fourfold in numbers since the beginning of the nineteenth century. That population explosion got into full swing after the mid century and reached its peak, evidenced in migration to the United States, around 1910. Almost half of this branch of the human family now lives outside Europe. The rapid increase was due to the fact that during the transition from the old pattern (high birth rate and high death rate, almost neutralizing each other) to a new fairly balanced stage (low birth and low death rates), the reduction in birth rate lagged several decades behind the lowering of the death rate. It is commonly assumed that the developing world will undergo an identical *demographic transition.* But there is no

---

*Sometimes called *crude birth rate.*

warranty that this will be the case. The demographic transition is not a law of nature, merely a description of a sequence of happenings.

The population explosion is usually attributed to medical advances and sanitary improvements over the past hundred years. This explanation is insufficient and overlooks the crucial fact that to survive those who were saved had to be fed, otherwise there would have been no population explosion. The European upsurge from 1850 to 1950 led to serious overpopulation and would have brought extensive famines and epidemics if the white man had not enjoyed the advantages of three simultaneous revolutions: (1) in agricultural techniques—seed control, irrigation, artificial fertilizers, (2) in transportation; and (3) in food handling and processing—application of refrigeration in storage and distribution, and improved preservation methods, in particular canning. These advances have so far only to a limited degree benefited the developing world.

But the white man had an additional option. He swarmed to all corners of the globe, taking possession of huge portions of the world's agricultural potentials (the North American prairies, the South American pampas, the African highlands, and the Australian grasslands). There the immigrants not only fed themselves but also organized a massive flow of food and feed to Europe, still continuing (Chapter 9).

To the developing countries of today no such option is available. The globe has few new lands left to settle and woefully small surpluses to trade. Emigration as a mechanism for easing population pressure therefore belongs to history. In addition, the cost for transferring one single family and establishing it on newly settled land amounts to at least $5,000, an expense the poor and hungry world cannot afford. To take one example: the total annual budget of Indonesia would hardly be adequate to transfer the added numbers of one single year from its people-packed main island of Java to its less populated outer islands.

Worldwide, therefore, population control is the only way to avert massive hunger and still more deepening misery. There is far too little food for far too many people, and the issue is to adjust people to resources and vice versa. To handle food apart from population will only exacerbate failure.

But even if we are successful in implementing worldwide population control, the full effect of such measures will not be clearly noticeable until the next generation, in other words, 20 to 30 years from now. As a consequence, we have to make a supreme effort in the area of birth control and while doing so must also work to the hilt to produce more food. What must be done is not *either . . . or* but is a mandatory *both . . . and*; and each item in the *both* requires drastic measures if mankind is going to enter the twenty-first century with a reasonably restored balance and the prospects of controlling its future destiny.

THE FOOD DEFICIT

Most experts agree that the world's food production needs to be doubled to eliminate the present hunger gap and give every human now living on earth an acceptable minimal diet. If we further take into account that the number of people in the world will double before the year 2000, the actual requirement is a fourfold increase of agricultural production, and this within the very brief span of three decades. The advancement far surpasses any the West has demonstrated in its history during a similar period of time.

The intimate and dynamic relationship between food and population is poorly understood in the current debate. Throughout history more food has as a rule meant more people. True, several examples equally support the notion that more people has induced more food. But it is overlooked that this latter applies only when there is a resource margin left in soils and water. A growing number of countries are crowding their geographical and ecological contexts and some have gone far outside. Few hungry nations could even attempt to copy Holland, England, or Japan in these respects, especially as massive depletion of water resources and soils now threatens the survival basis of hundreds of millions.

THE LAND SUPPLY

One key factor in the feeding of nations is obviously the availability of land resources suitable for food production. In this regard there are some striking differences.

1. The United States and the Soviet Union, in many ways the only two remaining "have" nations, dispose about equal agricultural acreage per inhabitant, but the United States has the good fortune of owning some of the best crop regions of the globe. The Soviet Union has nothing comparable in terms of climate and soils to the United States Midwest and its grain prairies. Soviet agriculture operates under much more adverse climatic conditions as to drought and frost, located as it is almost entirely to the north of the contiguous United States.

2. The United States, with 67 million fewer people than Latin America, has 139 million more acres of tilled land, or twice as much per person. Yet Latin America is exporting more than one-fourth of what its tilled land produces. The corresponding net figure for the United States is one-fifth.

3. Europe has not much more tilled land per person than India but has far more favorable climatic conditions. Europe is furthermore supplementing what its tilled land and pastures yield by huge net imports, besides being a

major recipient of the ocean harvests. Europe can thus be said to have vast supporting colonies for its survival. The fish and other aquatic products it consumes represent in animal protein the equivalent of the milk output of 42 million dairy cattle (or the meat from around 108 million cattle). If this number of cattle were raised and fed in the most efficient way in terms of acreage (through feed crops) and if this were done within Europe, it would take 125 million acres. If in the same way the food and feed of agricultural origin, now acquired from abroad, were produced within Europe, an additional 120 million acres would be needed.

The feeding base of Europe (1968)

	Million Acres
Tilled land	372.5
Pastures	227.5
Net importation (equivalent)	120
Fish and shellfish (equivalent)	125
Total	845

Judging feeding capabilities on the basis of traditional density figures, (number of people per square mile or number fed per acre of agricultural land or tilled acreage) is often misleading. Acre yields differ widely with climatic conditions and agricultural systems. In warm zones of the globe multiple cropping (the taking of two or more crops per year from one plot or field) is increasingly forcing itself into application, as a rule supported by added irrigation. Fallowing (leaving land untilled for one or several seasons) has been much reduced; today it remains significant only in major parts of tropical Africa, the outer islands of Indonesia, and parts of South and Central America. There techniques for permanent tillage have so far not been devised and people resort to various types of slash-and-burn agriculture. Earlier this was the prevalent method in major parts of the temperate forest regions which are now in permanent agriculture.

The most common fallacy in appraising agriculture capabilities is to overlook the degree to which countries are supported by acreages beyond sight; those who commit it neglect taking into account the acreages represented by the aquatic harvests and by the food and feed imported, often from distant lands. The urbanized millions on the whole lose sight and even awareness of their dependence on agricultural lands.

Acreage comparisons (1968)

Country	A Tilled land (million acres)	B Pastures (million acres)	C Population (million)	Acres per person A/C	Acres per person B/C
U.S.S.R	560	935	237.8	2.35	3.94
United States	440	649	201.1	2.19	3.23
Latin America	306	1,255	267.8	1.15	4.72
South America	222	1,040	180.5	1.23	5.77
Europe	372	228	454.3	0.82	0.51
Africa	510	n.a.	338.1	1.51	n.a.
Brazil	75	269	88.2	0.87	4.00
				(0.60)	(0.40)
Mexico	60	198	47.3	1.27	4.18
				(0.65)	(0.42)
Peru	6.6	66	12.8	0.52	5.20
		(7.1)			(0.56)
China	338	354	814.6	0.415	0.435
India	410	35	523.9	0.78	0.07
Japan	14.2	2.4	101.1	0.14	0.023
United Arab Republic	7.0	—	31.7	0.22	—
Netherlands	2.28	3.29	12.7	0.18	0.26
Jamaica	0.003	0.618	1.91	0.32	0.32

Figures in parentheses are harvested or usable acreages on the average per year.

n.a. = not available

Ghost acreages

Most urban Americans rarely give thought to the fact that each one of them is dependent for food on 1.8 acres of tilled land and 3.2 acres of pastures and grazing lands.* The British and the Dutch boast about their higher yields and pride themselves that they need far less, merely 0.34 and 0.18 acre of tilled soil and 0.55 and 0.26 acre of pastures, respectively. But these ratios are misleading half-truths. Both Britain and Holland depend on huge acreages in the North American prairies, in Argentina, in tropical Africa, and in Oceania. In the United Kingdom these nonvisible acreages represent, in terms of domestic yields, 0.75 acre per person, or more than twice the tilled land of England; in Holland about 50 percent more or 0.29 acre per person.

This author coined in 1965 the term *ghost acreages* for those lands beyond the boundaries. The term comprises the *trade acreage* and the *fish acreage* of a given country, that is, the area of tilled land which would be needed to raise in the country in question an amount of animal protein equivalent to (1) what is acquired through net imports, and (2) what the

---

*Of the 2.19 acres per capita of tilled land in the United States, indicated in the table above, the remainder is used for export crops.

oceans and freshwaters provide in fish and shellfish (whether harvested by their own fleets or imported). For the United Kingdom the ghost acreages per person thus amount to 0.98 acre, for Holland 0.78 acre. For Europe as a whole the total ghost acreage corresponds to 66 percent of its tilled land.

Acres per person, selected countries

	Tilled Land	Pastures	Ghost Acreage	Ghost acreage as percent of Tilled Land
Japan	0.14	0.03	0.84	610
United Kingdom	0.34	0.55	0.98	288
Holland	0.18	0.26	0.78	432
Italy	0.29	0.10	0.25	87

No major country in the poor world could attain the opulence of ghost acreages, huge food-supplying colonies, of the dimensions now enjoyed by Japan (6.4 times its present tilled land), the United Kingdom (2.9), Holland (4.3), and Italy (0.9). Yet none of these countries even approaches the rich soil resources of the United States with a considerably larger base for the feeding of its people.

The Caribbean, in particular the West Indies, has been forced to import protein ever since the seventeenth century, primarily in the form of dried and salted fish. This was paid for by sugar and rum, from a nutritional point of view an excellent exchange since high-quality protein was obtained with cheap calories. Today these islands have grown in human numbers to such a degree that more than half of what they eat has to be brought in from the outside, and most of these countries have a trade deficit despite some expansion of sugar cultivation.

The European prodigality

The European market, so much discussed today as a self-sufficient entity, is dependent as we have seen on vast lands overseas. With the addition of England, the most demanding partner in the world household, this trans-oceanic reliance becomes still more accentuated. Europe will, despite expanded internal trade, remain the chief recipient of most of the agricultural products moving through world trade.

How would the Europeans manage without these imports? If they had to produce within their own boundaries these additional amounts of food and feed: bread grains, feed grains, meat, butter, eggs, sugar, fats? One can be certain that this would not be feasible. Europe would be forced to reduce drastically its intake of animal products, fats, fruits, and vegetables. It would certainly not starve, but its present artificial affluence would need considerable adjustment, its intake dropping to a level corresponding roughly to the average intake of Greece and Italy, or that of present-day Japan.

THE GREEN REVOLUTION

In the 1960's much attention was focused on the introduction of high-yielding varieties of wheat and rice for cropping in hungry countries. Good results are reported from Mexico, India, Pakistan, the Philippines, and some other regions. It is far too early to judge whether these improved yields can be sustained against the hazards of new diseases, and in the long run return the huge extra costs involved in irrigation, fertilizers, spraying chemicals, and the like. But most important! Can the gains in food production match the concomitant increase in population? So far this has been possible only in a few instances. The involved area of Asia, now with some 830 million people, will add almost 400 million before 1985. Far more drastic brakes than any hitherto used need to be applied against population growth if this food-production advance is to achieve anything better than to expand more rapidly the numbers of hungry people.

REFERENCES AND RECOMMENDATIONS
FOR FURTHER READING

Appleman, P., *The Silent Explosion.* Boston: Beacon Press, 1965. 162 pp.

Borgstrom, G., *The Hungry Planet—The Modern World at the Edge of Famine.* 2nd rev. ed. New York: Macmillan, 1972 (1965). Paperback, Collier Books: New York, 1972 (1967). 552 pp.

Boughey, A. S., *Man and the Environment.* New York: Macmillan, 1971. 472 pp.

Day, L. H., and A. T. Day, *Too Many Americans.* 2nd ed. Boston: Houghton Mifflin, 1967 (1964). 298 pp.

Ehrlich, P. R. and A. N. Ehrlich, *Population, Resources, Environment.* San Francisco: Freeman, 1970. 389 pp.

Hardin, G., *Population, Evolution, Birth Control.* San Francisco: Freeman, 1969 (1964). 342 pp.

Hauser, P. M. (ed.), *The Population Dilemma,* 2nd ed. Englewood Cliffs: Prentice Hall, 1969. 230 pp.

Johnson, S., *Life Without Birth—A Journey Through the Third World in Search of the Population Explosion.* London: Heinemann, 1970. 364 pp.

Nicol. H., *The Limits of Man.* London: Constable, 1967. 284 pp.

Petersen, W., *Population.* 2nd ed. New York: Macmillan, 1969. 736 pp.

Pressat, R., *Population.* (transl. from French). Pelican Series. Baltimore: Penguin Books, 1970. 152 pp.

Sax, K., *Standing Room Only—The World's Exploding Population.* Boston: Beacon Press, 1969 (1955). 206 pp.

Snow, C. P., *The State of Siege.* New York: Scribner, 1969. 52 pp.

Stockwell, E. G., *Population and People.* Chicago: Quadrangle Books, 1968. 309 pp.

Stycos, J. M., and J. Arias (eds.), *Population Dilemma in Latin America.* Washington: Potomac Books, 1966. 249 pp.

Ward, B. (ed.), *The Widening Gap.* New York: Columbia University Press, 1971. 320 pp.

Wrigley, E. A., *Population and History.* New York: McGraw-Hill, 1969. 254 pp.

Young, L. B., (ed.), *Population in Perspective.* New York: Oxford University Press, 1968. 460 pp.

REVIEW AND RESEARCH QUESTIONS

1. What is meant by the population explosion? What are its main causes?

2. How large is the present size of the human family and what is its current annual increment in millions per year?

3. How many billions have been added to the world population in the twentieth century and how many more billions are anticipated?

4. Analyze the European population explosion in the period 1850-1950 and the key role of the North American prairies.

5. What is meant by "the demographic transition"?

6. Discuss present limitations to renewed migration of peoples.

7. Review contraceptive measures now and earlier in human history.

8. Discuss the plight of unwanted children and their lack of food in the hungry world.

9. Analyze the validity of population density data in view of massive

food and feed supplementation from distant lands through transcontinental and transoceanic trade and/or through ocean harvests.

10. Discuss the parts of the globe that were involved in the big swarming of Western man that reached a peak in its influx to the United States in 1912.

11. What are the prerequisites of the "green revolution" and to what degree are there tangible constraints in the overpopulated poor world? Can the hungry countries afford it in money (capital), water, soil, and other inputs?

Nutrition and Health 12

Terms such as *malnutrition, undernutrition, hunger, starvation,* and *famine* are swirling around in the debate about the world's food issue. Distinctions are not clearly observed and these words are used more or less interchangeably. Originally they each had a specific meaning. *Undernutrition* implies too low an intake of calories; *malnutrition* an imbalanced diet, either deficient in one or more nutrients or else distorted by excessive intake of one or several ingredients. When malnutrition becomes permanent and multi-faceted, its many combined symptoms constitute what medical experts call a *syndrome*, resulting in a general undermining of health and bodily strength. When the gap between needs and intake becomes big and persistent, the term *hunger* applies, in extreme cases sharpened to *starvation*, often resulting in death. When this happens on a major scale there is a *famine.*

THE HUNGRY WORLD IS SICK

Hunger may, in certain respects, be labeled a disease, often with terminal outcome. Since resistance is undermined, undernutrition and malnutrition pave the way for infectious diseases; and these are far more severe in an undernourished individual than in someone well nourished. In this category are malaria, tuberculosis, diarrheas, measles, and many others. They cost dearly in terms of reduced productivity and premature death.

More than half a billion people carry hookworms, and almost a billion harbor intestinal parasites. Typhus, cholera, dysentery, and other water-borne infections involve at least a half billion. The annual toll of these afflictions in human lives is greater than the combined losses in World War II of more than

50 million. But the worst aspect of hunger is the irreparable damage to the brain and nerve tissue caused by shortage of protein in the fetal stage and during infant years and resulting in mental retardation.

Most livestock in the hungry world is also undermined by a multitude of diseases, sometimes erupting into epizootics that ravage cattle, hogs, and poultry in the millions, as was discussed in Chapter 5.

THE HUNGRY WORLD IS POOR

The hungry world is poor as well as sick and is caught in a vicious circle: it is poor because hunger or malnutrition keep its energy and productivity low. Causes and effects are here difficult to untangle. It is one of those squirrel cages with constantly revolving wheels. To save the squirrel he must be freed from his treadmill. Whether we identify the developing world as hungry, sick, or poor is immaterial. We must recognize the basic conditions of its life: the inadequate resources of tillable land, water, and forests, which contribute to inadequate average income.

Most family heads in the hungry world earn during a whole year less than the average North American family would casually spend on a weekend vacation—around $80 to $100. In Indian villages the daily earnings average 15 cents; current development programs aim at doubling this income within 35 years—not too exciting a prospect for these villagers. Most Mexican families have an annual income below $120. These are only a couple of random examples. Even considering the extremely small needs, low prices, and other mitigating circumstances, there remains an almost unimaginable chasm between the hungry world and ours. Their standard is far below any acceptable minimum.

FOOD, GROWTH, AND EFFICIENCY

Anyone can easily establish for himself that inadequate food intake reduces general efficiency and affects the feeling of well-being. Too little food and an unchanged daily routine easily induce tiredness, even sleepiness. The greater the discrepancy between bodily activities and the amount of daily food intake, the less are the accomplishments. Mankind presumably experienced this simple truth early in history, yet many people talk condescendingly about lazy stevedores in Brazilian coffee ports and lengthy siestas in the banana-loading ports of Ecuador. These workers have heavy physical work, whether carrying 120-pound coffee bags or 80-pound banana stalks or boxes! But they get far less food, far fewer energy-producing calories, than the average North American. Even when fed well according to *their* national standards they stretch out over 3 to 4 days what a North American eats each day. Furthermore, their food contains only a fraction of the high-quality animal protein included in the United States diet. This basic relationship between food intake and efficiency, both mental and physical, is well acknowledged, yet little heeded in the public and international debate.

Stature

Too little food for the mother often affects the growth rate and size of both the fetus and the newborn child. The children weigh less than they should and show a slower, retarded growth. In Europe and North America most people have become taller and more sturdy over the past one hundred years. The same effect is discernible in Japan during the period since World War II. This is generally attributed to an improved nutritional standard. In present-day U.A.R. (Egypt) the exact opposite is reported. Children are born smaller and grow less tall than 10 to 25 years ago. Many people in the hungry world show this reverse effect and, in addition, subdued reactivity. This is often interpreted as cultural and technical backwardness, apathy, or even laziness. But modern study of nutrition has thrown new light on these phenomena and has established an intimate relationship between adequate food and mental acuity.

Mental effects

One of the most significant recent discoveries has been the establishing of long-range irreversible effects of prenatal and early-childhood malnutrition. Lack of proper food in early stages of life may stunt not only physical growth but also mental development. The malnourished child of 1970 will be the retarded, underdeveloped adult of 1990. Malnutrition is therefore by a wide margin the world's number one health issue. Brain and nerve tissues grow most intensely immediately after birth and reach full size before the age of five. Lack of protein during this period easily results in scars, dead tissue sections, within or on the brain. Such damages cannot be repaired later in life. In contrast to other body tissues, the brain is never renewed. Such permanent scars create mental retardation or affect learning capabilities.

THE HUNGER EXPERIENCE

Hidden hunger

Even serious hunger is not always clearly noticeable by the naked eye. This fact has led to the concept of *hidden hunger.* The most common deficiencies within this category are the anemias. They manifest themselves in a shortage of blood components. Anemias affect more than half the population of many malnourished countries and are especially common among women and growing children. Lack of iron is the most prevalent form, being common in southern India, tropical East Africa, and Nigeria. But shortage of other trace elements in the food—copper, manganese, zinc, and vanadium—may be conducive to anemic conditions. Several of them, in particular zinc, cannot be mobilized by the body. Inadequate amounts of folic acid, due to extreme cereal diet, cause widespread anemia in India and the Middle East.

Anemias may also result from a high load of intestinal parasites, in particular hookworms. They take a major toll of iron. Intestinal parasites are a scourge among the malnourished in many countries. Frequently they get and take the first opportunity to pick up crucial minerals from the food in the intestines. When the host's intake of food is scarce, this becomes disastrous.

Hungry periods

Periods of food shortage occurring when the stored crops cannot be stretched to provide food until next harvest are another health hazard. Hungry weeks and even months are regular features of key areas of Latin America, tropical Africa, and parts of Asia. Unfortunately this low mark in food availability may well coincide with the need for heavy work in the preparing and tilling of the soil or in harvesting. In many instances this seasonal hunger leads to massive exodus, as in drought years in Northeast Brazil, or to regular seasonal migration as in South Africa. Studies show that the length of period during which the family head seeks work in mines and cities is directly proportionate to the shortage of food in the villages.

Up to the mid-1800's the Western world, even the North American prairies, experienced these very same phenomena when hit by drought or other calamities—locust or other insect attacks, grain rusts, floods, or the like. Local famines became rare events only after modern transportation permitted the hauling of supplementary food and feed across continents and oceans. Presumably spring fatigue was more common and severe in its manifestations in those days, when preservation of fruits and vegetables was more limited in scope.

PROTEIN DEFICIENCIES

In the world at large, shortage of protein is much more common than lack of calories. As we have noted, it is basically fairly easy to provide the requirements for energy-supplying foods. Protein foods demand much larger acreages and are thus far more expensive to produce. This difference explains why protein deficiency has emerged as the most common and crucial aspect of the world's hunger crisis. The most sensitive age period is at weaning, when the child abandons the mother's milk and starts taking other food.

Shortage of protein, with or without lack of calories, has many symptoms and may lead to serious deficiency diseases. The most common among them is *kwashiorkor*, first discovered in tropical Africa, where the name originated. It has since been identified in the Caribbean, in Central and South America, and in many parts of the Middle East and the Orient. It has had many names. In Jamaica, where the children get as many calories as they might want through sugar but are chronically short of protein, the accepted designation became "sugar babies." The disease was thought to be some disturbance caused by sugar.

Shortage of protein combined with undernutrition, that is, with calorie shortage, causes *marasmus*, a disease much more difficult to cure. With the growing shortage of food, the risk is great that marasmus will become more prevalent than hitherto.

Protein requirements

As is the case with calorie requirements, man's needs for protein vary from individual to individual. As a good rule of thumb, a physically inactive man needs 1 gram of protein daily for each kilogram of body weight. That means 70 grams for a man weighing 70 kg (154 lbs.). Strenuous muscular activity wears the body and its tissues a lot more. As a result, people performing heavy work need more calories in the form of energy-rendering foods, and also need a more protein-rich diet to provide the building stones for repair and maintenance of the muscle tissues. Growing children and youngsters need more protein, as do elderly people, in the latter instance to compensate for the rapid wear and tear of the tissues as age advances. Recent research has further made the unpleasant discovery that these elevated protein requirements are chiefly in those amino acids which are most prone to shortage.

Daily protein requirements

Calories	Total Protein (grams)	Animal Protein, Preferably* (grams)
2,000	63	20
2,500	80	30
3,000	95	35

*Half these quantities may carry an individual through if the intake of plant protein is somewhat increased (26 to 30 percent).

Protein needs, both qualitative and quantitative, are reasonably well established. Variations depend on ethnic factors, climate, and occupation. To what degree the body utilizes the food consumed as compared with how much is removed through the feces is not equally well known. The intestinal flora, in other words the bacteria in the intestines, also has an influence which needs to be better established. So does its interaction with all the above-mentioned external factors. Observations from New Guinea seem to indicate that tribes still living on a Stone Age level may have adjusted to a very low intake of protein, seemingly half of what is considered normal, without exhibiting deficiency symptoms. It has been suggested that possibly their intestinal flora is different. Ruminants (cows, sheep, camels, and others) have their own microbial factories in the rumen and are capable of supplementing their protein intake through this source. As a result they manage with less protein and may even synthesize protein from ammonia. Yet the ruminants have the same body needs as man: protein has to constitute at least 12 percent of their calorie intake. The needs of man for amino acids coincide very closely with those for swine, poultry, and rats (the most common experimental animals). Man's need of methionine seemingly is slightly higher than what these animals require.

VITAMIN DEFICIENCIES

Vitamin-deficiency diseases have played an important role in history. They created great difficulties in conquering the oceans and made lengthy sea voyages as hazardous as prolonged warfare. Vitamin shortage determined the fate of many early scientific expeditions. The illustrious accomplishments of industrialization in the Western world had their dark shadow in disease and misery among the teeming millions of the cities. Calories were supplied primarily through fat and sugar, but protein was scanty; such foods were expensive. Even worse, knowledge was lacking about many other nutrients required, in particular vitamins.

Early nutritional literature was replete with descriptions of devastating diseases such as scurvy, beri-beri, and rachitis, which afflict man when he does not get enough vitamins. Gradually it was learned how to prevent and remedy such diseases by eating particular foods and later by intake of a few milligrams daily of these vitamins in manufactured form. In developed countries severe vitamin deficiency largely belongs to history, but shortage of vitamins has not disappeared.

Nutritional research has gradually revealed a number of disturbances which result from insufficient intake of vitamins. Long before clearly visible disease symptoms appear, vitamin shortage may manifest itself in reduced resistance to such infectious diseases as common cold and in lowered working and learning capabilities. The entire health picture may be affected and body efficiency impaired when amounts of vitamins and other functional compounds are below par.

Among the more than 2 billion under- and malnourished in the world, and still more among those who are starving, vitamin-deficiency diseases take tremendous tolls through *avitaminosis,* mirrored in poor health, extreme misery, and death.

From the long list of functional substances, only those vitamins and minerals will be discussed here which have turned out to be important in the hungry world. They are also significant in the developed world, most clearly evidenced in the extensive production and consumption of vitamin and/or mineral preparations and pills. Most of the vitamins manufactured industrially are not used to fill the desperate needs among the world's hungry but are largely employed in the well-to-do countries; they go primarily to provide complete feed rations for livestock, in particular hogs and chickens, and secondly to people.

Vitamins are of two major categories: fat-soluble and water-soluble. In the hungry world the fat intake is generally low and fat-soluble vitamins are therefore in short supply, in particular vitamin A; the result is serious vision disturbances and skin defects. Among the water-soluble vitamins, ascorbic acid (vitamin C) and thiamin (vitamin B_1) are the most critical. Scurvy is the final outcome of vitamin C shortage. Beri-beri (muscular defects) results from lack of vitamin B_1.

Beri-beri

Beri-beri was discovered at the end of the nineteenth century in Asia, where it suddenly became widespread among rice-eating people. Research gradually revealed that this irruption had a direct connection with the introduction of new and more effective methods for milling rice. The outer parts of the rice kernels were removed through abrasion. In this polishing process certain nutrients were lost, in particular vitamin B_1. Instead of abandoning polishing, yeast was added to the rice as a source of B vitamins and a sharp drop in the number of beri-beri cases followed. Countries that practice parboiling of rice (page 119) were not affected by this hazard.

Beri-beri nevertheless continues its ravages, particularly in Southeast Asia and parts of India, where beans and fish are commonly eaten as a protein supplementation to rice, the bulk of the diet. It has been found that rice and beans, and in many instances fish, contain a particular compound, an anti-thiamine, which reduces or entirely eliminates the benefits of vitamin B_1. Measures to counteract this negative effect have been taken in several countries, but encountered great difficulties when bacteria capable of destroying thiamine got a foothold in the human intestinal flora. In such cases even massive doses of thiamine do not cure the afflicted or remove the beri-beri symptoms; instead, they favor the further development of these marauders. Most of these bacteria originate from fish and are common in Japan and other Asian countries.

Antivitamins

Certain compounds which are directly antagonistic to defined vitamins and sometimes eliminate their wholesome effects entirely are collectively called antivitamins. They are much more common than was earlier realized, especially in plant products—primarily in beans, but also in grain, tubers, leaves, and others. Many such unfavorable ingredients are removed in food preparation in homes or industries. Others must be eliminated through special procedures or be compensated for by the addition of vitamins. Besides antithiamine, there are known antivitamins for niacin, riboflavin, biotin, pyridoxine, and others.

Pellagra

In many corn-eating countries a disease called pellagra was early encountered. Research showed that it could be induced experimentally by lowering the amount of niacin in the food. Most corn varieties contain adequate amounts of niacin, but bound and not utilizable by man without special pretreatment of the corn kernels. Such pretreatment is practiced in Mexico, where the backbone of the daily diet is tortillas, a kind of pancake made from cornmeal. In these regions pellagra is rare. The reason is that the corn is treated with lime in a chemical brining, releasing tryptophan, an amino acid that in turn provides niacin. A further gain from this treatment is an increased calcium content. Pellagra is still common in the Balkans and some parts of tropical Africa, where corn bread or other corn-meal dishes dominate the diet but the kernels are not lime-treated.

MINERAL DEFICIENCY-DENTAL CARIES

Caries is fairly common among the hungry and malnourished and is caused by the same factors in both the hungry and the affluent worlds: a high consumption of sugar and starch and too low an intake of protein, calcium, phosphorus, magnesium, and various trace elements. Oral infections may also induce caries. In general, primitive peoples have good teeth unless they are damaged through the introduction of a one-sided cheap diet of sugar and starchy foods, often due to overpopulation. The Pacific Islands are a case in point; adequate food can no longer be produced on the islands for the rapidly growing numbers of inhabitants, and caries is increasing. Greenland is another example of the devastating influence of white man's sugar and starch, but in those regions where the traditional diet of seal flesh still prevails, rich in protein fat, the people have retained their fine teeth.

In Latin America, Asia, and tropical Africa many poor have been forced to abandon their earlier diets, far better in minerals and protein, and abate hunger with "empty calories." Sugar and sweets have become coveted novelties in the slums to the detriment of dental health.

INTERACTION IN NUTRITION

No foods are as such dangerous, hazardous, or particularly wholesome. These qualities depend on the composition of the total diet, in other words on the balance between the various ingredients of the food consumed. As was indicated in Chapter 10, food from the four major categories should be part of each meal. The various nutrients interact with each other in the metabolism of the body. If one or more ingredients are missing, the total nutritive value of the food is not fully utilized. On the other hand, excessive intake of cereals, sugar, or fat may increase the body's need for several vitamins and other functional compounds. In acute or chronic malnutrition the need for particular nutrients may be elevated. A good example is the need for vitamin B_1 in the combustion of sugar. Vitamin E and several other compounds are required in the normal metabolism of fat and for its transport in the body. In order to utilize the protein in the food, man is dependent on a normal supply of calcium, sulfur, magnesium, iron, and zinc.

Many more examples could be given, but these may suffice to underline that this interaction between nutrients often is neglected in efforts to improve nutritional conditions in the hungry world. Individual nutrients in short supply have often been administered, variously protein, iron, or one or more vitamins. In such cases new deficiency symptoms or poor health have surprisingly emerged, depending on the shortage of other substances with which the added nutrients interact. A telling example can be picked from United States school feeding programs in Indonesia and Pakistan. Skim milk was provided in the form of reconstituted powder (nonfat milk solids), but due to the shortage of vitamin A, which otherwise would be provided through the fat of the milk, serious vision troubles emerged among the children, in extreme cases blindness. Another instance (1965) involved more than 100,000 children in Recife, Brazil. Here also the reconstituted milk was short of fats, and thereby the fat-soluble vitamins were lost or at least considerably reduced. Vitamin A was the most critical one—closest to the minimum level.

HEALTH ISSUES OF THE SATISFIED WORLD

Even in the affluent countries many people are suffering from poor health due to malnutrition. The United States, Canada and European countries have pockets of poverty and misery. Ignorance as to nutritional matters is another cause. Far more common, however, are disturbances due to overconsumption; most of these reflect too high an intake of calories, in particular of fat but also of sugar. To this group of diseases belong arteriosclerosis, heart infarcts, stones in the gall bladder and kidney, and conspicuous obesity. As a rule they are combined with fat deposits in the heart, arteries, and liver. These diseases hardly exist in countries with a low fat intake, and they are also quite rare among those in the affluent world whose economic circumstances force them to restrict their food intake.

Excessive consumption of sugar and sweetened foods is presumably the chief cause for certain types of diabetes and tooth deterioration, in particular caries. Not even the privileged Westerners, who have both knowledge and resources to maintain sound food habits, are protected from poor health due to nutritional imbalance. This category of so-called civilization diseases includes other disturbances which, as far as we know, do not directly relate to food habits but to the way of life, often under severe stress, typical of highly industrialized societies. Even the affluent world needs to make itself far better acquainted with the intimate relationships between daily food and general health.

REFERENCES AND RECOMMENDATIONS
FOR FURTHER READING

Bieler, N. C. *Food Is Your Best Medicine.* New York: Random House, 1965. 236 pp.

Borgstrom, G., *The Dual Challenge of Health and Hunger—A Global Crisis.* Population Reference Bureau, 1970. Spec. Publ. Selection No. 31, 6 pp.

Dubos, R., *Man, Medicine and Environment.* New York and Toronto: New American Library, 1968. 160 pp.

Dubos, R., *The Mirage of Health*. New York: Harper, 1970 (1959). 236 pp.

Grant, M. P., *Biology and World Health*. London, New York, Toronto: Abelard-Schuman, 1970. 242 pp.

Magee, H. E., *Nutrition and Public Health*. London: Pitman Medical Publishing Co., 1959. 152 pp.

Scrimshaw, N. W., and J. E. Gordon (eds.) *Malnutrition, Learning, and Behavior*. Cambridge: MIT Press, 1968. 566 pp.

Sigerist, N. E., *Civilization and Disease*. Chicago: University of Chicago Press, 1962 (1943). 256 pp.

Ward, B., *The Lopsided World*. New York: Norton, 1968. 210 pp.

REVIEW AND RESEARCH QUESTIONS

1. How does food shortage affect general working efficiency?

2. Why are Americans and present-day Japanese getting taller?

3. How does protein deficiency affect mental capabilities?

4. What is meant by "hidden hunger"?

5. What does the expression "hungry weeks" (*or* months) imply?

6. Which are the chief diseases caused by protein shortage in the diet and what are their distinctive features?

7. What are the dietary implications of the interaction between nutrients?

8. Which are the most common vitamin deficiencies in the United States and in the hungry world?

9. What is the role of antithiamine?

10. Which are the main categories of disease agents?

11. Discuss the significance of diseases with reference to crops, livestock, animals, and man himself.

12. Review major criteria for the void between the satisfied world and the hungry world, with reference to the kind of foods consumed.

13. What does poverty mean in terms of food patterns?

14. Review the main causes of obesity.

15. What is the causal relationship between food on the one hand and caries, gastric, and cardiac disturbances on the other?

Protein: 13
The Key Issue

The most critical and crucial aspect of the whole protein issue, the basic reason for its being an issue, is the fact that foods with high quality protein are the most costly part of man's diet. In a world where one-third of the people enjoy an annual income of less than $100 and two-thirds less than $200, animal proteins are rarely within reach in adequate amounts. Any supplementation toward improvement or novelty needs to fit within such a parsimonious budget. This poverty more than anything else, has limited the options for alleviating the protein squeeze under which so many hundreds of millions are suffering.

THE PROTEIN GAP

The graphs in this chapter as well as many of the tables illustrate how obliquely food is distributed on the world scene, particularly in regard to animal products. The hungry billions receive a fraction of what the well-fed enjoy. It is indeed no evidence of improved dietary conditions on Earth that the fortunate beneficiaries eat more eggs, steaks, pork chops, and poultry meat, and drink more milk than they used to do in the 1930's or in the 1950's. Most peoples on the other side of the hunger gap have less food available in major nutrients. Since the 1930's, the average person in the satisfied world has had a *gain* in available animal protein greater than the current *total* intake of the average person in the hungry world.

Japan has landed on the other side of this crucial gap, largely through its fisheries, which provide both human and animal food. The ocean catches contribute fish meal to its livestock and poultry, in quantity twice the

191

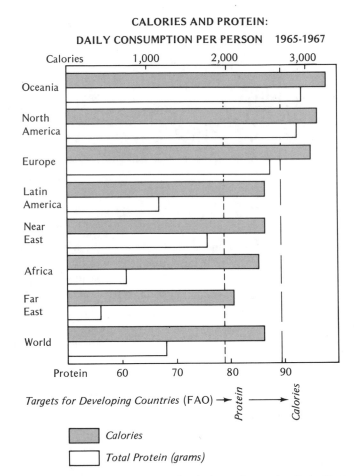

CALORIES AND PROTEIN:
DAILY CONSUMPTION PER PERSON   1965-1967

Daily consumption per person of calories and protein. Only Western nations surpass the desirable thresholds of calorie and protein consumption indicated by FAO. The protein shortcomings of the hungry world are greater than the calorie deficits.

amount that these commodities in turn convey to the Japanese people; one-third to one-half is lost in the feed conversion. Europe is masking its luxury in a similar way. Around two-fifths of its animal products originate in imported feed, primarily fish meal from Peru and West-Southwest Africa; other feedstuffs come from the North American prairie, Australia, Argentina, and tropical Africa.

Availability of animal protein (grams per day per person)

	Satisfied World	Hungry World
1936-1938	36	11
1963-1965	44	8

PROTEIN FROM LIVESTOCK

Protein produced through animal husbandry is by and large a luxury enjoyed by the well-fed world. Its improved level of living, particularly in the past hundred years, is to a considerable degree reflected in its growing intake of milk, meat, and eggs. The gap is mirrored in the fact that 65 to 80 percent of these commodities are consumed by less than one-third of the human family.

As was pointed out in Chapter 11, the Western world has much more land for tillage and in pastures, allowing its inhabitants this extravagance. Significantly, many countries, especially India, enjoyed a far more luxurious fare when they had far fewer people to feed—in other words, when the country was far less densely populated.

A couple of other salient points should be added. Meat was daily fare in the nomadic civilizations and still is for people that depend on grazing herds, whether on steppes or on the fringes of deserts (Central Asia, Arabia, Somalia, Mauritania). With 86 percent of all milk being produced in Europe, the Soviet Union, and North America, milk has become almost a Western monopoly. This is partly explained by the fact that only people that have acquired tolerance to milk sugar (lactose) can utilize milk as food. In major portions of Africa (except in regions with pastoral agriculture) and in the heartland of China the people show intolerance to milk. So do American Indians and Eskimos.

The Chinese miracles

There are some fundamental differences between the animal protein of China and India, reflecting their agricultural history. In China, meat dominates the scene; in India, milk, half of which comes from buffaloes. In a massive effort to augment the animal-protein supply, China has reinstalled the hog to its traditional place in the economy as a scavenger, feeding on plant wastes and human sewage. In this way a basis has been created for additional meat and fat (lard) production. It also provides raw material for the manufacture of

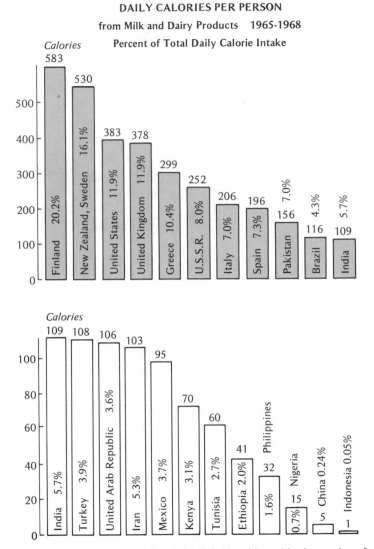

DAILY CALORIES PER PERSON

from Milk and Dairy Products   1965-1968

Calories   Percent of Total Daily Calorie Intake

The gap between the well-fed and the ill-fed is evidenced in the number of calories per person from milk and dairy products and in these dairy calories as percents of total calorie intake.

nitrogen fertilizers and special products like hormones and bristles. This has made China the number one producer of pork in the world, with three times as many hogs as the United States or the Soviet Union. A corresponding expansion of poultry raising has made China the second largest producer in the world. Droppings from swine and poultry are not infrequently collected in fish ponds and thus brought into another food chain to produce fish. This kind of extreme economizing, originating early in Chinese history, is a reminder that such recycling to regain nutrients as food is of fundamental significance (see Chapter 11). These Chinese miracles have raised the availability of animal protein in China to a level above that of India and Indonesia, though far below Western levels.

Rank of China in world animal production (1969-1970)

Rank	Pork		Eggs		Poultry Meat	
	Country	Percent	Country	Percent	Country	Percent
1	China	25.1	United States	20.1	United States	40.7
2	United States	17.2	China	16.2	China	18.5
3	West Germany	10.2	U.S.S.R.	10.5	U.S.S.R	5.8
4	U.S.S.R.	9.8	Japan	7.9	France	4.0
World production (millions of metric tons)		33.2		20.2		13.8

The huge discrepancies in animal-protein consumption become almost startling when the Asian giants are compared with the United States or even with their Japanese neighbor.

Animal-protein consumption (grams per person per day) 1968-1969

Country	Meat	Milk	Eggs	Fish	Total
China	5.3	0.3	0.9	1.4	7.9
India	0.6	4.3	0.1	0.6	5.6
Indonesia	1.5	—	0.3	3.4	5.2
Japan	6.1	3.7	4.4	15.5	29.7
United States	37.5	23.2	5.5	3.3	69.5

Only in countries where poultry raising has become commercialized and based on controlled feeding has the intake of eggs and poultry meat (broilers, fryers, and the like) reached a high level. When poultry is kept largely for subsistence, the consumption remains modest.

FISH PROTEIN

Fish is the main source of animal protein in major parts of the Asian continent and is also dominant in parts of Africa and the Caribbean. The relative significance of fish protein is best reflected in its share of the total intake of animal protein and less so in the data for quantity consumed. In

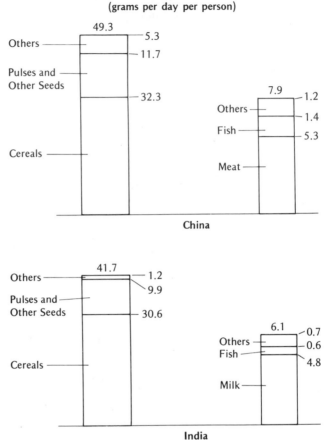

PROTEIN IN LOW-LEVEL DIETS
(grams per day per person)

China

Others — 49.3 — 5.3 / 11.7

Pulses and Other Seeds — 32.3

Cereals

Others — 7.9 — 1.2 / 1.4 / 5.3

Fish

Meat

India

Others — 41.7 — 1.2 / 9.9

Pulses and Other Seeds — 30.6

Cereals

Others — 6.1 — 0.7 / 0.6 / 4.8

Fish

Milk

Typical low-level diets (China and India). The average is slightly better in China than in India. Note the low intake of animal protein and the basic difference in that meat (pork and chicken) dominates in China and milk (cow, buffalo, and goat) in India. (FAO data)

Indonesia fish constitutes two-thirds of the animal protein, yet the total amount is exceedingly low, a mere one-fifth that of Japan. Nonetheless, for more than 1½ billion people, fish fills in the gap between starvation and subsistence. Freshwater fish is predominant in the hungry world, while in the satisfied world this source is losing out to pollution. Many other Asian countries are fish-dependent, and surprisingly so also are several African

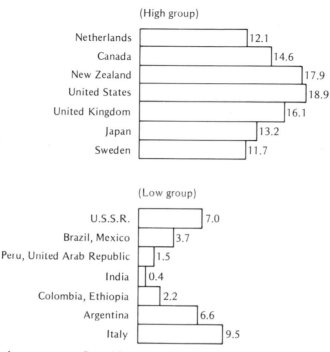

EGG CONSUMPTION   1967-1968

(kilograms per person per year)

(High group)

Netherlands 12.1
Canada 14.6
New Zealand 17.9
United States 18.9
United Kingdom 16.1
Japan 13.2
Sweden 11.7

(Low group)

U.S.S.R. 7.0
Brazil, Mexico 3.7
Peru, United Arab Republic 1.5
India 0.4
Colombia, Ethiopia 2.2
Argentina 6.6
Italy 9.5

The hunger gap as reflected in egg consumption.

nations. Most Caribbean islands rely on fish for much animal protein. (See table on page 227.)

PLANT PROTEIN

Cereals play a key role in the feeding of people on both sides of the hunger gap, being more than 67 percent of the diet. But grains have a low content of protein compared to pulses and oilseed, and the quality of their protein is inferior from the viewpoint of human nutrition. Therefore soybeans and other beans are highly important as an adjunct to the daily food of the poor in countries such as Mexico, Italy, and Brazil. The diet in the humid tropics is dominated by tubers (cassava). These are so poor in protein that they most be supplemented by animal products, in the hungry world most readily available in fish and fish products as a cheap source.

The next step

Proteins are in themselves not foods but food components, and they vary appreciably in their amino-acid composition and thus in their deviation from man's specific needs. The effort to overcome shortages and deviations has led to a wide range of proposals for filling the voids, implemented only in a few initial stages thus far. There are in principle two roads for achieving such greater perfection and improved nutrition. First is the long road of breeding such added amino acids into the proteins of cereals and leguminous seeds. This method is so far of limited practical application. The best-known examples are the high-lysine cereals (wheat, corn, triticale). The second alternative is to add to the cereals amino acids made either through chemical synthesis or microbial fermentation. Some twenty amino acids can now be manufactured by such procedures. Only four are of immediate practical significance: lysine, threonine, tryptophan, and methionine. Rice can be improved by lysine and threonine; corn by tryptophan, lysine, and isoleucine; and wheat by lysine.

NOVEL PROTEIN SOURCES

Experiments have shown that leaves could constitute a new source of protein. The process is adaptable to small rural units. The leaves are macerated, the juice pressed out, and the proteins precipitated; processing follows. Shortages of potable water or availability of suitable leaves are limiting factors.

Microorganisms such as fungi, yeast, bacteria, algae, and protozoa may all be multiplied in vats on suitable substrates and become sources of protein food. They can obviously be produced outside of any agricultural base such as a farm, as long as required minerals and organics (frequently wastes) are available. The difficulties may be in extraction and in unexpected side reactions after eating due to structural incompatibilities.

Finally, most traditional proteins may be concentrated and thus be made more versatile, even to the making of new foods. Such products have been made, and successfully tested, from meat and fish as well as from soybeans, peanuts, and other oilseeds.

The amino acids, concentrates, and the like need not necessarily be added to cereals or leguminous seeds but can also be transferred into the daily food through other vehicles such as tea, soft drinks, noodles, bread, even salt.

DEMAND AND DEFICIT

Economic analyses usually calculate the shortage of food or protein in terms of *effective demand*. Such calculations answer the question of how much more food or protein respectively can be moved in the market in view of anticipated improvements in purchasing power and expected increases in human numbers. But such figures in no way illustrate the *deficits*, namely the amounts actually required to fill the nutrition gap up to the level of minimum requirements.

These sizable protein inequities can be exemplified from almost every country on the other side of the protein gap. The *Indicative World Plan* of FAO illustrates the true magnitude of this protein shortage in the hungry world. The following figures refer to some ten key countries in tropical Africa, and not the most rapidly growing.

	Animal protein added demand (thousands of metric tons)	Plant protein added deficit* (thousands of metric tons)	Population	
			Million	As percent of Africa
1957	14	270	63	27
1985	27	290	68	22

*Assuming that animal protein is too expensive to consider, but filling the deficit through leguminous seeds (peas, beans, and other)

REFERENCES AND RECOMMENDATIONS FOR FURTHER READING

Lawrie, R. A. (ed.), *Proteins as Human Food.* Westport, Conn.: The AVI Publishing Company, Inc., 1970. 525 pp.

Milner, M. (ed.), *Protein-Enriched Cereal Foods for World Needs.* St. Paul, Minn.: American Association of Cereal Chemists, 1969. 343 pp.

Scrimshaw, N. S., and A. M. Altschul (eds.), *Amino Acid Fortification of Protein Foods.* Cambridge, Mass.: The MIT Press, 1971. 664 pp.

RESEARCH AND REVIEW QUESTIONS

The Research and Review Questions for Chapters 10 and 12 deal with the matter of Chapter 13.

Food and the Ecology Crisis

14

Most technical advances, including those in food production, have an ecological price. In many instances progress is worth its price, but under all circumstances a complete balance account should be made. With few exceptions we have registered only the gains—the credit entries—omitting the cost items and thereby neglecting to balance our books.

As a child I could hear the quaint creaking sound of the corncrake coming from the summer grainfields and meadows of middle Sweden. But big harvesters destroyed the nests of these birds and drainage reduced moisture; they vanished. For similar reasons the frogs are disappearing in North America and Europe. The blame has been directed to the reckless taking of frogs for use in experimental work in medicine, toxicology, and biology. More disastrous, however, is increased drainage, filling of dams, and changes wrought by urbanization and industrialization. The frogs have seen their habitat ruined. In both agricultural and urban areas they have been further decimated through massive spraying that has transmitted toxic compounds to their waters. In England and in continental Europe, insect-eating birds were deprived of their habitat in hedgerows as ditches were filled and the big fields required in modern agriculture were created. As these helpers of man were eliminated, the insect menace grew explosively.

THE FOOD QUEST

A major reshaping force

Man's quest for food has been a tremendous reshaping force on the face of the Earth. He has pulled down forests and broken land on plains and up the mountainsides. He has drained marshlands and burned the vegetation on grassy plains. He has made arid lands flourish by drilling wells or directing the flow of rivers and streams onto the fields and by creating dams to collect water for irrigation.

Oil refineries, car and truck industries, chemical industries for fertilizers and spray materials, and the packaging industry are to a large extent connected with the production and distribution of food. Vast tracts have been placed under concrete and asphalt for cities, industrial sites, shopping centers, highways, and airfields. Highways and railroads carry large volumes of food and feed, the most indispensable of all commodities. Supermarkets are primarily distribution centers for food to the consumer.

Food is thus via man a top-ranking ecological force. The price the Earth has paid for the privilege of accommodating the forthwelling millions and even billions of this "superanimal" is high. In his drive for survival, man has created more acres of desert than of new land placed under irrigation. He has pulled down more than half of the world's forest cover, thus exposing vast lands to the destructive forces of water and wind. He has destroyed topsoil through excessive cropping on acreages many times larger than he ever built up or created. In many parts of the world, coffee, banana, and sugar plantations have been abandoned after the land was stripped of topsoil. Such changes culminated in a large-scale ecological crisis in China some 3,000 years ago, and another in the Mediterranean area near the beginning of the Christian era. The consequences of these catastrophes are still severe.

The breaking of the prairie

Man gained little wisdom from earlier failures and created a repeat on a continental scale when ruthlessly pushing the frontier on the North American continent toward the Pacific. The breaking of the prairie with iron plows was one of mankind's greatest agricultural undertakings. It was pursued with shockingly little regard for Nature's limitations and vulnerable features. Technology was considered supreme and entirely capable of mastering any adversities.

One result was the big Dust Bowl catastrophe in the 1930's, when topsoil from the dry prairie descended windblown in huge clouds on eastern-seaboard cities and darkened their skies. This is history's third great ecological blunder and in many ways the biggest, because man was in this instance living on such an extravagant footing. Rarely have so few wrought so much havoc to the detriment of so many. The beneficiaries were few. In the conquest of the prairies more than half the forests were removed and one-fourth of the topsoil dissipated and forever lost, most of it to the Gulf of Mexico. The Mississippi is still being gorged with some 5 to 6 million tons of silt each day, much of it soil from agricultural lands.

The water squandering

Still more crucial is an ignorance of the fact that in ecological terms the United States is two countries—one humid and one arid—with the boundary between them largely following the hundredth meridian, a little west of the Mississippi River. Arid America has basically been living on a water capital accumulated through the centuries but tapped irretrievably and at a growing pace as human numbers grew. Falling water tables and vanishing ground-waters reflect this excessive mining of pleistocene water. The transfer of millions to arid regions in recent decades reflects the basic lack of awareness of man's water dependence and also proves the urgent need for a United States water and population policy. Both are greatly overdue.

Water availability has been greatly affected by the quest for food. In many regions, marshlands and flooding of farmlands due to poor drainage constituted a direct obstacle to effective cropping or grazing. Large-scale drainage was therefore a must to obtain food, but this expediting of the runoff meant loss of water desperately needed in other seasons. Thus immediate gains often led to unexpected losses. In general, higher farm yields have taxed and overtaxed the water resources and been a major desiccating force. Ponds, lakes, and streams have vanished in this process. Groundwater tables have fallen as vast volumes have been tapped and released to the oceans or atmosphere without replenishment. These effects have been thoroughly studied in major regions of Scandinavia, Central Europe, and eastern Canada.

Food is the big item in the water balance of all countries, irrespective of degree of industrialization. This is easily understood when it is remembered, as was discussed in Chapter 4, that most food crops require 1,000 to 5,000 lbs. of water for each pound of dry matter produced and that animal foods require many times more via the feed from pastures and fields. Nutritional standards can be gauged in such water terms.

Man is presumably no longer in a position to restore the hecatombs of water he has removed from under the ground into the oceans and the atmosphere, nor to restore the forests he has pulled down, nor to remake the topsoils he has squandered.

POLLUTION HAZARDS TO FOOD

Many other phases of agricultural production depend on protection of the environment. Air pollutants may kill off forests and crops and affect the quality of the harvest as reflected in levels of mercury, lead, DDT, and other harmful compounds. Water pollutants influence in a similarly dangerous way the composition of aquatic foods in terms of their content of radioactive compounds (from fallout and reactor effluents) or trace elements, such as cadmium, mercury, and others. Polluted water used for irrigation may transmit disease agents, a major consideration in the disposal of waste water. Water, heavily polluted by organic proteinaceous waste from dairies, slaughterhouses, and some other food-processing units, frequently harbors and propagates salmonella organisms, a growing food poisoning threat.

These random examples may serve to illustrate that if we wish to secure food we must protect the environment.

Chemical contaminants

Agricultural practices themselves may have detrimental effects. Among such hazards are residues in foods from (1) sprays used in cropping and animal raising, and (2) excessive application of nitrogen fertilizers. Some spray chemicals persist in the soil and find their way into crops, ending up in the prepared foods and also—via feed—in milk, meat, and eggs. At one time the demand was raised for zero tolerance in this regard. With added experience and through more refined analytical methods, it was found that many more chemicals find their way into food products than was earlier realized. Considerable effort therefore goes into establishing what are the hazardous amounts and how great the risks of a gradual accumulation in the body, up to dangerous levels.

Many chemicals are applied in livestock raising to fight diseases and control insect pests. Animals under medication are normally withdrawn from production until fully recovered. Yet penicillin, used to cure some udder diseases may accidentally enter into milk and cheese. This has become a major concern and requires constant surveillance.

The persistent depletion of the soil minerals has led to a vast counterstream of mineral fertilizers moving to the farms. Excessive use of nitrogen fertilizers is particularly harmful, for the runoff nitrate becomes a serious water pollutant, endangering groundwaters, wells, and quality and potability of water in general. Costly extra procedures in the waterworks are required to reduce nitrate levels. More critical is the build-up of nitrates in plant products, especially vegetables. Ingested nitrate is readily converted by intestinal bacteria into hazardous nitrite, which has great affinity for blood hemoglobin and in this way destroys its value for the regular oxygen transfer.

Sewage

Food is a direct part of the pollution picture in general through the waste it creates, primarily as sewage. The growth of our cities concentrates the out-takes of water to fewer localities and augments water needs through the congestion of increasing numbers of humans. Urban United States has five times as many people as at the turn of the century, but the flow of food to the cities has increased even more since the intake per capita is higher. These developments are to some degree inflamed by the emergence of food industries acting as major transformers along this lifeline of society. By trimming inedible and less digestible parts and through processing, they reduce substantially the amount of waste reaching the cities and the consumers. In return, however, they create new pollution points, as was discussed in Chapter 8. The food ends up as human waste, transported by water as sewage to plants for treatment. There the polluting matter is reduced to a varying degree, but at least one-third is released into adjacent waters (lakes or rivers) as raw sewage. The same happens through private septic tanks that overflow, due to overloading caused by higher population densities with more people in each building and more visitors (thanks to more cars).

United States population, 1900 and 1970 (millions)

Year	Urban	Rural	Total
1900	30	45	76
1970	155	50*	205
Increase (multiple)	5.2	1.1	2.7

*Includes some suburban areas.

In some sewage plants all organic matter is broken down through so-called tertiary treatment. But a major portion of the mineral salts remain. They constitute a strong polluting force, identical to that of mineral fertilizers. As the cities continue to bulge, there is only one recourse, namely to recycle the waste. Presumably it will become necessary to convert the sewage plants into food-producing centers. (See earlier, Chapter 8.)

RECYCLING WASTE

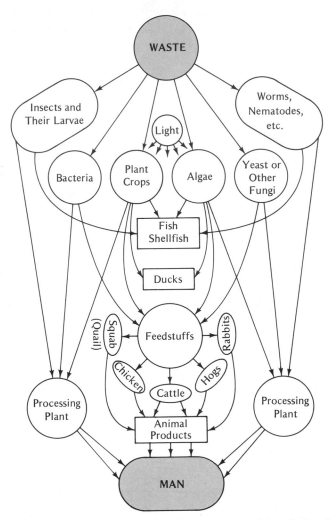

Various channels for converting waste (including sewage) into feed or food.

This gathering of humans into cities—urbanization—is consequently a major ecological factor, not necessarily because of the numbers as such but their concentration. A million people dispersed over wide expanses do not have a fraction of the polluting effect—in particular as to the recipient water bodies, whether lakes, rivers, or groundwater—that they have when restricted to a small area. This drastic switch in the congestion of man has its counterpart in the creation of huge animal-raising centers: hog and egg factories, cattle feeding lots, and big broiler-raising establishments. Their polluting effect has been rapidly compounded and now far exceeds that of man (in the United States corresponding to the sewage from more than 900 million people). This is a major ecological hazard generated by food. Most of this animal waste also needs to be recycled back into food via special centers.

Still another related factor is the abandonment and changed use of farmland, demanding more intense cropping and higher yields from remaining croplands with mounting use of fertilizers and in many instances more use of water. This puts a greater strain on the soil and its living world, but more importantly, it increases the risks of seepage of minerals into adjacent waters, particularly critical as to nitrogenous compounds.

The overworked waters

At the same time that man expects the natural waters to take care of mounting loads of sewage and other waste, he does his very best by massive water removals to reduce their capacity as receptacles. In the United States the use of water has climbed steeply since 1900, from around 20 gallons per person per day to an average of 175. Europe uses about half that figure. To a growing degree potable water—the number one food—has to be recovered from sewage for reuse, involving great sanitary risks. The chlorine barrier is not fully efficient, in particular with regard to several viruses.

IRRIGATION HAZARDS

The benefits of providing water to spur crop cultivation, especially in arid and semiarid regions, are obvious and often enumerated. But the ecological side effects of irrigation are mostly overlooked. We ought not to forget that the water also favors man's foes, whether microorganisms, weeds, or other pests. The spread of many tropical diseases is enhanced. This applies to scourges like malaria, river blindness, schistosomiasis, and others, despite intense countermeasures. A high price to pay for more food, frequently wiping out the gains in reduced malnutrition! These side effects are in particular critical from large-scale dams, involving millions of acres. Small-scale extensions through wells are easier to control with medical countermeasures. In this area coordination has been lacking.

THE MOUNTING INTRICACIES
OF FOOD AND ECOLOGY

Many other links between food and ecology have been discussed in previous chapters of this book. It deserves to be underlined once more that the relentless chemical warfare in which we are engaged to protect our food—the crops in the field, the animals we raise, and the food itself during storage, processing, and distribution—has no final victories. Our chemical tools are sooner or later outsmarted by our foes, be they insects, microorganisms, or other pests. They build up resistance or create biochemical pathways for detoxification. Among unpleasant surprises in this regard is the renewed resistance of the tse-tse fly and the mosquito to insecticides; another is the gradually increasing ineffectiveness of warfare against rats, established in England and Australia.

As we have seen in Chapter 6, the aquatic sphere has also suffered greatly from pollution, jeopardizing even the vast oceans as a dependable source of food. The most critical toxicants are DDT, the polychlorinated biphenyls (PCB), several radioactive compounds, and heavy-metal ions. DDT and mercury compounds directly affect the photosynthetic activities of the phytoplankton. If this poisoning is extended to global scale, man may in this way become a direct menace to life itself by striking a blow against the vital oxygen-delivery system of the oceans. Overtaxing of fish stocks and the near eradication of valuable whale species are other items on man's long list of ecological guilts. The foremost menace to the oceans seems, however, to be oil leaks from underwater drilling and spill from oil tankers. The general use of the oceans as direct dumping grounds for man's waste, to a large extent food-related, constitutes another paramount danger.

In the struggle to live and to obtain food, man has become the most influential force in Nature, including—absurdly enough since he is a terrestrial animal—the oceans. If mankind is going to survive and to secure food for this and future generations, much greater knowledge and awareness of the intimate relationships between food and ecology have to be implanted and acted upon.

REFERENCES AND RECOMMENDATIONS
FOR FURTHER READING

Innumerable books have been published covering various aspects of the ecological crisis. Few have focused attention on the specific aspects related to food. The references here given are selected papers of particular relevance in this context.

Audy, J. F., "Ecological Aspects of Introduced Pests and Diseases," *Medical Journal of Malaya*, 1 (1), 21-32 (1956).

Borgstrom, G. A. "Food and Ecology," in C. L. San Clemente (ed.), *Environmental Quality: Now or Never.* East Lansing, Mich.: Michigan State University, Continuing Education Service, 1972, pp. 58-70.

Borgstrom, G. A., "The Human Biosphere," in *Proceedings of UNESCO Symposium,* held in Stockholm, July 25-29, 1964. Uppsala: Almqvist and Wiksell. New York: Wiley, 1965, 599 pp.

Brown, L. R., "Human Food Production as a Process in the Biosphere," in *The Biosphere,* Scientific American book, 1964, pp. 93-104.

Commoner, B., "Damaged Global Fabric," in S. Novick and D. Cottrell (eds.), *Our World in Peril: An Environment Review.* Greenwich, Conn.: Fawcett Publications, 1971, pp. 9-20.

Deevey, E. S., "The Human Crop," *Scientific American,* 194 (4), 105-112 (1956).

Kuenen, D. J., "Man, Food, and Insects as an Ecological Problem," *Proceedings XVI International Congress of Zoology,* 7, 5-13 (1963).

REVIEW AND RESEARCH QUESTIONS

1. Analyze why man was and is such a major factor in reshaping the earth.

2. In which way did man's efforts to raise food basically affect the water and soil balance?

3. How does excessive tapping of groundwaters affect food production and to what degree is it explained by man's food requirements?

4. In which different ways may food affect water pollution?

5. Discuss the hazards of some water pollutants (microbial or chemical) entering into food.

6. How can nitrogen fertilizers influence the composition of food?

7. Discuss the role of sewage plants as contaminators of adjoining waters.

8. Why has the growing congestion of people through urban living aggravated man's role of water polluter?

9. What is the rationale for converting sewage plants into food-producing centers and through what channels can this be accomplished?

10. What are the benefits and hazards of man's extensive use of chemicals in fighting crop diseases, weeds, storage pests (fumigation), mold, and the like?

11. In which ways does man threaten the living resources of the oceans?

Supplementary

Tables

One meter (m) = 3.28 feet	One foot = 0.305 meter
One kilometer (km) = 1,000 m = = 0.62 mile	One mile = 1.61 km
One liter (ltr) = 0.264 gallon	One gallon or four quarts (4 qts.) = 3.785 ltr
One kilogram (kg) = 1,000 grams (g) = 2.205 lbs.	One pound (lb.) = 0.4536 kg = 453.6 g
One hectare (ha) = 100 ares = = 2.471 acres	One acre = 0.405 ha = 40.5 ares
One kg/ha = 0.89 lb/acre	One lb/acre = 1.12 kg/ha
One metric ton = 1,000 kg = 2,205 lbs.	

Potato availability—average 1967-1968

	Production (millions of metric tons)	Population (millions)	Production (kilograms per person)	Consumption (kilograms per person)
1. Poland	49.72	32.80	1,539.0	127.2
2. East Germany	13.36	16.00	835.0	140.3
3. Czechoslovakia	6.29	14.40	437.0	101.0
4. U.S.S.R.	98.82	237.80	416.0	138.5
5. Netherlands	4.95	12.74	389.0	90.5
6. West Germany	20.35	60.16	338.0	114.1
7. France	10.23	49.92	205.0	82.1
8. Sweden	1.36	7.90	172.0	91.3
9. Spain	4.47	32.40	138.0	101.9
10. United States	13.61	201.20	67.6	45.0*
11. Japan	3.85	101.10	38.1	na
12. China	20.00	815.00	24.5	na

*Includes sweet potato.
The excess production reflects the use of potato as animal feed and as raw material in starch manufacture. (In the United States corn is used for this purpose.) The amount actually eaten is in the right-hand column.

Cassava availability—average 1967-1968

	Kilograms per Person		Kilograms per Person
1. Paraguay	675.0	11. Tanzania	89.3
2. Togo	633.0	12. India	73.3
3. Dahomey	428.0	13. Central African Republic	70.2
4. Liberia	380.0	14. Kenya	59.7
5. Angola	280.0	15. Thailand	56.4
6. Burundi	258.0	17. Colombia	40.4
7. Uganda	233.8	18. North Vietnam	40.0
8. Ivory Coast	110.4		
9. Nigeria	103.5		
10. Indonesia	102.0		

Consumption hardly exceeds 200 kg/person. Excess production is traded, mostly as cassava flour.

Milk production—average 1968-1970 (millions of metric tons)

	1968	1969	1970	Annual 1968-70	Percent		Population (millions)	Kilograms per Person
					—	Sum		
World	394.7	396.7	397.4	396.9	—	Sum	3,538	112.1
Europe	150.7	150.8	150.6	150.7	38.0		455.0	331.5
—East	37.4	37.6	37.7	37.5	9.5		124.0	302.2
—West	113.3	113.2	112.9	113.2	28.5		330.0	342.5
U.S.S.R	82.3	81.5	82.9	82.3	20.7	58.7	238.0	345.8
North America	61.5	61.2	61.2	61.3	15.4	74.1	222.0	276.1
Asia	51.7	52.8	52.0	52.8	13.9	87.4	2,035.0	26.0
Latin America	23.1	23.9	24.1	23.7	6.0	93.4	268.0	88.6
Oceania	13.4	14.3	14.1	13.9	3.5	96.9	18.6	748.4
Africa	12.0	12.2	12.5	12.2	3.1	100.0	338.8	36.2

Note that most milk (three quarters of the total) is produced in temperate regions (Europe, the Soviet Union, and North America). In the tropical and subtropical areas milk production is very modest; lactose intolerance is also prevalent.

213

Milk production (by countries)—Average 1968-1970 (million of metric tons)

	Quantity	Population (millions)	Kg/person
1. New Zealand	6.52	2.75	2,370.9
2. Denmark	4.87	4.87	1,000.0
3. Finland	3.57	4.68	762.8
4. France	31.28	49.90	626.5
5. Australia	7.54	12.10	625.7
6. Netherlands	7.94	12.70	623.7
7. Norway	1.77	3.82	463.4
8. Austria	3.39	7.35	461.2
9. Poland	14.80	32.30	458.3
10. East Germany	7.34	17.70	414.7
11. Canada	8.40	20.80	404.4
12. Belgium	3.87	9.62	402.3
13. Sweden	3.15	7.92	397.7
14. West Germany	22.30	60.30	370.4
15. U.S.S.R.	82.20	237.90	345.8
16. Czechoslovakia	4.87	14.40	339.1
17. United States	52.90	201.20	263.0
18. United Kingdom	12.80	55.50	230.8
19. Italy	10.70	52.80	203.4
20. Argentina	4.58	23.60	193.9
21. Brazil	7.26	88.20	82.3
22. India	21.30	524.00	40.6
23. China	3.05	815.00	3.7

The top six countries export dairy products (butter, cheese, dry milk, and the like).

Meat—global production—annual average 1969-1970 (millions of metric tons)

	Quantity	Percent	Protein
Beef and veal	38.52	41.0	5.78
Pork	33.16	35.3	4.97
Poultry	15.15	16.1	2.27
Mutton, lamb, and goat	6.84	7.3	1.03
Horse	0.22	0.2	0.03
Total	93.89	99.9	14.08

Note the overall dominance of beef. (See also the graphs on pages 70 and 71.)

Use of commercial fertilizers—average 1967/1968-1968/1969 (millions of metric tons)

	Nitrogen	Phosphorus	Potassium	Total
Satisfied World				
Europe	8.34	6.70	6.42	21.46
—Netherlands	0.34	0.11	0.13	0.58
—Italy	0.50	0.47	0.18	1.15
U.S.S.R.	3.27	1.73	2.18	7.18
North America	6.52	4.49	3.72	14.73
Oceania	0.17	1.19	0.17	1.53
Japan	0.90	0.69	0.68	2.27
Sum, Satisfied World	*19.2*	*14.8*	*13.2*	*47.2*
World	23.6	17.0	14.4	55.0
Sum, Hungry World	*4.4*	*2.2*	*1.3*	*7.8*
Hungry World				
Latin America	1.03	0.72	0.49	2.24
Africa	0.65	0.49	0.23	1.37
Asia*	2.70	0.97	0.53	4.20
—India	1.18	0.37	0.19	2.74

*Excludes China and Japan.

Note the dominance of the satisfied world, using 86 percent of the total of commercial fertilizers.

Food and feed—world trade*—Annual Average 1967-1969 (millions of metric tons)

Cereals	99.2	Soybeans	8.64
—Wheat	50.6	Peanuts (groundnuts)	1.42
—Corn	27.9	Rape and mustard seed	0.83
—Barley	6.85	Sunflower seeds	0.54
—Rice	6.69	Oilseed cake and meal	9.21
—Millet, sorghum, etc.	5.88	Copra	1.17
—Bran and other		Beans, peas, lentils,	
milling products	2.45	and related	1.84
Sugar	19.8	Citrus fruits	4.85
Potatoes	2.80	Bananas	5.31
Onions	1.02	Apples	2.12
		Tomatoes	1.26
Vegetable oils	4.36	Grapes	0.84
Animal oils	1.58		
—Lard	0.46	Coffee	3.24
Cotton	3.83	Cocoa	1.07
Wool (greasy basis)	1.06	Tea	0.68
Jute	0.96		
Flax	0.33	Milk (evaporated,	
		canned)	0.68
Meat (fresh, chilled,		Butter	0.74
or frozen	3.88	Cheese	0.71
Bacon and ham	0.44	Nonfat milk solids	1.13
Fish meal	3.08	Eggs	0.31
Meat meal	0.24		

*Based on import data.

Cereals—world trade: Exports—annual average 1967-1969 (millions of metric tons)

Exporters	Exports	Percent	
		—	Sum
Continents			
1. North America	47.1	47.2	
2. Europe	19.0	19.1	66.3
3. Latin America	10.0	10.0	76.3
4. Oceania	7.2	7.3	83.6
5. U.S.S.R.	7.0	7.1	90.7
6. Asia	5.7	5.7	96.4
7. Africa	3.6	3.6	100.0
Total	99.6		
Countries			
1. United States	36.9	36.9	
2. Canada	10.2	10.3	47.2
3. France	9.9	10.0	57.2
4. Argentina	7.5	7.5	64.7
5. Australia	7.2	7.3	72.0
6. U.S.S.R.	7.0	7.1	79.1
7. South Africa	2.1	2.1	81.2
8. Thailand	2.6	2.6	83.8

Note that close to half the export is from the North American prairie.

Cereals—world trade: imports—annual average 1967-1969 (millions of metric tons)

Importers	Imports	Percent	
		—	Sum
Continents			
1. Europe	44.3	44.9	Sum
2. Asia	36.4	37.0	81.9
3. Latin America	7.9	8.0	89.9
4. Africa	6.5	6.6	96.5
5. U.S.S.R.	2.1	2.1	98.6
6. North America	1.1	1.1	99.7
7. Oceania	0.22	0.2	99.9
Total	98.5		
Countries			
1. Japan	12.7	12.8	
2. United Kingdom	8.6	8.7	21.5
3. Italy	7.3	7.4	28.9
4. West Germany	6.4	6.5	35.4
5. India	6.3	6.3	41.7
6. China	4.4	4.4	46.1
7. Netherlands	4.0	4.0	50.1
8. Spain	2.7	2.7	52.8
9. Brazil	2.6	2.6	55.4
10. United Arab Republic	2.3	2.3	57.7
11. U.S.S.R.	2.1	2.1	59.8
12. East Germany	1.9	1.9	61.7
13. Cuba	1.6	1.6	63.3
14. Pakistan	1.5	1.5	64.8
15. Switzerland	1.2	1.2	66.0
16. Ceylon	1.0	1.0	67.0

Note that more than half is received by Europe (45 percent) and Japan (13 percent).

Sugar—world trade: top-ranking countries—annual average 1968/1969
(millions of metric tons)

| Exporters | Exports | Percent | | Importers | Imports | Percent | |
		—	Sum			—	Sum
World Total	20.04			*World Total*	19.58		
1. Cuba	4.71	23,5		1. United States	4.48	22.8	33.7
2. Australia	1.85	9.3	32.8	2. Japan	2.13	10.9	44.4
3. U.S.S.R.	1.29	6.4	39.2	3. United Kingdom	2.10	10.7	52.3
4. Brazil	1.07	5.4	44.6	4. U.S.S.R.	1.55	7.9	57.0
5. Philippines	0.96	4.8	49.4	5. Canada	0.92	4.7	59.2
6. South Africa	0.84	4.2	53.6	6. China	0.44	2.2	61.0
7. France	0.65	3.2	56.8	7. France	0.36	1.8	62.8
8. Mexico	0.63	3.1	59.9	8. Malaysia	0.36	1.8	64.4
9. Dominican Republic	0.62	3.1	63.0	9. Ceylon	0.31	1.6	65.9
10. Mauritius	0.60	3.0	66.0	10. Spain	0.30	1.5	
11. Taiwan	0.60	3.0	69.0				
12. Poland	0.51	2.5	71.5				

Note that the main recipients, importing a total of 49 percent, are North America, the United Kingdom, and Japan.

Wheat—world trade—average 1967-1969 (millions of metric tons)

Exporters	Exports	Percent —	Percent Sum	Importers	Imports	Percent —	Percent Sum
Total	51.4			*Total*	50.6		
North America	26.0	50.7		Asia	21.1	41.8	
Europe	10.0	19.5	70.2	Europe	15.9	31.4	73.2
Oceania	6.2	12.1	82.3	Latin America	6.8	13.4	86.6
U.S.S.R.	5.9	11.5	93.8	Africa	5.3	10.4	97.0
Latin America	2.4	4.7	98.5	U.S.S.R.	1.4	2.8	99.8
Others	0.9	1.6	100.1	Others	0.1	0.2	100.0
Countries				*Countries*			
United States	16.8	32.8		India	4.78	9.5	
Canada	9.2	17.8	50.6	United Kingdom	4.34	8.6	18.1
Australia	6.2	12.1	62.7	Japan	4.18	8.3	26.4
U.S.S.R.	5.9	11.5	74.2	China	3.91	7.7	34.1
France	5.0	9.7	83.9	Brazil	2.50	4.9	39.0
Argentina	2.3	4.5	88.4	United Arab Republic	2.15	4.3	43.3
				West Germany	2.10	4.1	47.4
				Pakistan	1.39	2.7	50.1
				Czechoslovakia	1.28	2.5	52.6
				Italy	1.21	2.4	55.0
				East Germany	1.20	2.4	57.4
				Poland	1.20	2.4	59.8
				Cuba	1.16	2.3	62.1
				Netherlands	1.12	2.2	64.3
				South Korea	1.06	2.1	66.4

The global wheat trade amounts to 16 percent of the production.

Rice*—world trade—annual average 1967-1969 (thousands of metric tons)

	Quantity	Population (millions)	Kg/Person
NET IMPORT			
Continents			
Europe	546.9	455	1.20
Asia	933.0	2,034	0.46
Countries			
South Vietnam	589.6	17.40	33.90
Indonesia	552.8	114.00	4.90
India	454.6	524.00	0.87
Hong Kong	349.7	3.00	116.60
Ceylon	332.7	12.00	27.70
South Korea	339.1	30.70	11.00
Malaysia	335.6	10.30	32.50
U.S.S.R.	323.6	238.00	1.40
Singapore	192.1	2.00	96.00
Cuba	173.3	8.10	21.40
Senegal	161.5	3.69	43.80
Japan	157.4	101.00	1.60
Scandinavia	133.4	5.00	26.70
United Kingdom	114.5	55.30	2.10
NET EXPORT			
United States	1,888.8	201.00	9.3
Thailand	1,190.8	33.70	35.4
China	895.3	815.00	1.1
United Arab Republic	592.3	31.70	18.7
Burma	447.5	26.40	17.8
Cambodia	165.7	52.80	3.1
Italy	165.0	6.79	24.4
North Korea	93.7	13.00	7.2

*In milled equivalents
Only 3.9 percent of the production enters world trade.

Corn—world trade—average 1967-1968 (millions of metric tons)

Exporters	Exports	Percent		Importers	Imports	Percent	
		–	Sum			–	Sum
North America	14.0	52.9	73.9	North America	0.76	2.8	4.7
Latin America	5.6	21.0	87.6	Latin America	0.53	1.9	74.9
Europe	3.6	13.7	93.6	Europe	19.20	70.2	96.9
Asia	1.6	6.0	99.3	Asia	6.00	22.0	98.6
Africa	1.5	5.7	100.0	Africa	0.46	1.7	100.0
Others	0.2	0.7		Others	0.37	1.4	
World total	26.5			World total	27.3		
Countries				*Countries*			
1. United States	14.0	52.7	66.8	1. Japan	5.90	14.3	28.2
2. Argentina	3.7	14.1	74.3	2. Italy	3.80	13.9	41.4
3. South Africa	2.0	7.5	81.2	3. United Kingdom	3.60	13.2	50.2
4. France	1.8	6.9	86.2	4. Spain	2.40	8.8	58.6
5. Thailand	1.4	5.0	89.2	5. West Germany	2.30	8.4	66.7
6. Brazil	0.8	3.0		6. Netherlands	2.20	8.1	70.7
				7. Belgium	1.10	4.0	73.4
				8. Canada	0.74	2.7	76.0
				9. Portugal	0.71	2.6	77.8
				10. France	0.50	1.8	

Of the total production, only 10 percent enters world trade. The United States accounts for half of the deliveries. Europe receives three-quarters.

Soybeans—world trade—annual average 1967-1969 (millions of metric tons)

Exporters	Exports	Importers	Imports
1. United States	7.88	1. Europe	5.04
2. China	0.54	2. Asia	3.14
3. Others	0.32	3. Others	0.46
Total	8.74	Total	8.64

Net Import—Countries			
1. Japan	2.39	7. Taiwan	0.40
2. West Germany	1.48	8. Canada	0.38
3. Spain	0.92	9. United Kingdom	0.27
4. Netherlands	0.66	10. Belgium	0.25
5. Italy	0.61	11. Israel	0.24
6. Denmark	0.42	12. Norway	0.16

Note that the United States is the leading exporter and that only a pittance reaches hungry countries.

Soybeans—United States exports (millions of bushels)

Destination	1967-1968		1969-1970	
	Quantity	Percent	Quantity	Percent
Western Europe	150.1	54.2	226.7	52.7
Japan	71.8	25.9	102.1	23.7
Canada*	29.3	10.6	53.9	12.5
Total	276.8		430.7	
1. Japan	71.8	25.9	102.1	23.7
2. Netherlands	39.8	14.4	57.4	13.3
3. Canada	29.3	10.6	53.9	12.5
4. West Germany	31.3	11.3	47.4	11.0
5. Spain	30.3	10.9	37.5	8.7
6. Italy	15.6	5.6	25.7	6.0
7. Taiwan	13.6	4.9	20.4	4.7
8. Denmark	13.7	4.9	19.9	4.6
9. Belgium	9.5	3.4	14.7	3.4
10. Israel	8.0	2.9	10.7	2.5
11. France	0.5	0.2	9.1	2.1

*Includes transshipments to Japan and Western Europe.

The absence of the hungry countries is still more striking in the United States exports. Soybean products for food are not included in these data, but these constitute a mere fraction of the total. Soybean cake and meal used as feed are, however, in protein terms almost one-third that of beans. 86 percent of this goes to Europe and 7 percent to Japan (1969/70).

Peanuts—world trade—annual average 1967-1969 (millions of metric tons)

Top Exporters				
Continent	Quantity		Country	Quantity
1. Africa	1.22		1. Nigeria	0.57
2. Asia	0.13		2. Senegal	0.17
3. North America	0.06		3. Niger	0.16
World (total)	1.45		4. Sudan	0.09
			5. China	0.06
			6. United States	0.05

Top Importers				
Continent	Quantity		Country	Quantity
1. Europe	1.21		1. France	0.50
2. Asia	0.09		2. Italy	0.14
World (total)	1.42		3. Portugal	0.12
			4. United Kingdom	0.10
			5. Canada	0.05
			6. Japan	0.04

The chief exporters are the protein-short continents of Africa and Asia. The main importers are the European countries.

Peanut cake and meal—world trade—annual average 1967-1969 (millions of metric tons)

Top Exporters	Quantity		Top Importers	Quantity
1. India	0.60		1. United Kingdom	0.35
2. Senegal	0.22		2. France	0.18
3. Nigeria	0.16		3. West Germany	0.15
4. Brazil	0.13		4. Czechoslovakia	0.15
5. Argentina	0.09		5. Hungary	0.10
6. Sudan	0.04		6. Denmark	0.07
Total above	1.24		7. Japan	0.07
World Export	1.44		8. Sweden	0.05
			Total above	1.12
			World import	1.29

Note that India bears 40 percent of the export load. The United Kingdom and other European countries are the chief purchasers.

Oilseed cake and meal—world trade—average 1967-1969 (millions of metric tons)

Export			
Top Exporters	Quantity	Net Exporters	Quantity
1. North America	3.17	1. United States	2.81
2. Asia	1.92	2. Argentina	0.80
3. South America	1.45	3. India	0.76
4. Europe	1.29	4. Brazil	0.50
5. Africa	1.15	5. Turkey	0.28
Total	8.98	6. Senegal	0.22
		7. Sudan	0.19
		8. Nigeria	0.20

Import			
Top Importers	Quantity	Net Importers	Quantity
1. Europe	8.42	1. West Germany	1.96
2. North America	0.36	2. France	1.83
3. Asia	0.34	3. United Kingdom	0.92
Total	9.12	4. Denmark	0.59
		5. Netherlands	0.34

The chief recipients are European countries. The United States delivers one-third; half originates in Asia, South America, and Africa, and some 15 percent in Europe.

Food and feed—world trade: percent received by European countries—annual average 1967-1969

	Percent of World Trade	
Commodity	Overall	Intra-European*
Cereals	45.0	19.00
Corn	70.0	13.00
Bran	76.0	10.50
Soybeans	58.5	0.01
Sunflower seed	82.0	36.00
Peanuts	85.0	1.00
Peanut cake and meal	93.0	6.00
Oilseed cake and meal	93.0	14.00
Pulses (beans, peas)	57.0	20.5
Meat (fresh, chilled, frozen)	70.0	41.00
Butter	80.0	50.00
Marine oils	89.0	37.00
Meat meal	52.5	34.50
Fish meal	69.5	22.00

*Trade with European origin.

Japan's dominance of Asian imports of food and feed—average 1967-1969

Commodity	Japanese imports	
	Millions of Metric Tons	Percent of Total Asian Imports
Cereals	12.700	34.8
—Wheat	4.180	19.8
—Rice	0.280	6.5
—Barley	0.640	63.2
—Corn (maize)	4.860	91.0
Soybeans	2.390	71.8
Cottonseed	0.240	85.0
Rape and Mustard seed	0.250	89.0
Sugar	2.010	38.2
Cotton	0.810	56.0
Bananas	0.620	88.0
Meat	0.220	58.6
Milk, dried	0.090	26.7
Cheese	0.026	47.1
Meat meal	0.063	62.8
Fish meal	0.120	51.0

Agricultural population (1965) as percent of total population

Countries	Percent	Continents	Percent
United Kingdom	4	North America	7
United States	6	Oceania	19
West Germany	8	Europe	23
Canada	9	U.S.S.R.	32
Australia	10	South America	46
Sweden	13	WORLD	52
France	16	Central America	53
Argentina	18	Asia	64
Japan	24	Africa	74
Iran } Brazil	48		
Mexico	52		
Philippines	53		
United Arab Republic	55		
Ghana	56		
Algeria	60		
Tunisia	63		
Indonesia	66		
India	70		
Turkey	72		
Pakistan	74		
Thailand	79		
Nigeria	80		
Ethiopia	88		

Meat—quantities available per person—average 1967-1968

Country	Amount per Person		Country	Amount per Person	
	g/day	kg/year		g/day	kg/year
New Zealand	302	110.0	Brazil ⎫ Portugal ⎭	74.0	27.0
United States	299	109.0			
Australia	290	105.5	Peru	67.0	24.6
Argentina	256	94.0	Kenya	55.0	20.1
Canada	250	91.8	Ethiopia ⎫ Mexico ⎭	53.0	19.9
France	227	82.9			
United Kingdom	205	74.9	China	47.0	17.2
West Germany	200	73.0	Philippines ⎫ Tanzania ⎭	43.5	15.9
Denmark	166	60.6			
Netherlands	159	58.1	Guatemala ⎫ Turkey ⎭	39.5	14.4
Sweden	145	53.0			
Italy	129	47.1	Japan	37.0	13.6
Spain	115	42.0	United Arab Republic	35.0	12.9
Finland	110	40.7	Thailand	26.0	9.5
Chile	95	35.3	Nigeria	19.0	6.9
Colombia	83	30.3	Indonesia ⎫ Pakistan ⎭	11.0	4.0
			India	4.0	1.5

Intake of calories and proteins (grams per day) per person—1966-1968

	Calories	Plant Protein	Animal Protein (not Fish)	Fish Protein	Total Protein
Hungry World					
Far East[a]	2,080	43.8	3.0	5.2	52.0
—China	2,050	49.3	6.5	1.4	57.2
—India	1,940	42.3	5.0	0.6	47.9
Near and Middle East	2,310	57.8	10.8	1.2	69.8
Africa	2,170	47.6	6.9	4.0	58.5
Latin America[b]	2,350	43.5	20.0	4.1	67.6
Average, Hungry World	2,100	47.9	5.4	4.3	57.6
Satisfied World					
Europe	3,060	43.8	39.2	4.2	87.2
U.S.S.R	3,180	56.4	32.8	3.0	92.2
North America	3,250	29.3	63.8	3.2	96.3
Oceania	3,300	36.2	67.0	3.2	106.4
Argentina and Uruguay	3,120	42.0	60.7	1.0	103.7
Japan	2,450	45.4	15.5	14.2	75.1
Israel	2,930	46.6	40.4	2.7	89.7
South Africa	2,730	48.7	24.7	3.8	77.2
Average, Satisfied World	3,070	40.8	44.6	3.7	89.1

[a]Excluding Japan.
[b]Excluding Argentina and Uruguay.

Portion of fish protein in total intake of animal protein—1967-1969

	Animal Protein Intake (g/day/person)		F/A (percent)
	Total (A)	Fish (F)	
Hungry World			
Cambodia	19.1	16.0	83.5
Congo (Brazzaville)	16.0	11.3	71.0
Indonesia	5.2	3.4	65.5
Ghana	7.3	4.3	59.0
Philippines	20.0	10.0	50.0
Thailand	12.3	6.2	50.0
South Korea	8.3	4.1	49.5
Senegal	21.2	9.8	46.0
Malaysia	14.7	6.6	45.0
Ivory Coast	12.9	5.6	43.5
Jamaica	26.5	11.0	41.5
Venezuela	26.4	7.4	28.0
Trinidad	26.4	6.5	24.6
Satisfied World			
Japan	29.7	15.5	52.5
Portugal	32.1	12.2	38.0
Iceland	73.2	22.3	30.5
Norway	51.4	9.8	19.1
Italy	38.2	3.4	8.9
U.S.S.R.	35.8	3.0	8.4
United States	69.5	3.3	4.8

The protein gap—consumption of protein*—1965-1966 (grams per person per day)

Source of Protein	Satisfied World	Hungry World
Cereals	33.0	33.0
Roots and tubers	5.0	2.0
Pulses (peas, beans) and oilseeds	4.0	12.0
Fruits and vegetables	6.0	3.0
Meat	20.0	4.0
Eggs	3.0	0.4
Fish	2.0	2.0
Milk	18.5	3.0
Total	91.5	59.4

*Based on FAO figures.

Index*

---

*Figures in italics indicate pages upon which illustrations occur.